Wisconsin Uprising

Wisconsin Uprising

Labor Fights Back

edited by MICHAEL D. YATES

MONTHLY REVIEW PRESS

New York

Library of Congress Cataloging-in-Publication Data

Wisconsin uprising : labor fights back / edited by Michael D. Yates ;
foreword by Robert W. McChesney.

   p. cm.

 ISBN 978-1-58367-280-8 (pbk. : alk. paper) — ISBN 978-1-58367-281-5
(cloth : alk. paper) 1. Labor movement—Wisconsin—History—21st century.
2. Labor unions—Wisconsin—History—21st century. 3. Working
class—United States—Social conditions. I. Yates, Michael, 1946–

  HD8072.5.W57 2012

  331.89'309775—dc23

           2011045385

Monthly Review Press

146 West 29th Street, Suite 6W

New York, NY 10001

5 4 3 2 1

Contents

PART ONE:
ON THE GROUND IN MADISON

PART TWO:
MOVING FORWARD: THE LESSONS OF WISCONSIN

To all those who dare to protest

Acknowledgments

First and foremost, I thank the authors who have contributed essays to this book. It has been a pleasure to work with each of you. I also thank Martin Paddio and Scott Borchert at Monthly Review Press for first suggesting that we do such a book. My other comrades at Monthly Review—John Foster, Brett Clark, John Mage, and John Simon—have, as always, been supportive and encouraging. Thanks to Erin Clermont for another fine job of copyediting. Finally, let me give praise to all the people who rose up in Wisconsin, who by their brave and inspiring actions, have given new life to the labor movement. Already, we have seen working men and women, from our schools to our docks to Wall Street to towns and cities across the country, rising up too. They are beginning to say that their falling living standards, their growing insecurity, and a government run by the plutocrats who have gotten rich at their expense are no longer tolerable and will be met with an organized response.

Foreword

ROBERT W. McCHESNEY[I]

When Michael Yates approached me about writing a preface to this book, I feared it might be a hastily thrown-together operation, an effort to capitalize as quickly as possible on the events in Wisconsin before they were sucked into the black hole of America's political memory. As a resident of Madison who spent much of February and March participating in the protests at the state capital, I was concerned that the book would fail to convey accurately the Wisconsin uprising, and there would be a tendency to leap from a weak foundation into political flights of fancy. I thought my foreword might have to disentangle the reality of the Wisconsin uprising from what was to follow.

Boy, was I ever wrong.

Upon reading this book, I discovered the essays are by and large outstanding. The accounts of the events in Madison in the winter and early spring of 2011 are the best I have seen in writing, with context, detail, and analysis I have seen nowhere else. I learned more than I thought possible. Better yet, the connections of the Wisconsin revolt to the existential questions facing the labor movement are handled with a clarity, intelligence, perspective, and urgency that is exactly

appropriate to the task. Far from being a quickie, this book is a fundamental historical document in its own right and will stand the test of
time. The authors include some of the most accomplished writers on
the left, as well as a number of emerging young writers.

I have several related points I wish to add to the arguments and
observations made in this book. First, as one who was there much of
the time and who participated as one of the throng, not as a leader,
there was most definitely something special happening, and everyone
present knew it. For much of my adult life the actual prospects for
social change seemed slender, and political work was too often dis-
tasteful, with petty bickering and mindless egotism playing an out-
sized role—hence the common description of left-wing politics as a
"circular firing squad." I was there in the 1970s when being political
went from being in a community of friends, of comrades sharing
values and experiences, to being pointless drudgery, a form of
penance. No wonder so many people jumped ship.

The Wisconsin protests reaffirmed what many Americans had for-
gotten or never knew: that when people come together in solidarity
directed toward social justice they are capable of great sacrifice and
unrivaled joy. When there is a sense of solidarity, of hope, of
dynamism, everything changes. The feeling this engenders, this
bonding, is like breathing fresh air for the first time. I had experienced
this in a handful of political campaigns in my life, but absolutely
nothing came close to what was happening on the streets of Madison.
It reminded me why the right to assemble is a core democratic liberty—inscribed in the First Amendment to the U.S. Constitution—
and probably the one liberty those in power fear the most.[2]

Second, the Wisconsin revolt confirmed that the United States in
the second decade of the twenty-first century is not a reactionary
country. The participants, by and large, were the sort of folks the corporate media tell us inhabit Tea Party events. But though the Tea Party
and its billionaire benefactors could barely get a thousand people to
show up at one of their Wisconsin demonstrations—even flying in the
Koch Brothers' favorite union-hating worker, Joe the Plumber, to hype
the gate—tens and ultimately hundreds of thousands of Wisconsinites

came out to the protests. The demands and signs were overwhelmingly progressive and far to the left of what most political and labor leaders would countenance. There wasn't a scintilla of immigrant-bashing or racism to be found, or at least I did not see it. The signs and chants reflecting progressive positions on unions, taxation, social services, and military spending would never be found in the corporate news media. The cynical claim that the American people are a bunch of shop-till-you-drop airheads incapable of critical thought was purged from my system. People are far more complex, and beautiful.

Third, the Wisconsin revolt provided yet another case study in how atrocious and anti-democratic the corporate news media system is. I include public radio and television under the umbrella of "corporate," as they follow the same conventions. The second day of the demonstrations, when maybe five or ten thousand people surrounded the capitol on a weekday, provided a case study. Several local TV crews were huddled around a group of maybe five or six people. I wondered who on earth demanded all this attention. I soon got the answer: a few Republicans brought out pro-Walker signs for a counter-protest. They received coverage almost commensurate to the coverage of the demonstration itself. Lazy analysts and apologists write this off to professional journalism's obsession with presenting "both sides," but nothing is further from the truth. Take five labor activists with a sign to the next Tea Party or Republican Party event and see how many TV crews come over to get your side of the story. Don't hold your breath.

Political players who do not correspond to the range of legitimate debate (that is, the range countenanced by capital) simply disappear from the official record. Most working journalists have internalized this value so they are oblivious to it. That is why nearly any gathering of the pro-corporate Tea Party gets ample attention, yet when 15,000 progressives meet as they did in 2010 at the U.S. Social Forum in Detroit, the event received a near-total blackout in the mainstream news media. Had the head of the FBI ordered the news media not to cover the U.S. Social Forum under threat of death, it could not have been more effective.

So it was in Wisconsin. MSNBC did the best coverage on the corporate front, but it was the exception that proved the rule. Most devastating was a hack piece on the front page of the *New York Times* purporting to demonstrate how private-sector union workers supported the Republican attack on public-sector unions. The piece was played up by Scott Walker and the Republican Party as clear evidence that their campaign had broad support from workers and even the liberal media. The story was a fraud, however. The alleged union worker the story was based upon had never been in a union. Indeed, the true story, unknown in mainstream news, was the spectacular, almost unimaginable, solidarity of all Wisconsin workers with the protests.

Crappy media coverage matters. It did incalculable damage. People around the nation, even those sympathetic to the protests, were confused by the coverage. And as soon as possible the coverage stopped and Wisconsin fell down the memory hole. Political journalism effectively forgot the protests ever took place and returned to its conventional wisdom.

The lesson of the Wisconsin revolt for media is clear: Good coverage matters, which is why the work of independent media like *Democracy Now!*, The Real News Network, *The Nation*, *The Progressive*, Workers Independent News (WIN), the Center for Media and Democracy, and Madison's WORT-FM radio, to mention just a few, made an enormous difference. Locally, it helped activists compensate for the predictably lame coverage of the anti-labor morning newspaper, the *Wisconsin State Journal*. It points to why structural media reform must be a mandatory part of any democratic reform platform going forward.

Fourth, the political crisis in the United States today is not merely that corporations and billionaires own the government and have turned elections into a sick joke, or that the news media accept this state of affairs as a given, and woe be it for a journalist to question the status quo without appearing ideological and "unprofessional." The crisis is that public opinion is no further to the right on major issues than it was in the 1970s, and in some cases is moving to the left.[3] But the political system has moved sharply to the far right over the past thirty-five years, such that the range of legitimate debate in

Washington and in state capitals is the range countenanced by capital, and the system has very little to say to the majority of the people in the nation. The gap between the concerns of the masses and the solutions countenanced by the corporate-run political system are wider than at any point in generations. It is the defining political story of our times.

This is why the Republicans are presently obsessed with limiting the franchise as much as possible; they need to maintain the astonishing (and never discussed) class bias in U.S. voting, whereby the top income groups vote at around a 75 percent rate of the adult population and the lowest income groups vote at around a 25 percent rate, and there is a straight line from rich to poor that connects all income groups. Republicans know full well that they cannot possibly win a fair election where the turnout rate is the same for all classes; or even win an election with a turnout of 60 percent or more of Americans over the age of eighteen. At 65 or 70 percent, the United States moves decidedly to the left. If nothing else, this should provide a tremendous measure of optimism for progressives. *We have the numbers on our side!* Now we need a party to represent our interests.

This leads to my fifth point: the Wisconsin revolt brought home the political dilemma that labor and progressives have faced for decades: whether to work through the Democratic Party and attempt to get some support for progressive policies by making it possible for Democrats to win elections or throw support to a third party that is explicitly on the left and avoids the pitfalls of the two-party system. Both routes have well-known pitfalls. The Democratic Party has delivered next to nothing to labor for decades, except the knowledge that Democrats are not Republicans. Labor and progressives have been triangulated, because the Democrats know they can serve the corporate community and Wall Street and keep labor support because labor has nowhere else to go. The Democrats are now more closely attached to Wall Street and corporations than ever, or at least since before the New Deal. The third-party option seems a clunker, at least in the near term where everyone lives, because its immediate effect would be to give Republicans even more power. This is due to the way the two parties have written electoral laws to effectively give themselves a duopoly.

Both options, it is now obvious, are dead-end streets, and the Wisconsin revolt only crystallized the point. AFL-CIO president Richard Trumka, on the heels of the Madison protests, stated that labor would scale back its support for Democrats in 2012. "For too long, we've been left after Election Day holding a canceled check, waving it about—'Remember us? Remember us? Remember us?'— asking someone to pay a little attention to us," he recalled in an interview, sharing, among other things, his frustration with the failure of the Obama administration and Democrats in Congress to pass the Employee Free Choice Act and other needed labor law reforms. "Well, I don't know about you, but I've had a snootful of that shit!"[4]

But what to do? An emerging consensus connecting activists across labor and the entire progressive community is that labor and progressives need to develop an independent body, unattached to the Democrats, which will only support candidates who are on board with a progressive platform. It will run primary challenges, work with people not associated with the Democrats, and make electoral reform a mandatory part of its work, such that the two-party duopoly bankrolled by billionaires will be quashed. Every bit as important, the emphasis will be on year-round organizing—education, outreach, and general hell-raising—with electoral work getting a smaller percentage of the resources. Little or no money will go to idiotic TV political ads. The discussions are amorphous at this point, but the logic is pointing in this direction, and not a moment too soon. There is considerable risk, but what other option is there?

Along these lines, a fairly coherent platform of progressive policies is emerging, including issues like universal single-payer health care, sharp cuts in the military, guaranteed employment at a living wage, green jobs and conversion to a green economy, massive infrastructure spending, trade unions for all workers who wish them, expansion of public education, free higher education, and expansion of Social Security. It is, effectively, a left-Keynesian, social democratic platform that unites liberals, progressives, and socialists. The plan would be to cut down corporate power while working in a capitalist system. For some in the coalition, the reforms will stand to make capitalism work more efficiently and productively and in a more humane manner, a supercharged New Deal, if you will. For some, the social democracies of Scandinavia provide a model of what can be squeezed out of a capitalist system with sufficient political organizing.

This leads to my final point: although left-liberals and socialists will join forces to battle effectively for a progressive platform, we have to understand that the political crisis of our times is at its core an economic crisis. Political activists, like generals, routinely fight the last war, and the notion of battling for progressive reforms within capitalism has become *de rigueur* on the left. There is little doubt that progressives have exacted significant reforms within a capitalist system, and it has seemed throughout the neoliberal era that capitalism, for better or for worse, is here to stay.

But we need to be prepared for the possibility that this is not your grandfather's capitalism, and the sorts of reforms that high-growth rates made possible are unlikely going forward. Even the rosiest forecasts for U.S. capitalism for the next decade or two see the growth rate as little better than the first decade of the twenty-first century and that was the worst decade since the 1930s. Most forecasts are more pessimistic and that puts U.S. and global capitalism in the most precarious position it has been in for a very long time, or perhaps ever. And that is before we factor in the escalating costs of the environmental crisis. The downward pressure on wages is staggering. The attacks on necessary social services are unprecedented. To keep itself alive, capitalism is eating our future. We are moving in leaps and bounds back to the age of Dickens, except that was a time when the world had a future and now capitalism only allows us a past. While we work with reformers of all stripes in the here and now, we have to acknowledge that capitalism itself may prove to be a barrier to any meaningful reform. We may be at or approaching that point in history, with all that this suggests.

It should not surprise us. Marx, of course, zeroed in on capitalism's contradictions and understood that at some point in time— the sooner the better in his view—capitalism's disadvantages would far outnumber its advantages, and the system would be replaced. But it wasn't only Marx or socialists who understood capitalism as a system that had a necessary historical expiration date attached to it. John Stuart Mill and John Maynard Keynes—classical liberals of the first order, and staunch proponents of capitalism in their times—both anticipated that eventually capitalism would run its course and need to be replaced by a different economic system, one better suited to the needs of humanity. In such a world it would be necessary, as Keynes said, to break with the alienated moral code, in which "fair is foul and foul is fair," that governs the present society of greed and exploitation, dedicated above all to the accumulation of capital.[5] If that moment is at last before us, it is imperative that we put our minds to work on what comes next as we organize to get there.

There was a scene in the classic American television sitcom *Cheers*, where the bar's resident intellectual, Frasier Crane, grew frustrated with the dismal intellectual timbre of the bar's conversations and he leapt atop the bar to rectify the situation. Crane began reading aloud from Dickens's *A Tale of Two Cities*: "It was the best of times, it was the worst of times, it was the age of wisdom, it was the age of foolishness." Unimpressed with Crane's offering of high culture, Cliff Clavin barked, "That guy sure knows how to cover his butt."

One feels like Dickens when assessing these times, and that makes one susceptible to criticism like that of Clavin. Across the progressive community there is an understandable sense of dismay. "In forty years I've not seen a gloomier political landscape," writes Alexander Cockburn.[6] Mike Davis writes that "the United States is showing incipient symptoms of being a failed state."[7] On its own this can feed a demoralization that engenders a self-fulfilling pessimism about the prospects for social change.

But these commentators also know there is another reality and a truly revolutionary potential to U.S. society today. If this country does have a future, it began on those frozen snowy days on the streets of Madison in 2011, and it spread across Wisconsin to the point where hundreds of thousands of previously quiet Americans rose up and said, "We are the state."

Something Is in the Air

MICHAEL D. YATES

During the past year, I spent three months in my hometown. Ford City, Pennsylvania, was established in the 1880s by John Ford, founder of the Pittsburgh Plate Glass Company. Until the great Congress of Industrial Organizations (CIO) union drives of the 1930s, Ford City was a company town, with all that that meant in terms of the power of the workers who made the glass compared to the power of the men who owned the corporation. Then, matters changed dramatically, especially after the Second World War, when, through strikes and collective bargaining, the union forced the company to pay much higher wages and provide the benefits that made working in a factory at least tolerable. I grew up during Ford City's most prosperous period, which lasted for a little more than one generation after the end of the war. It was a hopeful and prosperous period for the white working class, and I couldn't imagine anything but good times ahead. I never thought, much less worried, about the future.

Today the good times are all gone. The population, a little over 3,000, is half what it was when I was a teenager. Jobs are scarce; drug and alcohol abuse are rampant; and wages are shockingly low. The glass factory and the pottery that once paid those union wages and benefits are shuttered. Every day, the local paper lists a slew of arrests, jail admissions, and fines levied. The sad affect of the shoppers at Wal-Mart and the crowds in the store at midday—retirees and younger men and women who in a more prosperous area would be at work—are symptomatic of what has been happening.

The nearest city to my hometown is Pittsburgh, about forty miles south. It is instructive to travel the back roads into Pittsburgh, through the old mill towns that surround it. These all look poor and run-down, victims not only of the demise of local manufacturing and mining but also more than two years of deep recession. Pittsburgh itself was dreary and dirty, with roads chock full of deep potholes. Gang violence and murders are appallingly common; public services are getting ever more scarce; and the city's finances are in disarray.

Western Pennsylvania may have features that make its economic misery unique, but I think in most respects it is not that much different than scores of other regions in the country. *New York Times* columnist Bob Herbert put it well in his final column early last year:

> So here we are pouring shiploads of cash into yet another war, this time in Libya, while simultaneously demolishing school budgets, closing libraries, laying off teachers and police officers, and generally letting the bottom fall out of the quality of life here at home.
>
> Welcome to America in the second decade of the 21st century. An army of long-term unemployed workers is spread across the land, the human fallout from the Great Recession and long years of misguided economic policies. Optimism is in short supply. The few jobs now being created too often pay a pittance, not nearly enough to pry open the doors to a middle-class standard of living.

High unemployment, enormous and growing inequalities in wealth and income, and endless wars are pestilences that stalk the land, leaving in their wakes a litany of woes: homicides, suicides, heart attacks, hypertension, arrests, prison admissions, mental illness, post-traumatic stress disorder, alcoholism, drug addiction, homelessness, family dysfunctions, and a host of others. Job growth is so slow that it will take nearly a decade just to get the unemployment rate down to 5 percent.

The U.S. economy and the economies of nearly every other country are under the firm control of financiers rich beyond comprehension, and these individuals and the firms they direct want a pliable and insecure worldwide labor force that will do their bidding. They stand ready to exert their enormous power to get their way, whether by shutting down plants, moving offshore, outsourcing jobs, disseminating propaganda through their media, or flooding politicians with money. They have no loyalty to any country, only to the expansion of their capital. If a nation tries to put in place policies that benefit working people, finance capital stands ready to attack its currency and move its resources elsewhere. Governments disobey their monied masters at their peril.

What all of this means is that the trajectory of working-class life is at best stagnant and at worst continuously downward, ever more pinched and insecure. The rich will get richer, and the rest of us will serve them in one way or another. It will not matter who is president or prime minister or what promises any aspiring politician makes. Whatever could be done to alleviate human misery will not be done. In the United States, there will be no "New New Deal," no universal health care, no concern for the poor, the aged, the infirm. There will be nothing but a deepening assault on the living standards of the working class.

The hope for a better future has been deeply ingrained in the American psyche. And this hope had some basis in reality, even if the "rags to riches" saga was more myth than truth. Today, however, hope is a pipe dream for most. Our best days are behind us. We have good reason to be anxious and depressed; the future looks bleak because it will be.

Unless, that is, we do something about it. At the end of *The Communist Manifesto*, Karl Marx and Frederick Engels said, "The workers have nothing to lose but their chains. They have a world to win. Workers of all countries, unite!" These words might sound like quaint, antiquated slogans of a bygone era. But they are as relevant as ever. One proof of this is that the enemies of the workers, the finance capitalists with all the power, have taken them to heart for a long time. As Warren Buffett famously said, "There's class warfare, all right, but it's my class, the rich class, that's making war, and we're winning." Perhaps it is time for us to wage class war in return. If much of what we had has already been taken, and what we still possess is under assault, we really don't have much more to lose but our chains.

Just last year, I would have said that the working class was not doing much to break its chains. But the rule of capital is fraught with contradictions, and rebellions can break loose at any time and be triggered by any number of events. We can never tell which spark will start a fire. Today, it seems that something is in the air. Perhaps the rattling of the chains. Perhaps the smell of smoke. For many months now, millions of people around the world have been rising up in protest against dictatorships that have not only denied their citizens basic democratic rights but have implemented the neoliberal agenda of attacks on workers. In Tunisia and Egypt, the masses said "enough is enough," took to the streets, and overthrew their governments. In Bahrain and Yemen, they bravely faced bullets to demand freedom. Civil war erupted in Libya, and protests spread to Syria. Chinese workers have been organizing, as have those in India and South Africa. Iran may soon once again see its streets full of anti-government demonstrators. What my friend and contributor to this book, Elly Leary, said about the top leadership of most U.S. labor unions applies in spades to the world's autocrats, "Everyone can and should be replaced."

Uprisings have also struck the rich countries, most dramatically in Greece, but also in Spain, Ireland, and Great Britain. In England, poor neighborhoods, frustrated by years of public neglect and police brutality, exploded in demonstrations and riots. There is no doubt that such events will happen again as capital and its government handmaidens continue to tighten the screws.

In the United States, the first notable uprising, and the subject of this book, took place last February and March, with the remarkable actions of public employees in Madison, Wisconsin. The massive protests initiated by public employees in response to the attack upon them engineered by Governor Scott Walker electrified the nation. There are excellent accounts in the essays that follow of what happened during those eventful days, and there are analyses of what those events meant and what lessons they might hold for the future of working-class struggle. There are also essays describing and examining other labor struggles in light of what took place in Madison. Working persons around the country have taken heart from this. Protests have erupted in other states, and ongoing struggles, in both the public and the private sector, have been given a boost by the Madison example. As living standards continue to deteriorate, what happened and continues to happen in Wisconsin will give others the courage to rebel. As this book goes to press, tens of thousands of workers, students, veterans, retirees, and others have joined the great Occupy Wall Street occupations and protests. Look for these to grow and deepen.

The upheavals in Madison and scores of other places around the world have been occurring at a time when the working classes of every nation have been weak and on the defensive for decades. Even the memory of past victories has been lost. Yet the past always weighs heavily on the present, as the authors in this collection understand. Capitalism and the labor movement have developed in specific ways in the United States, and these must be understood if we are to understand Madison and build upon it. In this connection, let me assume editorial privilege and make some observations. Readers sometimes ask me what I think should be done to reverse the collapse of the labor movement and the one-sided class struggle Warren Buffett and his ilk have been waging. I usually hesitate to answer, arguing instead that the people themselves will figure out what to do as they fight to improve their circumstances. Let me make an exception here and issue a call to arms.

First, we must educate ourselves so that we know what is going on in the world. We must not be taken in by the mainstream media, whose owners are more interested in making money than in telling us the truth. We must reject the hate-mongers who would have us believe that immigrants or Muslims or the Chinese are to blame for what is happening. They are not. It is the economic system and those who control it that bear responsibility. We must make common cause with all exploited people, no matter their race, ethnicity, or religion. We have more things in common than not.

Second, we must stop believing that political elections will make much difference for working men and women. They will not. President Obama says he is a man of the people. He is not. He is a war maker. He cares little for democracy and a lot for Wall Street. When he and his opponents tell us that taxes on the rich must not be raised, that deficits must be immediately cut, that we cannot afford Social Security and Medicare, that public services must be cut or privatized, that money doesn't matter when it comes to quality schooling, that Iraq and Afghanistan and Libya and all the new wars being planned are necessary to protect our freedoms, that all the things we think are good are really bad, remember that they are lying. Remember that it is better not to vote than to vote for the lesser of two evils. In politics, we must fight for programs not for people. We must begin to build an independent party for workers, based on an explicitly pro-working-class platform.

Third, we must organize our workplaces. We have no chance otherwise. Our employers do not have our interests in mind when they make decisions. We are not "associates" or "team members" or valuable and cherished human beings. To the boss, we are costs of production; the harder we work and the lower our wage, the more valuable we are. We will be scrapped like worn-out machinery whenever more money can be made with other workers in other places. The best way to organize our workplaces is to form a union. The weak and poorly enforced labor laws of the United States make this difficult. However, workers can often act in solidarity with one another and at least have some legal protection even when they do not have a union and even if they are not trying to form one. They can, for example, formally complain about working conditions, demand to meet as a group with supervisors, and picket their workplaces to make the public aware of conditions there, all with the protection of the law. They can file complaints with the National Labor Relations Board or appropriate state boards if the employer disciplines them for doing these things.

Fourth, if we are in unions, we must demand that we, the rank-and-file members, control them. We must reject all labor-management cooperation schemes. These are almost always initiated by union leaders with little member participation and they always end badly. Management only cooperates when it is in its interest to do so; when the owners or board of directors decide that an action adverse to the interests of the workers is necessary, they will take it. We must not abandon the strike. When circumstances are propitious, we must make our employers pay with the only thing that works: stopping the flow of profits. In general, we must make compromise a tactic and not a strategy. For a long time now, our union leaders have been nearly as bad as employers. They care for us just as little. We must show them the door as soon as they stop being one of us.

Fifth, if it is just for Egyptians, Syrians, and Iranians to demand democracy, it is for us, too. In our workplaces, in our unions, in our communities, in our country.

I am a writer and a teacher. It is my duty to choose sides when I write, to be allied to the working class. It is my duty to teach my students to think for themselves. We should use whatever skills we have to push our struggles forward. This might be a time when what we do matters. We must speak out. It is my hope that this book will be a useful resource for those who are speaking out and that it will inspire those who have not to do so.

PART ONE

On the Ground in Madison

* * *

The Madison revolt did not occur in a vacuum. Workers in both private and public sector workplaces had faced vicious assaults on their unions and working conditions for years. Then, Governor Scott Walker decided to defeat public workers' unions once and for all. This was too much for some employees, and their protests eventually mushroomed into the largest working-class uprising in the United States in decades. The essays in this section provide readers with the facts of the uprising, the historical background out of which it arose, and some insights into what might happen in its wake. All of the writers make it clear that the demonstrations did not arise out of thin air, that they had both a Wisconsin-specific and a more general character, that they were led by rank-and-file workers, that they had the potential to give rise to a more radical and democratic labor movement, and that, for the most part, union leaders and their allies in the Democratic Party ultimately gained control over the forces on the ground and channeled the revolt into safer—from the union bureaucracy's point of view—and less democratic actions. The writers also point out that what Walker and his allies are doing is going to continue, and become even more antagonistic to the economic well-being of working people. More Madisons are going to be necessary. Let us hope what we saw in Wisconsin is the birth of a new labor movement.

1—Disciplining Labor, Dismantling Democracy: Rebellion and Control in Wisconsin

CONNOR DONEGAN

> We had already built plans up but it was kind of the last hurrah before we dropped the bomb. And I stood up and I pulled out a picture of Ronald Reagan and I said . . . thirty years ago Ronald Reagan had one of the most defining moments of his political career . . . when he fired the air traffic controllers. And I said, to me that moment was more important than labor relations or even the federal budget. . . . I said this may not have as broad of world implications but in Wisconsin's history this is our moment, our time to change the course of history. . . . It's all about getting our freedom back.
>
> —GOVERNOR SCOTT WALKER (FEBRUARY 23, 2011)[1]

In the midst of the popular uprising to defeat Wisconsin Governor Scott Walker's Budget Repair Bill the newly elected executive received a prank phone call from a "David Koch," a billionaire campaign supporter. With the prompt of "How are things going in Wisconsin?" Walker spent twenty minutes divulging details of his political strategy. Among the more intriguing moments came when "David Koch"

baited the governor to admit that this was about "personal interest."
Yet Walker insisted, "It's all about getting our freedom back." What
spurious freedom is it that strips workers of their unions and the poor,
elderly, and disabled of basic, life-sustaining services? "It is," as Karl
Marx described this same "freedom" in the late nineteenth century,
"not the freedom of one individual in relation to another, but the
freedom of capital to crush the worker."[2] Walker's campaign slogan—
Wisconsin Is Open for Business—encapsulates his intentions to lib-
erate corporations from the restraints imposed on their profit-making
by environmental protection laws, public "monopolies," unions, and
workers' expectations for a decent standard of living.

So it is no surprise that Walker's crusade for "freedom"—busting
unions, privatizing education, deregulating industry, cutting corporate
taxes, and dispossessing the needy of publicly provided services—is
understood by the working people of Wisconsin, indeed of the world,
as not only a blatant transfer of wealth to the rich but as an attack on
democracy itself. Teacher sickouts, student walkouts, mass protest, a
popular occupation, and civil disobedience marked the return of
social movement politics—and class struggle—as they have not been
seen in the United States for upward of three and a half decades. In
this essay, I piece together a comprehensive view of the legislative
blitzkrieg under way in Wisconsin. I then follow the struggle over the
Budget Repair Bill through some of its defining moments, ending with
a picture of where this movement finds itself today. I draw mainly on
my own observations and discussions with other participants. Lastly,
with the U.S. and global economies mired in a prolonged slump, the
uprising in Wisconsin must be understood as only the first stage of a
much larger struggle over the restructuring of a political economy
threatened by instability and mired in deep crisis.

A Legislative Blitzkrieg

The Great Recession clobbered state budgets, Wisconsin included.
Between 2008 and 2009 Wisconsin state revenue dropped by 7 per-

cent, and by 2010's end revenue collection had only begun to tick upward. Increases in poverty and unemployment sent more residents to Medicaid and other social programs, while the bipartisan frenzy of tax cuts since 2003—costing $800 million annually—helped none but corporate profits. On Tuesday, March 1, 2011, Governor Walker delivered his biennial budget address to the legislature and members of the public. Citing high taxes (though two out of three corporate tax returns filed in Wisconsin in 2005 "showed a bottom-line tax of zero dollars"),[3] burdensome regulations, and a lack of "frugality and moderation" as the causes of Wisconsin's economic downturn—*not* the financial meltdown or global recession—and the state's $2.5 billion structural deficit, Walker unveiled a reduction of $4.2 billion from the biennial budget and promised more corporate tax cuts.

It was almost three weeks earlier that Walker introduced his Budget Repair Bill, expecting it to pass through the Republican-dominated legislature in a matter of days. It was a monstrosity designed to destroy public sector unions, expand executive power over all government agencies, and slash health and social services by $50 million while restricting eligibility, raising fees, and excluding undocumented immigrants. He also aimed to privatize public utilities in no-bid sales.[4] Though the last item was removed before signing, the rest remained intact: the entire public sector will be "right to work," the state will no longer deduct union dues from paychecks, contracts will expire if union representatives fail to receive support from a majority of members in annual elections, employees' contributions to pensions will increase to half the actuarial cost, and collective bargaining will be strictly limited to wages. Certain university and health care workers will have no right to unionize whatsoever. The legislation promises to land a deadly blow to all of Wisconsin's public sector unions, on top of an immediate drop in take-home pay totaling roughly $1 billion each year.

At the same time as the administration attempts to strike a mortal blow to collective bargaining rights, an equally monumental offensive on public education is pushing its way into law. It's a two-step political maneuver that will de-fund public schools while establishing a parallel system of private schools, funded by the state. Students and teachers at Milwaukee Public Schools (MPS) already suffer from chronic underfunding, despite depression-level unemployment and hunger rates in Milwaukee's African American neighborhoods.[5] On February 15, 150 parents and teachers of MPS gathered to discuss how to respond to the loss of the SAGE program (which supports smaller class sizes), as well as six teachers, two teachers' aides, and a librarian. That night, they learned that Walker's budget would cause MPS to lose $233.5 million—25 *percent* of the district's revenue. "This may be," remarked MPS school board president Michael Bonds, "the death of MPS."[6] School districts across the state face a similarly bleak future thanks to Walker's plan to cut $823 million from the general education fund and to eliminate entirely Title 1 Funds, which provide millions of dollars to support students in poverty-ridden districts.

The first step, then, in the administration's offensive will severely impair the capacity of public schools to serve students. The second step—creating the legal and financial infrastructure for a privatized school system—likewise has been under way in Milwaukee for at least two decades. Milwaukee's school voucher program, a national model, began modestly in 1990 to provide low-income, mostly African American students with vouchers to attend private schools at no cost. All along, supporters of privatization in Milwaukee, as elsewhere, have used the rhetoric of civil rights to gain support, allowing them to characterize opponents as in favor of a racist status quo. The financial and ideological backers—including the Milwaukee-based Bradley Foundation, Wal-Mart heir John Walton, and a host of corporate executives—"have had a strategic game plan," reports Barbary Miner, for expanding Milwaukee's voucher program.[7] The program has grown from 300 to 20,000 students to become, as the Milton and Rose D. Friedman Foundation described, a "beachhead . . . in the long march to universal school choice." As of the fall of 2005, sixty-seven private schools—many of them lacking "the ability, resources, knowledge or will to offer children even a mediocre education"—had opened in Milwaukee to capture the growing market in poor children, siphoning $65 million from MPS in 2004 alone.[8]

The Walker administration's offensive marks the culmination of a long-standing elite project to privatize the school system, in which bashing educators and their unions is only one part. The voucher program will be expanded to Racine County while every Milwaukee child will become eligible—regardless of income—to attend any private school located in Milwaukee County. The cost will be deducted from the MPS budget, which will shrink further as enrollment declines. A separate piece of legislation will institute an appointed, statewide charter school authorizing board. Charter applicants will then bypass the authority of democratically elected school boards and instead appeal to an executive board. The bill also removes the limit on the number of students who can attend "virtual charter schools"—online classes that require no school buildings or teachers at all. When, on March 23, the Senate Education Committee held a public hearing on the bill, parents, teachers, and other residents from across the state came to Madison to express their disapproval and dismay. For nine hours parents and teachers spoke against the bill. "What you're introducing," a resident of rural Schofield inveighed, "is going to destroy my district. This is not about education, it's about money and control and you're trying to take it away."

The barrage of legislation being fast-tracked into Wisconsin law—much of it tied to the corporate lobbying group the American Legislative Exchange Council and strongly supported by Wisconsin Manufacturers and Commerce—is tantamount to a legislative blitzkrieg, with attacks coming from every direction at once. The bombs are still falling, but when the dust clears the state itself will be fundamentally restructured. First, the systematic exclusion of poor and working people from electoral politics will be nearly complete. Destroying public sector unions will abolish the only means the working class has, meager and limited as it is, to influence electoral politics. Individually, working people have no capacity at all to contend with corporate donors. On top of that is a new, highly restrictive voter ID law that will disenfranchise countless thousands of voters, particularly the poor, students, people of color, and seniors. Second, the state is withdrawing even further from its responsibilities for social reproduction. Essential, life-sustaining tasks now provided by the state—like child services and health care services for the poor, elderly, and disabled—will be drastically reduced and available almost exclusively on the market, for a price, or from unpaid, mostly female family members. Education will still be paid for publicly, but its quality and content will increasingly be decided and administered privately.

Lastly, the government, as an employer, has long been a haven for decent benefits and compensation in an ever-more brutal labor market. Now, the public sector is exerting *downward* pressure on wages and benefits, curtailing the bargaining power of workers in the job market. In all, these changes amount to a structural adjustment of Wisconsin's political economy, something akin to the "Structural Adjustment Programs" imposed by the IMF and World Bank on the entire Third World, enriching the few and immiserating countless millions. But the attempt to discipline Wisconsin workers sparked the greatest backlash in decades, one that may yet revive progressive and left movements in Wisconsin.

Rebellion and Control

I arrived in Madison to find a line of hundreds of people snaking out of the capitol building. Police guarded the doors, allowing only one person in for every few that left. The game lasted for only an hour before the doors were closed and those still inside were told to leave. I stood outside in curiosity-cum-frustration as a small group of students spoke to the growing crowd from behind a line of police officers, flanked by AFL-CIO trained "marshals" in bright orange vests, urging everyone to comply with police orders to give up the capitol occupation. Later, I would wince as protesters chanted "Thank you" to the officers sent there to control the movement. Yet, that night around one hundred protesters defied police orders to end the occupation, and two weeks later the police would be forced to cede control of the statehouse to the people. These conflicts and contradictions within the movement—between union workers and union bureaucrats, between the promises of liberalism and the reality of class domination, and between differing interpretations of the attack—both constrained the struggle and propelled it forward. How did this mass upsurge of popular struggle occur? Is its energy now contained by electoral politics? And what has it achieved?

On Tuesday, February 15, four days after Walker announced the Budget Repair Bill, over 700 students from East High School walked two and a half miles from their classes to join 10,000 protesters at the statehouse. In Milwaukee, teachers had already been organizing demonstrations at the governor's house with the Wisconsin Education Association Council (WEAC) and the Educator's Network for Social Justice (ENSJ); some were using personal days to travel to Madison; and one school had already organized a sickout. Milwaukee teacher Joe DeCarlo spoke through a megaphone to a group of teachers rallying in Madison: "Even before the governor put forth this budget, we were losing our specialties, we're losing our art programs— we're here with art teachers today—we're losing our phys-ed programs, we're losing so many paraprofessionals."[9] Students rallying outside schools voiced not only their solidarity with their teachers but also anger that their own education is under continued assault.

This is not the first time that teachers in Milwaukee have struggled against an aggressive governor. The previous governor, Democrat Jim Doyle, sought to dissolve the school board and impose mayoral control on the district, a reform that is becoming common in major cities. ENSJ and the local NAACP organized the Coalition to Stop the Mayoral Takeover with community groups and labor unions, including the Milwaukee Teachers' Education Association (MTEA). Their public campaign included mobilizing Milwaukee residents to attend protests at legislators' homes and community hearings and forums. Doyle eventually revoked the proposal.

Many of those same activists from ENSJ gathered on those first Wednesday and Thursday nights to call other teachers about the next day's sickout. By the time Mary Bell, president of WEAC, called for a statewide sickout the rank and file was already mobilizing. Twenty-four school districts closed on Thursday, and by Friday that included

Milwaukee, Madison, Racine, and Waukesha—among the largest districts in the state. Just as the student walkouts inspired teachers, the mass strike by teachers infected workers, university students, and others around the state with a sense of urgency and militancy. By then, the capitol was occupied twenty-four hours a day, providing a space for essential movement building activities like communication, planning, and a visible presence. When the Senate prepared to vote on the Budget Repair Bill, protesters quickly organized blockades in stairways, hallways, and the Senate antechambers to stop the legislators from voting. This not only was the fire that compelled the Democrats to break the Senate's quorum by leaving the state, it also is why they were able to escape the Senate's sergeant at arms. Police, who were scouring the building for the minority party members, were stopped by an ironworkers' blockade while the Democrats fled the building.

Police responded carefully to the occupation and the protests so as not to inflame them. Outside the statehouse, law enforcement personnel patrolled in groups and were generally uninterested in intervening in demonstrations and rallies. Inside, police built relationships with a small group of unofficial leaders of the occupation. These police-appointed spokespeople acted as conduits for police orders to protesters, who generally complied. For two weeks the police slowly increased their control over the building until they finally moved in, locked the doors, and demanded that the occupation end. Most reluctantly vacated the building, though eighty would remain for two more weeks before finally being cajoled to leave by authorities.

The success of this soft-power strategy revealed as much about the protesters as it did law enforcement. There were competing conceptions of the struggle, and the "middle-class" perspective quickly became hegemonic. Defending the middle class was a common refrain in speeches, homemade signs, and conversations. These protesters drew from the progressive roots of Wisconsin politics and tended to personalize the struggle (that is, blame Walker). Many argued strongly for respecting and obeying police orders (to thwart any direct action) and even thanked the police for their hard work. For them, victory meant returning the Democrats to power. There were others—mostly from unions, immigrant rights groups, and leftist organizations—who understood this to be a broader struggle of the working class and oppressed groups. They made more militant demands, like "No Concessions" and "Tax the Rich," that drew on the history of class struggle in the United States, and placed this battle within the context of a transatlantic fight against austerity. These groups aimed to build a broader movement independent of the Democrats and pushed for more direct action while seeking to build solidarity between public sector workers, community organizations, students, immigrants, and people of color.

On March 9 the Senate Republicans reintroduced a slightly revised version of the Budget Repair Bill that, at least by their estimation, was void of fiscal items and therefore did not require the Democrats—still out of state—for a quorum. As they quickly passed the measure, angry protesters returned, passing one by one through police checkpoints. Once the senators were escorted away, protesters renewed the popular occupation, vowing to stay the night in preparation for the assembly vote scheduled for the following morning. Capitol police locked the doors at 8 p.m., but with protesters pushing against police lines, from both inside and out, the police became overwhelmed and ceded control of the building to the people. There was incredible excitement as tens of thousands rushed triumphantly inside, but by morning the numbers had dwindled. Eighty of those who remained inside, committed to stopping the assembly vote by blocking entrance to the chambers, were forcefully removed by state troopers before the assembly passed the bill.

Back in Milwaukee, teachers called a late-night union meeting after learning that the bill was moving through the legislature. They hotly debated their next move, with a majority seeming to be in favor of a strike. As Milwaukee teacher union steward Stephanie Schneider recalls, "Everyone's enthusiasm deflated" upon hearing that WEAC president Mary Bell was calling for teachers to go to work the next day and that Madison teachers planned to do so. The next call sent to teachers was "to turn in your protest signs for a clipboard" to collect signatures for recall elections. "I see why recalls are important,"

Stephanie told me, "but it is a serious de-escalation. . . . To really win this we're going to need all the new and best tactics."[10] Students across the country staged walkouts on the day after—including Wisconsin, New York, Illinois, and Oregon—but this time the teachers did not follow. The Saturday after the signing of the Budget Repair Bill, the AFL-CIO, with many others, called a mass demonstration at the capital. It was the largest to date, with roughly 150,000 protesting. The message from the AFL-CIO leadership was clear: leave the streets and direct your energy to electoral politics. Most saw no alternative course of action.

Throughout April and May the movement followed the Democrats out of the streets and into electoral politics. In this sense the Democratic Party was successful in containing the boiling pressures from below by pretending to express them. Since the labor movement and nearly all other social movements had been largely dormant for over three decades, local union leaders, workers, and most other participants lacked the skills and organization necessary to take the fight in any other direction. But Walker's budget was moving through the legislature well in advance of the recall elections. The withdrawal of the state and national union leadership, and their refusal to even consider workplace actions, signaled that they were still uninterested in leading a wider struggle for social justice.

But as the AFL left the scene other groups began taking leadership. On June 2 the immigrant rights group Voces de la Frontera organized a civil disobedience action, disrupting the proceedings of the Joint Finance Committee. Voces and the immigrant rights movement in Wisconsin began gaining momentum just as protests in Madison subsided. The first indication of this was the record turnout—100,000—for the May Day march that Voces has led in Milwaukee for five years running, this one cosponsored by the state AFL-CIO. Voces membership was mobilizing against cuts to education and particularly against a measure that excludes undocumented Wisconsin students from in-state tuition. Then on June 6, in protest of impending austerity measures, came another civil disobedience action in Madison—workers and students shut down an M & I Bank with a demonstration and attempted to blockade streets on the capitol's square. This was organized by a "Solidarity Roundtable" consisting of two AFSCME locals, Madison firefighters, National Nurses United, UW teacher's assistants, Union Cab Cooperative, and community organizations. These demonstrations were significantly smaller, reaching only two thousand strong on June 6, and many of these unions expect to be destroyed by the Budget Repair Bill. Nonetheless, this "Solidarity Roundtable" and related community coalitions represented the kind of independent organizing necessary to turn the rebellion into a movement.

The Wisconsin rebellion was the result of accumulated grievances—declining wages and benefits, cuts to education, unemployment and underemployment, bank bailouts, and record corporate profits—pushed over the edge by an assault on the only remaining organized segment of the working class. Student walkouts inspired teacher sickouts. Their courage in turn energized mass protests and an internationally celebrated occupation that turned into direct action to kill the bill. Workers pushed the union leadership to call mass demonstrations in the streets. All of this failed to stop the Budget Repair Bill, but attacking public sector unions was only the next logical step in the offensive against labor. The backlash, however, marks an energetic start to what appears to be a new era of struggle.

Disciplining Labor

Here is the opening remark in radical economist Andre Gender Frank's 1980 summary of the political response to economic crisis in the West: "Capital and the state under its influence in the West have responded to the deepening economic crisis through political policies of deliberate unemployment in order to weaken labor unions and to reduce labor's wages in particular, and to impose belt-tightening austerity measures 'in the national interest' on the population in general."[11] As the Organization of Economic Cooperation and Development dryly but bluntly described its own position, it "envisioned . . . a sizeable shift in income distribution . . . from labor to capital" to be achieved through a "special effort" toward restraining public and private consumption.[12] As then chairman of the Federal Reserve Paul Volcker more famously stated, "The American standard of living must decline." While these statements were made in the late 1970s, they summarize just as well today's ruling-class consensus regarding capitalism's current crisis.

This "special effort" would include the "Volcker Shocks"—Volcker cranked up interest rates for two years, restraining economic activity to such an extent that the official unemployment rate reached 11 percent. It was then that President Ronald Reagan broke the air traffic controllers' strike by firing the controllers and replacing them with scabs. As David McNally writes in his book *Global Slump*, "The shock of mass unemployment was thus joined to the trauma of union busting."[13] He continues: "Volcker and company were in the business of instilling fear" so that workers would accept the serious concessions—including a greater workload for lower pay and with fewer benefits—that would be forced on them in the coming years.[14] In a very real way, then, Walker was not far off in comparing his attempt to break the public sector unions with Reagan's own union busting. Walker's budget proposal is a political instrument designed to, besides destroying social programs, beat down wages. As the Department of Administration's Budget in Brief explains, "Over one-half of the budget goes to cities, counties, towns, villages, and school districts . . . most of the general fund budget supports the compensation costs of public employees."[15] This biennial budget reduces spending by $4.2 billion while *disallowing* subordinate levels of government—including school districts—to compensate for the loss of funding by raising local property taxes. Thus, municipalities, counties, and school districts, including K-12 and technical colleges, will be *compelled* to reduce benefits and wages. They will otherwise cease to operate anywhere near their current capacity. That is why Walker argues that his Budget Repair Bill is integral to the budget—without it, or without otherwise implementing the same drastic cuts, "local government and school district leaders [will have] no choice but to lay off public sector servants who teach our children, plow our streets, and deliver a multitude of other critical services."[16] But even the $1 billion of "savings" to be wrenched out of public servants will not cover the total loss of funding, so those who rely on the public sector will nonetheless confront significant cuts to those critical services.

The contracts of some public workers in Wauwatosa, a Milwaukee suburb, have already expired, making the city among the first to confront the administration's ultimatum. Since contract negotiations began in November, the unions had refused to accept concessions requested by the city. But once it appeared that the Budget Repair Bill would become law, the unions conceded *even more* than the bill was going to require them to, including a one-year wage freeze. On the night of the vote, conservative citizens, encouraged by a local radio pundit, filled the room and demanded that the contracts be voted down. The atmosphere was vicious—the unions offered significant concessions to get a contract that would secure their existence for the next two years. The conservatives understood this well and argued that the city should wait for the bill to pass so that they could take advantage of the new "tools" to force more concessions, like sick time, from their public servants. The City Council gave in and voted not to sign the contracts.

But even the quiet suburban residents of Wauwatosa were not immune from the unrest across the state. With pressure coming from the other side, the council held a second hearing and vote. The room filled to capacity an hour before the meeting's scheduled start time. The atmosphere was highly charged and emotional as neighbors and family members took opposing positions. Dozens of residents spoke from both sides, with registered comments evenly split. One councilperson who voted against the contracts commented that with so many unemployed workers he is certain that the city would have no problem replacing any office workers who found the contracts to be intolerable. Most of the residents who spoke in opposition expressed frustration with their own declining standard of living and described public workers as the only ones still "sheltered." The City Council reversed its vote, but the mayor vetoed the decision.

A number of teachers' unions also moved quickly to sign new contracts. Green Bay teachers, for example, agreed to $15 million worth of concessions in a contract that even includes a suspension of collective bargaining rights. As Green Bay Educator's Association President Toni Lardinois stated, "This was not an agreement, this was an ultimatum."[17] Across Wisconsin, workers have similar battles to look forward to.

Subjecting public sector workers to such conditions is a central component of the ruling class's strategy to manage capitalism's crisis. The unstated premise is that corporations and the wealthy will *not* pay for the bailouts or for loss of revenue due to recession. Union busting makes this possible without contradicting the sacrificial fervor that insists we spread the pain to "everyone." The drastic spending cuts by states and the federal government (as well as by governments across Europe), by simply removing trillions of dollars worth of investment and spending, will be sure to increase unemployment even further. The labor market will do the real disciplinary work as competition for jobs becomes ever more frenetic. In the meantime, these public sacrifices stand as official endorsements of the mantra that working people must submit to an austere existence, buttressing the bargaining position of *all* employers seeking concessions from workers. Ultimately, the purpose is to cheapen labor in general and to get rid of the fight in us so as to achieve a "sizeable shift in income distribution from labor to capital."

Conclusion: Global Crisis, Global Struggle

The continuing global economic crisis that erupted in the 2008 financial meltdown forced the ruling class—of investment bankers, corporate executives, the International Monetary Fund, politicians and state functionaries—to intervene in the markets in a most pronounced fashion. They chose, conveniently, to distribute trillions of dollars of public funds to the banks and auto industry to avert the imminent threat of a global depression. Prolonged depressions, however, are endemic to the capitalist economy. Such crises are caused by the over-accumulation of capital—that is, capitalists accumulate more productive capacity and money-capital than can be profitably put to use (causing speculation, military complexes, and other dangerous means of soaking up excess capital). Crises and slumps cause massive *devaluations* of capital—of money, assets, and inputs to production, especially labor. By pushing the masses of humanity into a state of misery and desperation, and by dampening competition among capitalists, depressions eventually relieve the system of the problem of overaccumulation.[18] Today, the ruling class is attempting to manage the crisis so as to shelter themselves from the destruction that their system has wrought, by subjecting humanity to the blunt ax of austerity.

But labor is not a throwaway commodity. The struggle over the Budget Repair Bill began just as the Egyptians began celebrating the fall of the U.S.-backed dictator Hosni Mubarek. And it was just as the mass demonstrations in Wisconsin were subsiding that the call for "Real Democracy Now" sparked a mass movement of *"indignados"* in Spain, itself inspiring anti-austerity protests across Europe. In the face of a series of offensives that further concentrate the power of capital, and as millions of youth find themselves "indignant" and without a future under capitalism, hope is found in the struggle for a better world. The uprising in Wisconsin highlights the tasks ahead—popular education and independent political organization, which are at historic lows in the United States, must be undertaken. The Wisconsin rebellion may mark a changing tide. As Rosa Luxemburg aptly wrote: "The organization does not supply the troops for the struggle, but the struggle, in an ever growing degree, supplies recruits for the organization."[19] This is only the beginning.

2—Capitalist Crisis
and the Wisconsin Uprising

ANDREW SERNATINGER

Throughout February and March of 2011, I couldn't help but wonder if I were living in a folktale: in a flash tens of thousands of people rallied at the state capital in Madison; teachers shut down public schools in a statewide "sick strike"; and union workers physically blocked the legislature doors. I remember being at work listening to the radio when we all stopped to cheer at the breaking news about the fourteen state senators fleeing the state to halt a vote on the governor's anti-labor bill.

And for over a month it kept going like that. A prank phone call revealed the governor's unflinching resolve to break the protests as well as his personal ties with the notorious billionaire Koch Brothers. High school students marched out of class chanting "Thank you, teachers" with teachers returning "Thank you, students!" The South Central Federation of Labor (SCFL), a regional AFL-CIO council, put forward a motion endorsing education about a general strike. Life reached a truly bizarre point when, walking on the street, you weren't sure if the guy passing out strike pamphlets was from the Industrial Workers of the World or the labor council. In the face of massive protests, Governor Walker snuck in and out of the capitol building through a series of underground heating tunnels, owned by M&I Bank. And after police locked the public out of the building, protesters took to opening windows with screwdrivers to get right back in, smuggling pizza for the remaining hundreds who refused to go.

The social sense of time sped up and the limits of the possible seemed to be blown open. But even as workers walking down the street in green AFSCME shirts were cheered and thanked by pedestrians, the reality was that the scope of attacks on working people was the broadest and deepest in recent memory.

While volumes could be written about the incredible moments that people experienced, outside the confines of alienated routine, I'd like to take up two tasks that I feel are of great importance for understanding the Wisconsin moment. The first is to explore the conditions that created an upsurge of working-class anger that, while it may seem tame relative to anti-austerity movements in other countries, was profound for working people in the United States. The heightened class consciousness in this moment popularized slogans such as "Blame Wall Street" and "We Won't Pay for Their Crisis," so to start I will look at how the capitalist crisis that began in 2008 persisted and laid the foundation for Wisconsin.

The second part of this essay will look at how the protests themselves actually progressed, examining the key dynamics at work. I have been surprised in the months since the protests concluded to find that most people don't know much about what happened and why the energy and potential of the movement ultimately fizzled just at the moment when it was needed most. Some accounts paint the situation as if it could have gone on forever, and seem to blame workers for missing a strike moment. The account I am offering has a different view—that after the first week's explosion of activity, the protesters had to contend with both the political maneuvers of the Republican government *and* forces inside the movement, namely the trade union bureaucracy and the Democratic Party, that swept in and frustrated the movement's potential. But far from just laying blame, it is important to point out the way history set limitations on the movement despite the best intentions.

From Financial to Public Debt Crisis

After the financial crisis in 2008, many scholars and activists in the United States hoped that a renewed left would emerge as part of a broader fight back. With the notable exception of Republic Doors and Windows in Chicago, this did not happen. So why, nearly three years later, would there be such an upheaval in Wisconsin to confront the state government? I think the answer is in how capital managed its crisis through two waves of austerity.

In 2008, a crisis in the capitalist economy exploded in the form of a financial meltdown. The Great Financial Crisis was then met with the Great Bailout, and the financial system was saved when governments around the world took on "toxic debt" and other liabilities. In essence, the financial crisis was transferred onto the state, taking away private debt but leaving the underlying crisis of overaccumulation in the capitalist economy.[1]

Coinciding with this, U.S. auto companies also demanded state aid to keep them from collapsing, using the opportunity to attack the United Auto Workers (UAW), cutting workers' wages in half. Instead of pointing out that workers should not pay for capital's crises, the UAW leadership accepted the concessions. This signaled that trade unions would not fight the coming assault on workers, and in turn sparked a crisis of legitimacy for trade unions in the eyes of the public. For the two years following the bailouts, working people were disciplined by massive permanent unemployment and foreclosures (a first wave of austerity),[2] and the public debt crisis that would hit the country state by state was deferred by the federal stimulus.

The purpose of the stimulus was not to create new jobs or public relief, but to patch up state budgets with federal funding and give tax breaks to businesses to right the capitalist economy. As a result, a second crisis was looming and getting deeper as states had greater demand for social services and relief due to joblessness at the same time that state revenue was decreasing with less taxable income—fewer sales and less employment, as well as a string of tax cuts beginning with Bush.[3] Ultimately, the stimulus money dried up in November 2010, just in time for the midterm elections and the next round of state budget proposals. The second wave of austerity would come in the form of budget cuts and state restructuring in 2011.

Wisconsin in 2010:
Contract Crisis and the GOP Victory

Two major political events, both informed by the general crisis, set up the Wisconsin uprising. The obvious one was the Wisconsin midterm election, in which Republican majorities were won in the state assembly and senate, as well as Scott Walker's gubernatorial victory over Democrat Tom Barrett (the difference between the two was cut or cut more). This did not so much represent a shift to the right among working people, but a frustration with Democrats who, while in power, oversaw huge transfers of income and wealth from bottom to top as they let workers become immiserated. Republicans ran on a platform of job creation while scapegoating public employees (who were somewhat cushioned from the crisis with stimulus money, while others were left to feel the full weight of the recession). With no other option, voters either stayed home or voted to remove the party in power, which was largely responsible for the preceding two years.

The second, less mentioned event was a contract crisis for Wisconsin state workers. In the summer of 2010, public employee unions submitted their contracts to the state legislature for renewal. Despite large concessions from public sector unions, the Democrat-controlled state legislature stalled the approval process month after month, until finally voting them down on the very last day of the session in December. State workers were then left in the lurch, anxious and vulnerable. An even more hostile party was coming into power with contracts set to expire three months down the road, on March 13, 2011.

The Wisconsin Winter

Walker came into office ready to hit the ground running, but he had a problem. Much of the Republican election campaign was based on the premise that Wisconsin was broke, when in reality the state had a $121.4 million surplus.[4] So both to reward his political supporters and to manufacture the crisis that he said had been there all along, Walker and the Republican government wasted no time, paying over $140 million to special interest groups in January through tax deductions, credits, and reclassifications.[5] They could then say that there was actually a budget crisis (keeping quiet that they themselves created it) and move forward with measures to "correct" it.

On Friday, February 11, 2011, Walker announced the introduction of his now infamous "Budget Repair Bill," which would effectively eliminate collective bargaining rights for all public employees except police and firefighters, to be voted on in the senate and assembly the following Thursday. To add insult to injury (or maybe injury to insult?), Walker announced that he would lay off thousands of state workers if the legislature did not adopt his bill, and further, he was placing the National Guard on standby. The rapidity of the proposal, plus the heavy-handed threats by Walker, enraged people in Wisconsin.

The First Week

No one expected that protests would erupt as they did. In the first few days, some local progressives demonstrated at the Governor's Mansion and unions prepared for a lobby day. The Teaching Assistant Association (TAA), an AFT local of graduate students at the University of Wisconsin, called a rally on Monday, February 14, at the capitol to deliver valentines to legislators, imploring them not to make cuts to the university, and then set aside time for their members to meet with representatives. Similarly, AFSCME state councils and the Wisconsin AFL-CIO planned for two identical rallies on Tuesday and Wednesday (with the same set of speakers repeating their speeches both days) in order to gather public workers to lobby their representatives to save collective bargaining for public employees.

But as labor officials prepared to give their rehearsed speeches, things blew up when firefighters showed up in their helmets with signs that read, "Firefighters for Labor," signaling their opposition to the bill despite being exempted from its union-busting provisions. Almost simultaneously, hundreds of high school students walked out from class and arrived at the protests, calling out support for their teachers and brandishing their own signs calling out Walker.

People gathered on the square (four streets form a square around the capitol) and made their way into the capitol to get out from the cold, lobby their legislators, and sign up to give testimony to the Joint Finance Committee, whose members were taking public comment on the bill before voting on it. As the list of people grew longer, thousands of people, many of whom were not union members, waited inside the building for their turn to speak and be heard about what it would mean to lose collective bargaining rights. Testimonies continued, and members of the TAA put out a call to get sleeping gear to stay in the building and keep testimonies going all night long. Protesters quickly got the sense that with such a critical mass their testimonies might be used to delay the bill, since the committee was not supposed to vote until the end of public comment.

The level of excitement grew on Tuesday night (February 15) as a public forum organized by local labor activists took up the question of what kinds of militant activity would be necessary to stop the bill, with newspapers broadcasting hot bulletins about workers discussing the need for strikes. At the same time, Madison Teachers Inc. (MTI), the city's local teacher union, announced that their members were all calling in sick the next day to be part of the protests, prompting the district superintendent to close area schools.

Every development seemed to encourage another in kind, and the Wisconsin Education Association Council (WEAC), a Wisconsin state National Education Association (NEA) affiliate, then announced that they would follow MTI's lead and "sickout" on Thursday and Friday. I remember watching television on that Wednesday night and seeing a ticker at the bottom of the screen announcing school closures as if there had been some kind of weather emergency, but in fact they were announcements for schools closed by teacher absences.

All this grew and built upon itself at an astonishing rate. While the first few days had the air of appeals to institutions of power, by Thursday confidence had grown and demands had become more assertive. Workers inside the capitol posted their handmade signs with blue masking tape (a building code for "do not remove") and filled the building with unison calls of "We Are Wisconsin" and "Union!" On the capitol square, union workers sang out "Recall Walker" to the tune of Queen's "We Will Rock You," and signs depicted epic battles from movies and television shows in place of an indigenous memory of struggle.

On Thursday morning, as the state senate was supposed to meet to vote on the bill, WEAC teachers marched into the capitol intending to get arrested in a symbolic show of protest. With such a mass inside the capitol, they instead took to directing students, iron-workers, and whomever else they could find to pack themselves in front of the senate chambers, elevators, staircases, and any other place where policymakers might come through to hear the bill. Realizing that they were in a moment of serious political crisis that could make or break their careers, fourteen state senators used the delay to exit the capitol and flee the state, breaking quorum and preventing a vote on financial legislation. Senate Republicans in a rage demanded, to no avail, that the Wisconsin State Patrol pursue them and force them back to the session.

Struggle for the Movement

Notably absent in that first week were trade union officials and the Democratic Party. The former had expected that this would be a routine lobby and demonstration to air a grievance and that people would march right back home; the latter continued to search for compromises, even telling crowds of workers inside the capitol to quiet down so that they could work out some amendments. In their absence, an extraordinary movement exploded onto the stage and pushed harder than anyone expected.

But by Friday, things began to change when major institutional players showed up to take ownership of the spontaneous rebellion. AFL-CIO president Richard Trumka gave a rousing speech calling the budget crisis a fraud, but began to shift the discourse from that of working-class people to an attack on the middle class. Shortly after taking protesting high school students back to class, Jesse Jackson spoke about the "Superbowl of Workers' Rights," making reference to the recent Packer victory.

The weekend cooled down some when the legislature announced that it would recess until Tuesday, February 22, but here the movement from below started to come into conflict with the conservative institutions above. On Monday, despite Trumka acknowledging the false deficit, AFSCME Council 24 Executive Director Marty Beil and WEAC President Mary Bell had announced that they would offer even greater contract concessions if collective bargaining provisions were removed from the Budget Repair Bill. Bell also ordered her teachers back to work, leaving MTI teachers alone in their "sick strike" on Monday and Tuesday until they too went back to work. Similarly, Democratic senators and assembly representatives assured the media that they were looking for a compromise to end what appeared to be a political stalemate (where the bill could not pass so long as the fourteen senators were absent). And, of course, both groups began to direct their constituents into preparation for senate recalls, a demand that was first put forward by the movement but then used to dismantle street protests.

Despite these powerful measures taken to end the protests, there are three reasons why they continued. The first was that Republicans simply refused to compromise; instead they drew up measures to fine the missing senators and looked to the courts to rule that their presence was not necessary for quorum after a session had started (which did not pan out). More revealing was a prank phone call on February 23 between Scott Walker and a radio host pretending to be billionaire David Koch, in which Walker candidly said that he would never cave and that he would crush the protests in the end. Republicans made a Democratic Party compromise impossible.

The second important development was that even as union officials tried to end major confrontations, calling home striking teachers and directing union members to staff phone banks for more lobbying, local trade union activists prepared and won a motion calling for education around a general strike at the South Central Federation of Labor (SCFL), an AFL-CIO central labor council. The media again took up the story and misrepresented (to the movement's benefit) the motion as calling for a general strike, and the international AFL-CIO broadcast the news through its channels as well. The effect was to renew much of the enthusiasm among protesters, display a weapon that workers had at their disposal (which suddenly seemed possible), and to put pressure on the trade union leadership to move in a more militant direction.

Lastly, enough time had elapsed to investigate what was actually in the Budget Repair Bill. Local newspapers, blogs, and magazines published details of the January tax breaks Walker had issued, which had created the crisis, as well as the cuts to Badgercare (state low-income and emergency health plan), to transportation, environmental services, and civil rights programs, among others. The University of Wisconsin School of Law hosted a packed-to-overflowing teach-in at a gymnasium, explaining just what the bill would do. Perhaps more important, UW professor Bill Cronon explained on his blog that this bill and the other nearly identical bills introduced in Ohio, Michigan, Florida, and Tennessee were all written by the American Legislative Exchange Council (ALEC), which pointed to a larger political project. Consciousness about the bill then moved from a trade union issue to a greater, if implicit, class issue, and community groups refused to accept a compromise that would benefit trade unionists while leaving others vulnerable.

Though all these elements managed to keep the struggle afloat, they could not produce labor actions out of unions that had been steeped in business unionism for so long. Still in a stalemate, a kind of "war of maneuver" began between the Walker camp and the movement. By February 24, Walker announced that if unions did not back down and allow the bill to pass, he would lay off thousands of public employees. The UW Hospital then began investigating doctors who issued sick notes to sickout teachers in order to pressure them to withdraw support from the protests, and the Madison Schools Superintendent took MTI to court for an illegal strike (which he lost).

On the workers' side, activists began picking targets to disrupt in the absence of job actions. In the second week of protests, firefighters and community activists picketed outside M&I Bank and rallied at meetings of the Wisconsin Manufacturers and Commerce and outside the Koch Brothers lobbying office. Disability activists from ADAPT occupied the downtown office of the Republican Party and students inititated solidarity petitions to counteract pressure at the hospital. Actions like these continued into March, but were not able to sustain and take hold of the movement, eventually losing out to recall petitioning and phone banking sponsored by unions and the Democratic Party.

The Capitol Contest

As all this went on, the capitol remained the home base for protesters. Inside the building, thousands of people came in to see what newspapers started to call "the workers' cathedral," with posters and decorated pizza boxes along every wall, chanting and dancing in the central rotunda, and hallways on five floors filled with sleeping protesters with pillows and blankets. Early on the basic needs of that many people demanded organization, so an "information station" arose as a central site for communication and updates about the legislation and the protests. As protesters realized that they would be there long-term, anarchist collectives began to staff food and medical tables and organized a childcare space.

Strategically, packing the capitol was a basic defense against the legislature continuing business and moving the bill through. But in the absence of any offensive push by labor, the capitol occupation could not go on forever, and plans were being made to get people out.

Soon after firefighters arrived in the first week, a number of off-duty police officers joined the protests, carrying signs that read, "Cops for Labor." The majority of the movement was quick to identify with what they believed were friendly "labor cops," and in turn deferred to police in uniform, whom they now believed were "on our side." The Capitol Police inside the building used the image of "labor cops" to their advantage, identifying people inside that they could depend on to support a gradual push to clear out a floor of the building each night. This eventually led to an order by the Capitol Police on February 27 to vacate the building. The TAA, which had kept an office inside the capitol, agreed to leave without incident, and police then began ushering protesters outside. For those who questioned the evacuation, Democratic assemblyman Brett Hulsey and other Democratic legislators made a number of speeches imploring people to leave the building to allow the real business to begin, until only about a hundred protesters remained.

Police then locked the capitol on the orders of the Department of Administration (DOA), removing this central meeting ground and site of grassroots networking. In response, a number of AFSCME locals filed a lawsuit stating that the DOA's order violated the Wisconsin constitution, and at the beginning of March union workers flocked to hearings for four days hoping for a judicial order to reopen the building. Instead, the court ruled that the DOA could take security measures and limit entry, and allowed the building to stay closed another week.

With the capitol locked down and no labor actions in sight, the only obstacle that remained to passing the bill was the absence of the fourteen senators, still holding out in Illinois. But despite this, Republicans finally decided to split off eight pages of their 144-page bill to reclassify it as nonfinancial legislation, bypassing the higher quorum that had halted the process, and pass it on the evening of Wednesday, March 8. A furious crowd made their way into the building, opening the side doors to let in over 7,000 protesters who celebrated their momentary return. By morning, the protesters trickled out, and Walker signed the bill the next day.

Making Some Sense of This

Rosa Luxemburg noted that events that seem spontaneous actually come out of a set of historic conditions, even if we are not aware of them at the time. This suggests that we have to start by seeing the Wisconsin moment as a continuation of the capitalist crisis of 2008. Wisconsin happened when it did because a set of policies delayed the effects of the capitalist crisis for state governments until November 2010. When stimulus money finally dried up, an austerity program had already been drawn up with language written up by groups like the American Legislative Exchange Council (ALEC) and various chambers of commerce.

But it is not that "things have to get worse before they get better." We should view this eruption of working-class anger more broadly, sparked by the combination of the unusually aggressive attack by Governor Walker, which was perceived as a *political* abuse of power, and a failing of the usual venting mechanisms. Both opened up the space for this movement to come together. Not only did the trade union bureaucrats and the Democrats underestimate how working people would react, but when they tried to regain control they found themselves blocked by the Republicans who were not playing the usual game of "one hand washes the other." When their command of groups that are normally meant to stop struggle before it gets started failed, masses of people creatively turned conditions of necessity into spectacular plays of resistance, transforming our ideas of what might be possible.

As the struggle progressed, it became clear that though working people were fighting Walker and the state legislature they would also have to confront the trade union bureaucracy and the Democratic Party. Union officials made greater concessions instead of pressing demands on Walker in return for creating a fake crisis and did not contest the bill's swift passage, though many had hoped for contingency job actions. Democrats similarly channeled energy into more acceptable electoral activity and played a part in clearing out the capitol and demobilizing angry students.

Still, if it is certainly true that both parties played troublesome roles, they also held a certain amount of power that working people were not organized to exert. Mass rallies do not happen on their own. They need the infrastructure that unions provide; and similarly, the only reason the bill was halted for so long was because fourteen senators fled the state, giving the Democrats a certain amount of control over the protests. Living questions confronted activists at every turn as to how they might assert independent politics while acknowledging the real balance of power within the movement.

So why was the movement defeated? More than anything this is an issue of historic capacity. After decades of neoliberal attacks and union demobilization, there was a serious lack of working-class organization, historic memory, and collective experience. Most people who showed up in February and March had never been to a protest in their lives, and fewer had been part of a strike. If there had been another strike of any kind, it would have been miraculous, but a general strike was solely a point of agitation; even so, it should give us pause that throughout the struggles in France and Greece the mass strikes that did materialize were not capable of repelling austerity measures. In the Wisconsin moment, there were no standing networks of rank-and-file unionists who could agitate to make it more likely that their unions would do what was needed to navigate a militant course for the movement. Nor were there channels for community members and unorganized workers to meet and develop their own plans.

Conclusion: Austerity and the Battles Ahead

A basic consensus across the spectrum of ruling parties has been that in order to manage the continuing crisis of capitalism the road ahead is going to be austerity for the vast majority of people. The experience of the last three years suggests that there is no win-win solution for workers and capital, as capital rolls back decades of rights and protections to open new avenues for profit.

Wisconsin is one part of a global struggle. In the past two years we have seen major mobilizations in Greece, France, the United Kingdom, Tunisia, Egypt, Algeria, Yemen, and into Spain, with more sure to follow. Despite setbacks and defeats, each struggle informs the next in kind, and statements of solidarity are sent from place to place in an understanding of common struggle. If we learn something from these places, it is that a radically democratic, "from below" orientation is not just a good idea or something we would like to see, but critically necessary for success in the battles to come. There is no simple move or strategy to take us out of this situation, but clearly we will have to prepare ourselves for patient, committed organizing and movement building.

3—Who Were the Leaders of the Wisconsin Uprising?

It was another day, another demonstration in the midst of Wisconsin's dramatic, nearly month-long labor mobilization against anti-union legislation. But the protest that took place March 1 was different.

The unions, following a 100,000-strong protest on Saturday, February 26, had broken down their soundstage and dropped the twice-daily rallies that had become a focus of national attention. Days earlier, union officials had—according to the chief of the Capitol Police—collaborated with authorities as the police ended the occupation of the building that had been a focus of activism.[1] Union leaders apparently believed that they had made their point by mobilizing masses of people to Madison, and that Republican Governor Scott Walker would sit down to negotiate a compromise, as even Wisconsin's previous Republican governors had done.

Instead, Walker pressed ahead with legislation that would gut the unions' membership and finances as well as eliminate meaningful collective bargaining. So when the governor prepared to give his budget address at the capitol building in Madison, as required by state law, thousands turned out to protest, even though no union or organization had called for any action.

Thus as union members gathered that afternoon—in what had become the usual gamut of teachers, firefighters, social workers, highway repair crews, electrical workers, and more—the union officials who had presided over previous protests were nowhere to be seen. The sound system that had made speeches on the capitol steps audible from several blocks away was gone. The only amplified speeches this day came via the small loudspeaker belonging to the University of Wisconsin's Teaching Assistant's Association (TAA), whose members offered an open mike for anyone who wished to speak.

But rank-and-file union members had organized themselves to get to the capitol anyway. They were determined that Walker's budget speech would not go unchallenged. Many were private sector workers who had seen their own wages and benefits cut—and often, jobs eliminated—in recent years. Among them was Jerry Thompson, who had been a pipefitter at the now-closed Janesville plant operated by General Motors. "I've been a card carrying member of a union for fifty-two years," he said, but he'd never seen anything like the protests in Madison. "I am retired but I want to be here because of solidarity."

Madison teachers, who had returned to work the previous week following their sickout, were also scattered throughout the crowd. It was part of the union's tradition, explained teacher Joan Shahrani. "We have always been concerned about teachers' rights."

Suddenly, around 4 p.m., the crowd—furious at a police lockdown of the capitol and the isolation of the few-dozen protesters still occupying the building—surged forward, tearing through the orange plastic safety fence set up that day to keep protesters away from the northwest entrance. About a dozen Wisconsin state troopers, alarmed, sprinted toward the main door to the capitol, racing demonstrators who were determined to get there first. In the scuffle that ensued, one trooper was visibly shocked to find himself squaring off against Ben Gall, a hardhat-wearing member of Ironworkers Local 8 in Milwaukee, as scores of others tried pushing their way into the capitol.

The dozens of police officers posted inside the entrance finally managed to get the doors closed, and the two shaken troopers who had been stranded outside nervously threaded their way through a crowd that was pounding the doors, chanting, "Whose house? Our house!"

Gall was asked if the police had roughed him up. The compact but powerfully built ironworker said simply, "I don't get pushed around."[2] He was angry, he said, because "Scott Walker kicked us out of our house," referring to the end of the occupation two days earlier. "This is a union-busting thing."

Gall's Local 8 veteran union brother, Ron Moore, explained why the two men, like many other workers in the building trades, had made the trip to Madison that day despite the absence of any official call to action. "All we have, this is it. Right here. This is the epicenter for the working person's future."

After the shoving match with state troopers, the marchers gathered around and discussed what do. Word came that a bigger crowd was protesting outside the door on the opposite side of the capitol. TAA members carrying the sound system led the crowd in a brief march around the building, where they found other groups of union workers and supporters using the steps to the eastern entrance as a stage. The TAA loudspeaker was again opened up to anyone who cared to address the hundreds gathered nearby while thousands more milled around the capitol building.

Steve Tippel, president of Professional Fire Fighters of Wisconsin Local 1440, in the North Shore suburbs of Milwaukee, took the microphone. Speaking clearly but not shouting, he soon commanded the raucous crowd's attention. He took his union card from his wallet and held it aloft. He'd got that card on his first day on the job eighteen years earlier, he said. Ever since, it had meant solidarity, dignity, and mutual support. That is what the struggle in Wisconsin was about to him, and other firefighters who'd driven across the state that day, he said.

"We've made the trip up here almost every day in support of union rights," Tippel said after his speech. "We may be exempt from this bill, and we are grateful for that," he continued, referring to the exclusion of firefighters and police from the collective bargaining ban, which many believed was payback for the Milwaukee firefighters' union endorsement of the Republican in the 2010 governor's race. "However," Tippel added, "we are not in favor of anyone losing their right to collectively bargain."[3]

If members of Tippel's local could identify with other public sector workers facing cuts, it was in part because they had already experienced some painful concessions themselves. A year earlier, Local 1440 agreed to reduce minimum staffing from twenty-nine to twenty-seven firefighters per day, down from thirty when the North Shore fire district was organized in 1995. That made it all the easier for the members of his local—like other firefighters from around the state—to identify with public sector workers who were in Walker's crosshairs. Asked if he thought the governor's attacks would spark job actions, he said: "Whenever you back someone into a corner, don't underestimate what they're capable of doing."

The leaderless March 1 protest highlighted a key dynamic of the Wisconsin revolt. It was a groundswell by almost every sector of organized labor, not just by public sector workers directly targeted by the legislation, but by their counterparts who worked for private employers as well. The action was driven at first by fear and anger and then sustained by the inspiration from solidarity and mass action that went beyond the plans of union officials. Indeed, labor leaders often had to scramble throughout the nearly month-long protest to provide leadership to a movement that transcended organized labor to mobilize tens of thousands of non-union workers and students.

Thus when union leaders hesitated to take the fight forward March 1 and for several days afterward, a central question came to the fore: Who were the leaders of this fight, and what was their aim? Was defense of collective bargaining the only issue, or was this a challenge to economic concessions as well? Was the goal to use workers' power to block Walker's anti-union legislation, or was the mobilization simply a pressure tactic for the unions' negotiators? If the bill were to be passed, should labor use job actions and strikes to fight back? Or should unions accept legislative defeat and turn to long-term electoral remedies?

Labor militants, and activists and community groups had already been grappling with those issues when top union officials abandoned the protests February 26, so they didn't hesitate to take the initiative in organizing their own actions.[4] That put pressure on Wisconsin's main public sector unions, which called another 100,000-strong protest—the biggest, and last, demonstration on March 12. But that demonstration came a day after Walker had signed the anti-union bill into law. With the implementation of the law delayed in the courts, labor leaders used the protest to redirect the movement into an unsuccessful effort to mount recall elections of eight of Wisconsin's Republican state senators and install a Democratic majority in that chamber. While another large labor demonstration May 16 provided a coda, the mass union mobilizations came to an end, their goals unmet.

Further discussion of the character of the demonstrations can be found elsewhere in this book. The subject here is the conditions that laid the basis for the transition from protest to mobilization, and from demonstration to occupation. For although Walker's attack on public sector bargaining rights sparked the mobilization, the resistance immediately gathered mass support from unionized workers in the private sector, too—workers who had taken devastating concessions themselves in a series of recent contracts. Indeed, it is impossible to understand the breadth and depth of the working-class mobilization in Wisconsin without taking into account the scale of the corporate rollback of decades of gains in what had been bedrocks of the state's industrial union strength, as well as a previous series of attacks on public sector employees.

This essay will also look at how different currents in the labor movement developed during the struggle. It will focus on the attempt to create a network of union members and supporters who rejected top union leaders' calls to separate labor's issues from the broader fight over Walker's austerity budget as well as union leaders' repeated offers to accept all of the economic concessions demanded by Walker in exchange for maintaining collective bargaining rights. These activists focused instead on organizing a labor-student-community alliance that could challenge the wider attacks on working people, both those carried out by Walker and employers in the state.

The Long War on Wisconsin Labor

If Scott Walker thought he could roll over Wisconsin's public sector unions without a fight, it was likely because the traditional bastions of the state's union strength had already been decimated over the years by plant closures and concessions by union leaders in an effort to save jobs. A labor movement known for its pioneering advances in the nineteenth century and for achieving a good standard of living for workers in the decades following the Second World War was unable to resist the national trend of declining union strength.

Wisconsin's union density was above 14 percent in 2010, compared to 11.9 percent in the United States overall. But union density in the state is less than half the level of 1964, when one in three workers was unionized. Just 8.4 percent of workers in the private sector in the state were unionized in 2010, less than half the level of 1983.[5]

The radical reduction in union members at Briggs & Stratton is emblematic of labor's decline in Wisconsin. This maker of small engines and generators saw an epic strike in 1983 that highlighted labor's resilience. In the early 1990s the company still had 10,000 employees in the Milwaukee area before a wave of outsourcing.[6] By October 2010, the company's contract with its main union, now affiliated with the United Steelworkers (USW), covered just 350 workers and cut take-home pay as the result of increases in health care costs. Wages are $17 per hour—about one-third lower than the level of the mid-1990s, after inflation is considered.[7]

Since 2003, following national contracts, automakers and auto parts suppliers in Wisconsin began cutting wages for new hires before closing plants altogether. The plant shutdowns included the Delphi plant in Oak Creek,[8] the Chrysler engine plant in Kenosha,[9] and the GM assembly plant in Janesville.[10]

The paper industry saw a similar pattern. The NewPage paper mill in Kimberly closed in 2008, eliminating jobs paying around $28 per hour—twice the amount of non-union jobs in the industry. Wisconsin has lost 16,000 paper industry jobs since 1997, about a third of the total.[11]

Meatpacking, another key Wisconsin industry, also saw a decline in wages in the aftermath of the defeat of the Hormel strike in Austin, Minnesota, in 1985–86. In 2011, wages at Hormel's Beloit facility represented by the United Food and Commercial Workers (UFCW) union were $16.75 per hour—some 30 percent lower than in the 1980s, after inflation.[12] At Madison's Oscar Mayer meatpacking plant, also represented by the UFCW, wages were lower still.[13]

The downward push in the Wisconsin meatpacking industry wasn't enough for Tyson Foods Inc. In 2003, the company, despite being profitable, demanded that workers at its Jefferson plant take a one-third cut in wages, to $9 per hour, pay higher health care costs, accept a freeze on pensions, and eliminate that benefit for new hires. The workers struck on February 28 of that year, and got widespread support that anticipated the outpouring of labor sympathy in Madison."[14]

Many Tyson strikers saw their struggle as part of a larger fight. "Big corporations are trying to take advantage," Chuck Moehling, a twenty-two-year veteran of the plant, said on the picket line. "Let's face it— there are not a lot of jobs out there, and corporations know it. If they were losing money, maybe we could live with some part of this. But they're not losing money. This plant here made $24 million. It makes you feel all the more committed to keep going, because you know that they don't have any legitimacy in their proposals since they're making profits and increasing CEO pay as much as they are."[15] After nearly a year on the picket line, the workers accepted the company's offer.[16]

The recession that began in December 2007 saw a new wave of attacks on unions. At the Woodman's grocery chain, a company that is nominally employee-owned but controlled by the Woodman family, management seized the moment to try to decertify UFCW Local 1473 as the workers' bargaining agent. Despite a multi-union, statewide solidarity rally in May 2008, the company succeeded.[17]

Wisconsin Teamsters also found themselves under intensifying pressure. In August 2008, drivers for Waste Management Inc. in Milwaukee waged a month-long strike that ended largely on the company's terms—a five-year contract that replaced defined-benefit pensions with a 401(k) account.[18]

Other corporate employers also used the recession as a weapon to inflict greater, even decisive blows, against the unions. At the Mercury Marine boat engine plant in Fond du Lac, the parent company, Brunswick Corp., used a threat of a plant closure in 2009 to obtain a contract that froze wages for seven years and cut pay by 30 percent— to about $11.50 per hour—for both new hires and laid-off workers recalled to their jobs.[19] The workers, members of the International Association of Machinists (IAM), initially rejected the deal before accepting it.[20]

Motorcycle manufacturer Harley-Davidson took a similar approach the following year. Members of the IAM and the USW agreed to concessions at Harley's two Wisconsin plants, as did their counterparts in Pennsylvania and Missouri, including a seven-year wage freeze, higher health care costs for workers, and the hiring of casual workers who will be paid less than permanent employees for identical work and receive no medical or retirement benefits.[21]

Another storied Wisconsin industrial powerhouse, the plumbing and fixture maker Kohler, in 2010 obtained similar concessions from UAW Local 833, which represents about 2,300 workers in two plants. The contract freezes pay for upper-tier workers at $22.54 an hour for five years and provides them with $1,000 signing bonuses. Lower-tier workers will receive wages that are one-third lower, and will have to pay more for health care.[22]

By early 2011, a concessionary statewide pattern in manufacturing had been established across Wisconsin. Appliance maker Sub-Zero got members of Sheet Metal Workers Local 565 to accept a seven-year agreement that imposes a 20 percent cut in wages and benefits for all 350 workers.[23]

Meanwhile, another mainstay of Wisconsin private sector unionism, the building trades, suffered their worst wave of unemployment in decades. After reaching a peak of around 130,000 in 2006, the number of statewide jobs in the industry was less than 90,000 as 2011 began.[24] The president of Plumbers Local 75 reported a 20 percent jobless rate in his local in mid-2011.[25] The number of idled union construction workers helps explain the building trades' large and consistent turnout during the Madison mobilization. Overall, joblessness in Wisconsin when the uprising began in February 2011 was at 7.4 percent—better than some states but still well above the pre-recession figure of around 4.5 percent.[26]

Thus, by the time Walker declared war on public sector unions, their counterparts in private industry were already embittered by three decades of retreats and humiliating setbacks in recent struggles. Moreover, the progressive leadership of the Wisconsin AFL-CIO under longtime president David Newby and of the Madison-based South Central Federation of Labor (SCFL) under Jim Cavanaugh had played an important role in promoting such cross-union solidarity efforts.

Wisconsin's unionized workers in the private sector, therefore, were primed to respond to public sector workers' call for labor solidarity in February 2011—and in large numbers.

Public Sector Unions Get Squeezed

While corporate employers were pounding unions, public sector workers were also suffering from stagnant and declining wages and, in recent years, the assumption of a portion of health care costs. A twenty-year-old effort toward partnership-style collective bargaining had already unraveled by the time Walker took office. If Walker concluded that he could move decisively against public sector unions, it was in part because his Democratic predecessor in the governor's mansion had already extracted major labor concessions.

Walker's move to eliminate meaningful public sector collective bargaining turned back the clock half a century, when the state legislature came to terms with the reality that municipal workers and teachers were organizing, irrespective of their legal status. Public sector unions in Wisconsin were first recognized under state law in 1959, but the process wasn't fully formalized until 1962 in a tumultuous period of organizing, struggle, and strikes.[27] The state legislature extended collective bargaining rights to state employees in 1966, and amended the law to allow bargaining on wages and benefits as well.[28] The laws banned public sector strikes, but couldn't prevent them. Despite a 1971 law explicitly barring teachers' strikes, the next few years saw a wave them, including the 1974 battle in Hortonville that saw eighty-four teachers fired[29] and a long 1976 strike by Madison Teachers Inc. (MTI).[30]

The high-water mark of public sector worker struggle in Wisconsin came in 1977 with a fifty-day wintertime strike by teachers in the industrial town of Racine[31] and a fifteen-day successful strike by state employees in 1977, a showdown in which the governor mobilized the National Guard to do the jobs of corrections officers who were walking picket lines.[32]

Labor relations in the Wisconsin public sector were quieter in the 1980s as the collective bargaining process became institutionalized. In 1991, the Republican administration of Tommy Thompson initiated "consensus bargaining" with the Wisconsin State Employees Union (WSEU), also known as the American Federation of State, County and Municipal Employees (AFSCME) Council 24. The negotiation model explicitly rejected the proposition that labor and management are adversaries, and instead focused on the discovery of supposed common interests. Marty Beil, executive director of Council 24, was an enthusiastic participant. In 1998, the project was bolstered by a grant from the Federal Mediation and Conciliation Service which funded labor-management training classes around the states that involved 750 people and culminated in a "graduation" ceremony at the governor's mansion. When the federal grant expired, Working Together became formalized, with funding partly provided by a grant from AFSCME International. "The Wisconsin experience and the success with the Working Together project should be a national model," AFSCME president Gerald McEntee said at the time.[33] For his part, Beil saw labor-management partnership as extending to the ballot box, and broke with most union leaders to support Thompson.[34]

But when the recession of 2001 left the state with a $1 billion budget shortfall, Thompson's Republican successor, Scott McCallum, set aside consensus bargaining for a more confrontational approach, demanding that workers contribute to health care coverage for the first time. That didn't sit well with workers, who had seen wages eroded by inflation over the previous fifteen years—including a 20 percent decline in the pay of University of Wisconsin (UW) custodians. In response, Beil of WSEU/AFSCME Council 24 organized a rally of more than 1,000 state workers in March 2002, perhaps the largest protest by that union since the 1977 strike. AFSCME president McEntee was among the speakers.[35] The final collective bargaining agreement wasn't reached until May 2003, barely two months before the contract was set to expire. State employees held the line on health care and won 5.5 pay increases retroactive to 2001—a significant gain, even if insufficient to overcome the losses due to inflation. Republican legislators approved the deal on the promise that the new Democratic governor, Jim Doyle, would seek employee contributions to health care insurance premiums in the next round of talks.[36]

AFSCME Council 24 leaders may have hoped that a Democratic governor would return to the consensus bargaining of the Thompson years. But Republicans had good reason to trust Doyle to take on public employee unions. During the Democratic primary race for governor, Doyle had antagonized labor by promising to eliminate 10,000 state jobs, prompting Council 24 to back his Democratic primary opponent.[37]

In his two terms, Doyle cut some government jobs, but not total employment by the state.[38] He did, however, keep his promise to Republicans to impose a portion of health care insurance premiums on state employees, first requiring non-union employees to pay a share.[39] Next came a three-tier health care plan with premiums initially paid for by the state, but with workers accepting only a token raise.[40] In their next contract, Wisconsin state workers had to pay a portion of health care premiums for the first time—an amount that increased in the following agreement. In the 2007–9 contract—which was extended until Walker canceled it in mid-2011—members of AFSCME Council 24 in the most common family plan had to pay nearly $1,000 per year in insurance premiums that just a few years earlier had been entirely covered by the state. Though this may seem modest, the impact was significant because of the long-term decline in real wages. Participants in the top-tier health insurance plan had to pay much more.[41]

Doyle's shift of health care costs to workers didn't prevent him from winning reelection in 2006, once again with labor support. But by dragging out negotiations with contract extensions and keeping pay raises to a minimum, the eight-year Doyle administration steadily shifted the balance of power in labor relations in favor of management.

"In the last ten years, our wages have barely increased, usually only about at the rate of inflation," said Eric Robson, a twenty-three-year mailroom worker at the University of Wisconsin (UW) and a former president of AFSCME Local 171, which is part of Council 24. "There haven't been a lot of formal changes in the work rules. But there has been a constant speedup through attrition, as they split up people's work when they leave without replacing them. I've gotten part of the work of two or three other people."

At the same time, the union has atrophied, added Robson, who continues to serve the local as a shop steward. "The union used to fight for having more money in the state budget, so we could challenge management when they said, 'We can't fund this.' But now bargaining waits until the state budget is done, and then seeing what's in it. The approach became, 'The budget is in, how do we make the best of it?'"

When the impact of the recession hit the Wisconsin state budget, Doyle tossed aside consensus bargaining and made harsh demands on the state employees' unions. Besides foisting health care costs on state workers for the first time, Doyle cut their pay by 3 percent in 2009 by mandating sixteen unpaid furlough days over the following two years and instituting state worker contributions to pensions for the first time. Though the amount was relatively small—0.2 percent—the move legitimized Scott Walker's later demand that workers pay more into pensions. Overall, state employees averaged annual pay increases of just 1.21 percent per year under Doyle, well below the rate of inflation and the lowest level of any governor since 1971. "I've made deeper cuts than any governor's ever made and I've had to impose tougher cost controls on state employees than anybody's made," Doyle declared to reporters in the aftermath of the 2010 elections.[42]

Doyle's hard-line stance prevented AFSCME Council 24 from gaining a contract for more than eighteen months. This would later give Walker the opportunity to cancel the contract extension in place, thus enabling him to void bargaining rights for Council 24 as soon as his anti-union law came into effect.

Although Walker didn't declare his intention to attack public sector unions until after the 2010 election, his anti-labor record as head of Milwaukee County was well known. But that didn't provide much of an edge to his Democratic challenger in the 2010 race, Milwaukee Mayor Tom Barrett. That's because in 2009 Barrett himself threatened to eliminate up to 1,400 union jobs and impose twenty unpaid furlough days unless the unions agreed to concessions. The final deal included a two-year wage freeze and a limit of four unpaid furlough days in exchange for no layoffs.[43]

Despite Barrett's attack on labor, most unions endorsed him in his race against Walker, with the exception of Milwaukee's firefighters' union, which backed the Republican candidate. But the enthusiasm for Barrett's candidacy from rank-and-file union members was limited: some 37 percent of voters from union households voted for Walker.[44]

"State Workers Haven't Had to Sacrifice"

When Scott Walker formally unveiled his budget repair bill on February 11, 2011, Wisconsin public sector union leaders saw a mortal threat to their organizations. The bill restricted collective bargaining to wages, which would be limited in any case to the rate of inflation. It also prohibited the automatic deduction of union dues from workers' paychecks, known as dues checkoff, potentially crippling labor financially. The unions would also be forced to recertify annually as the union's bargaining agent, an onerous and expensive requirement for the union staff. But Walker was able to justify it as a

budget measure because of its impact on the paycheck of public
employees, who would be required to pay 5.8 percent of their pay to
their pensions while covering at least 12.6 percent of the cost of their
health care premiums for new, lower-quality health insurance.[45] The
result would be a sharp cut in workers' take-home pay, ranging from
6.8 to 12.9 percent, depending on their insurance plan.[46]

To state workers already saddled with paying health care premiums and still suffering the effects of furlough-induced pay cuts, further reductions would be especially painful. But according to a television advertisement by the right-wing Club for Growth, which had
strongly backed Walker, this was only appropriate, given that unionized workers in the private sector had also accepted concessions at
Harley-Davidson, Mercury Marine, and Sub-Zero. The ad's narrator
concludes: "But state workers haven't had to sacrifice. They pay next
to nothing for their pensions, and a fraction of their health care. It's
not fair. Call your state legislator and tell them to vote for Governor
Walker's budget repair bill. It's time state employees paid their fair
share, just like the rest of us."[47]

Labor leaders sounded their own call to action. Yet they focused
not on economic issues, but exclusively on bargaining rights, eventually offering to swallow Walker's demands on pensions and health care
in exchange for dues checkoff and continued collective bargaining.
But there can be little doubt that the squeeze on paychecks was a powerful motivator for public sector workers already battered by three
years of economic crisis.

As the Club for Growth made clear, Walker's economic aims were
simply an adaptation of the Wisconsin private sector anti-union
agenda in the public sector. Though much has been made of Walker's
ties to the notoriously anti-labor Koch brothers, who control a major
energy conglomerate, the governor's aim to cut workers' benefits
reflects the consensus of big capital in the United States. It was also
part of a wider bipartisan campaign in many states to squeeze public
sector workers: Walker and his Republican counterparts in Ohio and
Michigan captured attention in their attempt to roll back public sector
union rights, but their economic objectives were shared by

Democratic governors in California, New York, Illinois, and elsewhere, along with Democratic mayors.[48]

The threat to union rights and the cut in union pay spurred a labor protest of some 20,000 on February 15, far beyond the expectation of union leaders. Labor demonstrations were perhaps more common in Madison than in most state capitals, thanks in part to the activist traditions of the local labor council, the South Central Federation of Labor (SCFL), and the state AFL-CIO leadership. But this protest reached far beyond the usual networks of Madison-area trade unionists.

Mike Imbrogno, a food service worker at UW and a shop steward and executive board member of AFSCME Local 171, described the scene that day: "The mood was angry, but also optimistic—almost jubilant. More than one person said to me, 'The whole country is looking at us now. If this happens here, it will go everywhere else.'"[49]

The protest set for the following day, February 16, was bigger still. The transformation from union protest to worker uprising began that day with the sickout by Madison schoolteachers. It soon spread, compelling the Wisconsin Education Association Council (WEAC) leaders to call for spreading the action statewide. Suddenly industrial action, all but abandoned by union leadership in recent years, became central to a key labor struggle, turning a small-state political conflict into a national test of labor's resolve in a widening battle over the rights, wages, and benefits of public sector workers. The occupation of the capitol building, initially a short-term union tactic to prevent the Wisconsin state senate from voting on the legislation, was the key to sustaining the struggle. The blockade of state senator Chris Larson's office that day, for example, helped him exit the capitol and take his place among the fourteen senators who crossed state lines. Over the next several hours, the capitol became the "people's house" in more than name—a 24-hour center for political debate, strategy discussions, and refreshment for protesters seeking a break from the winter cold.[50] After years of setbacks and defeats in apparent isolation from one another, Wisconsin workers, both union and unorganized, discovered they were not alone. Problems that had seemed like a personal burden—difficulties making ends meet, the lack of secure employment—were now seen as social and political issues shared by workers of all backgrounds. The anger and frustration dammed up over years had been released, and transformed into hope based on the inspiration of a common struggle. The result was the emergence of networks spanning several organizations that pushed to both broaden the movement to challenge Walker's entire budget agenda and to escalate the struggle beyond protests to include job actions.

Not About the Money?

At first, the novelty and excitement of a mass labor upsurge eclipsed any debate over the objectives of the struggle. After the February 17 sit-in that led to the full-scale occupation of the capitol, the protest settled into a routine: weekday noontime protests rallies by the Wisconsin AFL-CIO and evening protests anchored by a range of left-wing and progressive organizations such as Wisconsin Wave. Among the most popular labor speakers was Mahlon Mitchell, a Madison firefighter who had just taken office as the first African American president of the Professional Fire Fighters of Wisconsin (PFFW). The previous leadership had been forced to resign as the result of scandal surrounding union expense accounts.[51]

The firefighters' leader cut a very different figure from his predecessor. "Our house is burning down, ladies and gentlemen," Mitchell said to a crowd of more than 20,000 at the February 16 rally on the capitol steps. "And we're here to lead the charge. We're going to go in first. And if that house burns down, we will be right here beside you to help you rebuild that house," he concluded as cheers nearly drowned out his speech.[52]

Mitchell's speech borrowed the words of Joe Conway Jr., president of the PFFW's Madison affiliate, Local 311 of the International Association of Fire Fighters. Conway had used that image in an email to PFFW union locals across the state, announcing that an emergency meeting of his local voted unanimously to donate $20,000 to organizing resistance. Conway was a voice of authority in the union: he had taken the lead in cleaning up the PFFW's scandal, and his backing secured Mitchell's ascension to the PFFW's presidency.

In a press release, Conway explained why firefighters would be on the front line of the struggle, despite their exemption from the law: "It is unsettling that the governor has chosen to carve out protective services and treat them different from every other employee in public service. We are no different than the teachers, public works employees, office staff and municipal workers; we provide a service to our community, support the local economy and provide for our families just like all public workers."

Conway was a low-key but constant presence at every labor rally and among the handful of leaders pressing to widen the demands and take bolder action. Son of an activist in the 1969 Madison firefighters' strike, Conway had studied labor history at UW and dedicated his life to the union, passing up an opportunity to become the city's fire chief and remaining a full-time firefighter even as serving as local union president. When the legislature passed Walker's anti-union bill March 9, Conway called for a general strike.[53] Weeks later, Conway told a group of graduate employee union activists at the University of Chicago that he had disagreed with the union's sole focus on bargaining rights while neglecting concessions, citing the plight of a janitor who makes just $25,000 per year.[54]

Conway's views were in a minority among top Wisconsin union leaders. Even after the passage of the anti-labor bill, Mitchell was opposed to any industrial action by firefighters.[55] And although the SCFL, Madison's labor council, had earlier passed a resolution in support of a general strike, Wisconsin AFL-CIO president Phil Neuenfeldt said, "We don't have the authority to call that."[56] As Madison-based journalist and editor Matt Rothschild observed, "Many senior labor leaders in Wisconsin were reluctant to call the mass protests in the first place and pooh-poohed the importance of continuing with them. . . . Just as the crowds were swelling, all of a sudden the labor leadership seemed to lose interest in mass action. It may be that the labor leadership in Wisconsin, which didn't know quite what to do with all those people in the streets, has now missed its main chance."[57]

After acclimating to retreat and defeat over the last thirty years, it isn't surprising that Wisconsin labor leaders were opposed to taking the risk of calling a general strike or even a campaign of job actions to assert the relevance of the unions after the legislation passed. Yet from the beginning, most Wisconsin public sector labor leaders showed more interest in preserving their union apparatus than defending the interests of rank-and-file members. They accepted at the outset Walker's case that major cuts in public sector health care and pensions were necessary to balance Wisconsin's budget deficit, and confined their demands to the preservation of collective bargaining and dues checkoff. Thus union leaders were mostly silent on the other anti-worker provisions of the bill—such as severe cuts in Medicaid and BadgerCare, the state health program for low-income people, and the privatization of the University of Wisconsin's flagship Madison campus.

The key issue, according to Marty Beil, still executive director of the 22,000-member AFSCME Council 24, was the preservation of collective bargaining. "It's not about the money," was AFSCME's slogan. "We are prepared to implement the financial concessions proposed to help bring our state's budget into balance, but we will not be denied our God-given right to join a real union," Beil said. "We will not—I repeat we will not—be denied our rights to collectively bargain."[58] In fact, AFSCME Council 24 offered to take not only economic concessions, but also floated the idea of a two-year "freeze" on collective bargaining—as long as the unions could continue to collect dues through payroll deductions.

In short, the union leaders were prepared to see members take what would amount to at least a 6 to 12 percent pay cut and be without effective representation for two years in exchange for the flow of dues that cover union officials' own pay and benefits. Beil and other Wisconsin public sector union leaders saw Walker's attack on dues checkoff as a threat directed mainly at their own livelihoods—and they pushed workers to accept concessions in a bid to protect their own positions and incomes.

The unions' willingness to retreat did not go unchallenged. But from the beginning of the mobilization, a layer of rank-and-file union members, organizers, and activists, as well as a new crop of militants, began organizing to push for a strategy based on the widest possible working-class solidarity and a commitment to escalating the struggle. Out of this effort came the Kill the Whole Bill Coalition, which brought together activists like the socialist Sam Jordan, rank-and-file members of AFSCME locals of state and city workers, and graduate employees, members of the TAA at the University of Wisconsin.

The coalition issued a statement outlining its argument: "Walker's bold and shameless attack on labor has woken a sleeping giant. Our struggles and ever-growing mass rallies over the past week have captured the imagination of workers in this country and across the world. To walk away from this battle with only our bargaining rights intact would be a hollow victory. It's here in Madison that we can take a stand for labor and turn the tide of the last four decades in our favor."[59] The coalition made an appeal based not just on Walker's immediate attack but the experience of defeats like Harley-Davidson and Mercury Marine and the suffering that would be caused by cuts in public health care.

Among the participants in the Kill the Whole Bill Coalition (later renamed Wisconsin Resists) was J. Eric Cobb, who had recently taken office as executive director of the Building Trades Council of South Central Wisconsin. Cobb was among those at the February 21 meeting of SCFL arguing in favor of endorsing a general strike.

Cobb and his allies found a receptive audience among SCFL delegates. "There was virtually no debate on whether we should endorse a general strike—only how to prepare for one," wrote Robin Gee, a delegate from American Federation of Teachers Local 3872. "No one argued for accepting concessions. We have already made concessions for many years, and we've gotten to the point where we've got nothing left to give."[60]

Cobb successfully mobilized building trades union members to the demonstrations, workers who, as in the rest of the country, are generally considered to be among the most conservative sections of the labor movement. And when most union officials looked toward a concessions-based compromise with Walker, Cobb pushed building trades workers to embrace what he calls "the revolution." He wasn't surprised at the objections he encountered from the labor hierarchy. "The AFL-CIO isn't going to lead" such struggles, Cobb told a meeting of Chicago labor activists weeks later. The key, he argued, was organizing the rank and file.[61]

The Kill the Whole Bill Coalition found an ally in National Nurses United (NNU). Two NNU organizers, Jan Rodolfo and Pilar Schiavo, came to the scene to offer support despite the lack of members of their union in the Madison area. As the struggle unfolded, NNU Executive Director Rose Ann DeMoro published a statement opposing any further concessions. She wrote:

> Working people did not create the recession or the budgetary crisis facing federal, state and local governments, and there can be no more concessions, period. It should be apparent that the right wants to scapegoat workers and their unions, and is trying to exploit the economic crisis for an all-out assault on unions, public employees, and all working people in a campaign that is funded by right-wing, corporate billionaires like the Koch brothers.[62]

DeMoro's article and demands became the basis for a leaflet along with "Blame Wall Street" signs during the mass protest of February 26. While the no-concessions contingent was small, its demands and literature were popular. An effort to organize on a "no concessions" platform was put forward the following day at the SCFL building. The speakers included Rodolfo, Cobb, SCFL president Jim Cavanaugh, MTI executive director John Matthews, journalist John Nichols, and Jesse Sharkey, vice president of the Chicago Teachers Union. Among the crowd of nearly a hundred activists were a number of rank-and-file members who were frustrated at the lack of direction from union leaders about what to do beyond turning out for demonstrations.

Sharkey explained how the rights of union teachers were under attack in Illinois as well—but by Democrats—in an attempt to solve the economic crisis on workers' backs. "There is a consensus among the political class in this country that public sector workers have too

much, and we have to have less, and we have to give up the living standards that we have and work harder so that the system can run better.
Both parties don't want to look at the four and half trillion in debt that
was moved from the private books onto the public books." He added:
"To say that we want to save our rights but that we are willing to sell
out our dignity is a demand that makes no sense to me. I would rather
not be the vice president of the Chicago Teachers Union and teach in
the classroom rather than sell that injustice as something progressive."

Cobb criticized union leaders for trying to trade workers' income
in exchange for maintaining collective bargaining. "It really disappointed me when I heard that some of these larger [union] bosses—
and I may be putting my head on the chopping block here a little bit—
made these concessions without talking to the negotiating committee," he said. "In my opinion that's a horrible mistake. I want to see
this power pushed down to the membership. And I want the membership to step up."

He added: "These economic concessions [offered to Walker], they
are not going to cut it. I know too many people that work in these
offices, who work as nurses, work as teachers, that, if they were to take
these hits that he's asking for, it would absolutely devastate them."

Rodolfo, summing up the discussion, criticized "Democrats and
those who represent workers [and] get up publicly and say, essentially
we're willing to concede pensions, we're willing to concede pay." She
added, "We run the risk in Wisconsin of deep concessions [being
defined as] a victory as long as we hold on to a little bit."

Besides NNU and Kill the Whole Bill Coalition, other activists
opposed to concessions and favoring militant action pressed ahead
with similar efforts. The Industrial Workers of the World (IWW), a
well-established part of the Madison labor left, hosted a community
meeting on a general strike that drew about one hundred activists.
Activist and attorney Ben Manski, who was nearly elected to the
Wisconsin assembly on the Green Party ticket in the 2010 elections,
worked with the group Wisconsin Wave to bring together progressive
labor unions, community organizations, environmental justice groups,
and others into an alliance that could challenge the range of Walker's

agenda. Religious groups and immigrant rights organizations made similar attempts. Individual union activist sought to build rank-and-file networks in their union to better coordinate action and organize in the workplace.

Compared to the mass protests mobilized by the big unions, such efforts could appear paltry. But then the big union operations—AFSCME, WEAC, and the state AFL-CIO—literally pulled the plug on mass protests after February 26 and turned their backs on the occupation of the capitol. It fell to a thin layer of activists to try to sustain the mobilization, starting with the improvised budget protest March 1 discussed at the outset of this chapter. On March 3, the Kill the Whole Bill Coalition and the NNU organized a New Orleans jazz funeral march of several thousand to the capitol steps. Eric Cobb was emcee, and several speakers spoke against concessions and argued for the continuation of the struggle.

Among the organizers of the rally was Sam Jordan, an African American longtime organizer and labor activist in Madison who helped found Kill the Whole Bill Coalition. "We organized this rally just to show that there is a union voice out there that says it is about the money" as well as union rights, she said.

Still, the leading figures in labor were silent. With no mass Saturday labor protest scheduled, Manski worked through Wisconsin Wave and its allies to organize a demonstration on three days' notice. By then, the pattern of weekend worker mobilizations to Madison was well established, so the Wave activists could be confident of an audience of at least thousands of people—and they had filmmaker Michael Moore as a featured speaker. Labor leaders, realizing that they had left a vacuum to be filled by others, also made a last-minute call for their own action, building on a rally called by the International Brotherhood of Electrical Workers. But union officials were determined that the protest remain "on message" and refused an offer by Wave to collaborate. The unions rejected Moore as a speaker, apparently out of fear that he would call a general strike.[63]

It was apparent that the protests would continue, with or without the blessing of top union officials in WEAC, AFSCME, and the

Wisconsin AFL-CIO. So after May 5, union leaders stepped on the accelerator again, providing money and resources to mobilize another 100,000-strong demonstration for March 12. Forced to contend with the fact that Walker wouldn't compromise, and that Wisconsin senate Democrats couldn't stay out of state indefinitely, the unions directed the protest movement's energies almost exclusively into recall elections.

But before throwing their weight into the recall campaign, the unions sought to postpone the effects of Walker's law as long as possible by extending union contracts. They did so by offering local governments and school districts essentially the same economic concessions that Walker had demanded.

For their part, Madison Teachers Inc., which sparked a four-day job action by teachers statewide with a sickout February 17, responded to the passage of Walker's bill by narrowly ratifying a two-year contract that also included practically all of the economic concessions demanded by Walker. They were under heavy pressure to do so by WEAC, which pushed local teachers unions around the state to extend contracts and delay the impact of Walker's bill by locking in contracts—and dues income.

The argument for making concessions was that it preserved the union for a few years until Democrats could retake control of the state government. Yet it wasn't at all clear that elected officials would take a pro-labor stand. For example, Madison Mayor Dave Cieslewicz, a Democrat who had publicly supported the protests against Walker, didn't hesitate to take advantage of Walker's law by extracting major concessions from AFSCME Local 60, which represents Madison city workers. The deal increases health insurance premiums and implements a 50 percent contribution to retirement benefits in January 2012, and rolls back a pay raise at the end of 2011 from 3 percent to 2 percent. The result: $2.8 million more for the city's budget at workers' expense. The deal, said Cielsewicz, "proves again, [and] I want to underscore this, that collective bargaining works."[64]

Moreover, the recall campaign didn't become a referendum on labor and workers' rights that union leaders had promised. Instead, the issue of collective bargaining rights in the recall elections was side-lined by Republicans and Democrats alike.[65]

Conclusion

Could labor have won in Madison? If you shake off the defeatism of the last decades, step back, and look at the dynamics and potential of the struggle, the answer is clearly yes. A month-long mobilization showed that despite the retreats and atrophy of the unions in what had been long considered a "labor state," there was a rebirth of activism and debate over politics and industrial strategy that involved tens of thousands of Wisconsin workers, and thousands more who came to Madison in solidarity delegations from around the country. The idea of a general strike, usually confined to the pages of labor history books and discussions by socialist and anarchist militants, was suddenly a practical concern, with the SCFL carrying out education and prepara-tion for such an action. The chant of "general strike" was taken up by the thousands who protested in the capitol March 9 when Walker's allies in the legislature suddenly rammed through the collective bar-gaining bill on its own.[66]

Ultimately, union members weren't confident enough in their own capacity and organization to reject concessions. Furthermore, rank-and-file militants were too small in number and were insufficiently organized prior to Walker's attack to be able to turn the struggle back to workplace action when union leaders turned decisively toward the recall strategy. In the 1970s, such networks of militants existed within key industries and unions, and drove strike levels to their highest level since the Second World War, often in defiance of union leaders.[67] As we have seen, this militancy was central to the establishment and growth of public sector unions in Wisconsin. But nearly forty years later, industrial restructuring, a relentless corporate offensive against unions and a demographic transition had all but eliminated such rank-and-file union organization in corporate America. And the decline in union strength in the workplace wasn't unique to the private sector, as

public sector employers mimicked corporate "lean" production tech-
niques in a constant push for greater productivity. The Wisconsin
public sector was not immune from this trend.[68]

The consequences of this long decline in rank-and-file organization were clearly seen in Madison. Nearly four decades later, one of the
lessons of the 1970s—that trade union officialdom is more interested
in institutional self-preservation than taking risky actions to defend the
interests of the rank and file—was made clear once more. For that
reason, organizations such as Kill the Whole Bill/Wisconsin Resists
have attempted to rebuild networks of union militants and dissident
union officials who want to revitalize organized labor on the basis of
class-struggle unionism and broader working-class solidarity. Such
developments will be critical to successful outcomes in the struggles
and inevitable clashes generated by the drive to austerity.

Indeed, despite the shrinkage and debilitation of labor in
Wisconsin, rank-and-file union members showed that they still exercise enormous potential power because of their strategic location at
the point of production. The sickout by teachers in Madison quickly
became a statewide movement carried out by the rank and file and
endorsed by union leaders only after it was already under way.
Without that show of workplace power, it was highly unlikely that all-
night participation in legislative hearings by a few dozen activists
could have morphed into the occupation of the capitol, winning the
active support of private sector workers who were still reeling from the
harsh concessions their unions had accepted.

Without the occupation of the capitol, the Wisconsin labor
struggle also would not have become a broad popular movement that
attracted non-union workers, students, and even small business
owners. And if the capitol hadn't been turned into a round-the-clock
meeting and organizing center, labor would not have been able to sustain the political pressure to keep the fourteen Democratic state senators out of Wisconsin. The sustained occupation made repeated mass
protests possible, making Madison into a mecca for union militants
around the nation. Wisconsin thus became a touchstone for workers
who were searching for both inspiration and strategies for their own

similar struggles, whether against Republican copycat legislation in Ohio, Indiana, and Michigan or against less draconian but still severe attacks on public sector workers by Democratic governors in New York, Illinois, California, and Connecticut.

At the time of writing, some seven months after the last mass labor protest in Madison, it's too soon to draw any definitive conclusions about Madison's immediate impact on labor struggles. However, it was evident that the Wisconsin struggle opened the way to the outpouring of labor support for Occupy Wall Street and Occupy struggles around the U.S., an alliance with great promise for the renewal of a wider working-class resistance to austerity and economic inequality. After a thirty-year anti-union offensive by corporate America and its public sector counterparts, there is at last a two-sided class war.

4—A New American Workers' Movement Has Begun

DAN LA BOTZ

Thousands of workers—sometimes as many as 100,000—demonstrated at the capitol building in Madison during February and March of 2011 to protest plans by that state's Republican Governor Scott Walker to take away the state workers' union rights. The massive protests were accompanied by strikes by Wisconsin school teachers and by the day-and-night occupation of the capitol building by as many as 3,000 workers. Once the movement had begun, hundreds of workers from other states flew in or drove in to join the protests. The United States had not seen such a massive worker uprising in years—indeed, in decades. This was in fact the biggest public and political fight over labor union rights since the Taft-Hartlley Act of 1947.

Walker had cleverly attempted to divide the public workers by excluding police and firefighters from his anti-union law, and the media worked to divide public employees against private sector workers. Yet both firefighters and private sector workers showed up at the statehouse to join public workers of all sorts, and then students and local residents joined as well until a roiling, roaring river of demonstrators, carrying signs and banners, some festooned in union regalia and others in the Wisconsin football fans' cheese-head hats, marched down State Street, and then into and around the capitol. Only California has seen worker demonstrations as large as these in recent years. This was the beginning of a new American workers' movement.

The Wisconsin events gained an added significance because they happened to coincide with the beginning of the democratic revolution sweeping the Arab world. Many demonstrators in Madison, taking a clue from the rebellions against authoritarian and anti-worker governments in the Middle East, carried signs saying, "Let's negotiate like they do in Egypt" and "Walk like an Egyptian." Demonstrators in Cairo's Tahrir Square responded by carrying signs in solidarity with Wisconsin workers. For a moment it seemed as if there was one revolutionary movement stretching from the Nile to Lake Michigan. Though the situation in Madison was hardly comparable to the revolution in the Arab world, what we witnessed in Wisconsin was a working-class upheaval larger than any since the rank-and-file upsurge of the 1970s. Because this movement is so different than what many of us expected, it took us by surprise.

Not What We Expected

Many of us, myself included, had for years expected a rank-and-file workers' movement to arise out of shop-floor struggles in industrial workplaces, out of the fight for union democracy, and out of the process of working-class struggle against the employers. That perspective still has validity, but something different was happening. The new labor movement that arose did not start in the industrial working class (though it will get there soon enough); it did not focus on shop floor issues (though they will no doubt be taken up too); it was not primarily motivated by a desire for union democracy (though it will have to fight for union democracy to push forward the leaders it needs). And it did not, as so many American labor movements of the past did, remain confined to the economic class struggle (though that too will accelerate). It was from the beginning an inherently political labor movement.

The new movement that has arisen does not focus on the usual issues of collective bargaining—working conditions, wages, and benefits—but focuses rather on the political and programmatic issues usually taken up by political parties: the very right of workers to collective bargaining, the priorites of state budgets, and the tax system that funds these budgets. The new labor movement, because it has begun in the public sector, will not be so much about the process of class struggle as it will be about how class struggle finds a voice through political program. This will have tremendous implications for the traditional relations between the organized labor movement and the Democratic Party, especially since the Democrats, from Barack Obama to state governors like New York's Andrew Cuomo and California's Jerry Brown, are also cutting budgets and demanding that public employees give up jobs, wages, benefits, conditions, and rights.

Not Your Grandfather's Working Class

We have for decades in this country thought of the working class as being made up of those who labored on the railroads, in the mines, and in the mills, whose calloused hands produced the material wealth of this nation over two hundred years; that is, since the first factories were opened in the Northeast in the 1790s. Industrial workers have been declining as a percentage of the population since the 1920s, however, and have diminished at an accelerating rate since the 1950s. Since the 1980s the decline of industrial workers as a proportion of the wage-earning class has been dramatic.

In the old days, skilled workers, almost all white men, came as immigrants to the United States from Western and Northern Europe, whereas unskilled industrial workers immigrated from Southern and Eastern Europe. Southern whites came North from Appalachia, as did African Americans from the South's plantations. Though most of those industrial workers were male, millions of women also toiled in textile mills, garment shops, and other workplaces. Those workers created the Knights of Labor in 1869, the American Federation of Labor (AFL) in 1886, the Industrial Workers of the World (IWW) in 1905, and finally, in the great labor upsurge of the 1930s, when they won the legal right to organize with the Wagner Act of 1935, built the Congress of Industrial Organizations (CIO).

Since the 1950s, however, the industrial working class that had been at the core of those labor movements has been in decline. The key factor in the decline of the American working class as a social force has been above all the dramatic reduction in the size and weight of industrial workers; that is, those engaged in manufacturing. The industrial working class includes construction workers, electric power and other utility workers, warehousemen, dockworkers, and truck drivers—altogether about 20 percent of the U.S. working class—but at its core is the factory worker. Factory workers, because they produce commodities for sale on the market and are concentrated in great numbers, have economic power unlike any other group of workers. Though manufacturing employment has been declining as a percentage of all employment since the 1920s, it was the period of deindustrialization and runaway shops in the 1970s and 1980s that marked the most significant decline. The new balance between manufacturing, services, and public employment began to fundamentally reshape American capitalism and the working class.

The manufacturing worker core had been declining for some time, a result of both new technology and offshoring, and now its decline had become precipitous. The statistics tell the story. In 1960 out of a total non-farm workforce of 54,274,000, there were 15,687,000 manufacturing workers, representing 29 percent of the total. By 2009 out of a total of 134,333,000 non-farm workers, there were only 12,640,000 in manufacturing, representing only 9 percent of the total. That is, manufacturing workers fell in the last fifty years from almost one-third of all workers to less than 10 percent.

Manufacturing workers, especially those in heavy industries such as steel, auto, rubber, glass, and electrical industries, had been among the most highly unionized workers in the country. These industrial workers often had higher wages than other workers, even those in professions like teaching, in health care, or in services. The industrial shakeouts and manufacturing relocation to the South or offshore, together with lean production's speed-up, devastated the unions, reducing union density and weakening union power. In 1973, 38.8 percent of manufacturing workers were in unions; by 1979 that percentage had fallen to 32.3; by 1990 it was only 20.6 percent; and by 1995 just 17.6 percent.

The Rise of Service and Public Sector Workers

The postwar period saw two related employment trends develop: the growth of the service sector and the rise in public sector employment. Millions found jobs not only in streets and sanitation and at the water works, but also as teachers and social workers, public health nurses, and college professors. Some former industrial workers, young workers entering the workforce and immigrants, found other jobs, particularly in the private service sector. Once again, the statistics tell the story. In 1960 there were 26,476,000 service workers or 44 percent out of a total non-farm workforce of 54,274,000. By 2009 they numbered 91,666,000 or 68 percent of a total workforce of 134,333,000. That is, in half a century service workers went from making up less than half of the workforce to constituting more than two-thirds of the workforce. The change was important.

The growth in public employees led to a another labor upsurge in the 1960s and 1970s with the establishment and rapid growth of public employee unions of all sorts: the American Federation of Teachers (AFT), the National Education Association (NEA), the American Federation of State County and Municipal Employees (AFSCME), and the American Federation of Government Employees (AFGE). Wisconsin was in fact the first state to win public employee collective bargaining in 1959. These public workers were far more racially and gender diverse than many of the private sector unions, with relatively more African American, Latino, and women workers. Public employees in the 1960s and 1970s won the right to union recognition, collective bargaining, and the strike through hundreds of strikes, large and small, during those two decades. The front page of newspapers often carried the photo of some teacher or social worker, nurse or secretary, sanitation worker or park employee being carried off to jail for striking with the union. The most famous of these strikes, perhaps, was the AFSCME Local 1733 strike by African American sanitation workers in Memphis in 1968. Dr. Martin Luther King Jr., by then the outsanding leader of the civil rights movement, brought national attention to that strike shortly before he was assassinated.

The public sector continued to expand throughout the latter half of the twentieth century and into the twenty-first. Public administration workers—government clerks, welfare workers, police officers, and many others—numbered 8.0 million in 2006. Health and education employed 19 million workers. In education there are over 4 million preschool, kindergarten, elementary school, middle school, and secondary school teachers (excluding special education). Health care work (not all done by public workers) was designated the largest industry in the country, providing 14 million jobs—13.6 million jobs for wage and salary workers and about 438,000 jobs for the self-employed.

As the public sector expanded, so did its unions. Building on the foundation laid by the strikes and organizing campaigns of the late 1960s and early 1970s, public sector workers came to represent the most unionized sector of the working class. In 2008, unions represented only 7.6 percent of workers in the private sector, but they represented 36.8 percent of public sector workers. Though many states in the South and West denied some or all public employees the right to organize, bargain or strike, from the 1970s to today public employees have been the most dynamic, fasting growing, and now largest sector of unionized workers, larger than the private sector. Yet because of the nature of public employment they do not have the same leverage as the private sector unions once did.

Public workers' power is different than that of manufacturing workers. Manufacturing workers have power because their labor produces the commodities sold in the marketplace that generate the profit that enriches the corporations. The manufacturing workers' power exists at the point of production, in the concentrated numbers of the huge workforce of the factory, and in the organization of that force in the union with its capacity to strike. Service workers might provide important services of various sorts, but their work is less central to the production of commodities and wealth in a capitalist society. Consequently, service workers often, though not always, receive lower wages and fewer benefits than industrial workers.

Public sector workers have a weaker position than private sector workers not only for economic reasons but also because of social expectations and legal restrictions. Public workers provide public services, often essential services, and consequently public workers might hesitate to strike. Medical workers reluctantly strike because a work stoppage may affect patients; teachers may hesitate to affect children and parents; water workers recognize the essential nature of the service they provide to all. Moreover, an ethic of professionalism and sense of status may inhibit some public employees. And, if they do strike, the result is often that they save their employers money since while on strike they are not paid. And they cannot take personal or sick days or accumulate time toward vacations while on strike.

In legal terms, even before the current wave of attacks, most public employees did not enjoy the same basic labor union rights as workers in the private sector, and could be denied the right to strike or have their collective bargaining rights limited. Since they form part of large government bureaucracies, bargaining for public sector workers tends to take place in the public arena and in the city, state, or federal legislatures, usually under the pressure of clients, public advocacy groups, and political parties as well as labor unions. Yet public workers also have some important advantages. Public employee unions, unlike most private sector workers, have opportunities and the necessity to form worker-client or union-community alliances that can give them a natural political platform that private sector workers do not necessarily have.

The Labor Movement at a Turning Point

Today we in the labor movement are at a turning point. American employers, political parties, and government at all levels have decided that the time has come to move against what is the last bulwark of American unionism: the public employee unions. Right-wing foundations, employers associations, the Republican Party, and its Tea Party right wing understand the vulnerability of the American labor movement, and have decided to make a move to reduce the unions to irrelevance.

To understand just how vulnerable we are, and why public employee unions are the target, we need only look at the statistics. Only 11.9 percent of all workers belonged to a union in 2010. In the private sector only 6.9 percent of workers have unions, while 36.2 percent of public employees had unions. In 2010 there were only eleven strikes or lockouts involving 1,000 or more workers, while in 1970 there were 270 such large strikes. Most American workers have never participated in a union, a strike, or a protest demonstration—but among the most active unions of the last thirty years have been the public workers' organizations. The goal of conservatives is to weaken and ideally to eliminate public employee unions which today constitute the majority of unionized American workers.

Behind this effort are wealthy businessmen, right-wing think tanks, and conservative legislators. Two industrialists, David and Charles Koch, have financed much of the effort to destroy public employee unions through their contributions to think tanks such as Americans for Prosperity, the Cato Institute, the Competitive Enterprise Institute, the Reason Foundation, and the Republic Governors Association. The Kochs were also big contributors to Governor Scott Walker of Wisconsin, who spearheaded the attack on public workers' unions.

The right-wing think tanks developed the arguments against public employee unions that were taken up by Fox, CNN, and the rest of the corporate media. The argument was made that American government at all levels faced a budget crisis and the only way to meet the crisis was to cut taxes. Taxpayers were thus pitted against public employees who worked too little, earned too much, and had "Cadillac" health plans. Schoolteachers in particular were targeted as responsible for many of the nation's ills. Playing upon public anxiety during the economic crisis, the media promoted a politics of resentment between private sector workers and public employees. Yet when Scott Walker pushed the attack on public employee unions in Wisconsin, they found surprising resistance.

Wisconsin: A Unique History

Wisconsin, like many midwestern states, has a historic tension between its liberal large cities and its conservative rural hinterlands. Politically it has alternated between reactionaries like Republican Senator Joseph McCarthy, the notorious anticommunist witch hunter, and liberals like today's liberal Democratic Senator Russ Feingold. Besides the alternation of right-wing Republicans and left-wing Democrats is a profound history of a progressive, socialist, and labor movement. In the more distant past, Wisconsin in the 1910s was both the center of the Progressive movement and a stronghold of the Socialist Party. Milwaukee had a Socialist mayor until 1960. And, as already mentioned, Wisconsin was the first state to grant collective bargaining rights to public employees in 1959.

Modern Madison during the 1960s and early 1970s had been the scene of enormous antiwar protests by University of Wisconsin students. Many current residents of Wisconsin grew up taking part in those demonstrations and never gave up the notion that there was power in the streets. Many subsequently found jobs in Madison at the university or working for state, county, or city government, and they raised their children and grandchildren in a liberal and radical ethos. Wisconsin has also always had independent political parties, from the Farmer-Labor parties of the 1920s to the Progressive Dane and Green Party today. Given this history of mass protest and political independence, when Walker and his Republican legislators pushed their anti-union agenda, they met with a massive popular reaction by unions and their allies. America's political and economic elite had been looking for the final solution to the labor problem—but discovered that in Wisconsin they were not getting on the trains and going to the camps.

The New Workers' Movement Faces the Old

When in mid-February Walker attempted to push his anti-union legislation through the Wisconsin legislature, threatening the collective bargaining rights, the right to strike, and the very existence of unions, he set into motion a tremendous upheaval from below. Local labor public employee unions, joined by the entire labor movement and then by students and the capital's residents, created for a week or two a movement that almost completely escaped the higher levels of the union officialdom. With their union's backing teachers called in sick and later struck the schools. Students and parents marched in support of their teachers. Workers, students, and townspeople engaged in radical tactics of confrontation that shattered the complacency of decades and captured the imaginations of union members and workers throughout the country. Unions with large African American memberships and Latino organizations in Milwaukee sent delegations to swell the numbers in demonstrations. Unions around the country sent members in a show of solidarity, including an entire planeload from the Los Angeles teachers' union.

Feeling a sense of power and at the same time a need for greater force if they were to defeat Walker and the Republicans, Madison's South Central Federation of Labor put the issue of a general strike on the table. The *Capitol Times* asked "Could a General Strike Happen Here?" and answered that it seemed possible. Yet, as became clear, the consciousness, sense of solidarity, organization, and will to risk a fight were not there. Key groups like teachers and firefighters declined the challenge, and many private sector workers had not yet come to see the public employees fight as their own. Nor had African American workers and Latino immigrants come to see the public employees' fight as their own. The raising of the prospect of a general strike, however, affected the consciousness of the strike activists and leaders, leading them to explore just how far they could push the resistance.

Yet, within a week, the AFL-CIO, the Service Employees International Union, the national leadership of AFSCME, and the AFT were sending national leaders and staff to attempt to take control of the movement and channel it into political action and support for the Democratic Party. While some union officials in Madison, including local leaders of the AFL-CIO, talked about expanding the strike action of the teachers and even talked about the possibility of a general strike, most upper-level union officials worked to put the brakes on the movement. Union officials worked to get protesters out of the capitol building, while at the crucial moment the teachers' union leader told teachers to get back to work.

From Mass Movement to Union Mobilization

Union officials, working with the Democratic Party, channeled much of the Wisconsin movement's energy into a recall effort. Union members were organized to circulate petitions to recall Republican state legislators in order to change the balance of power in the legislature by electing Democrats. Similarly, in Ohio, where there was no such upheaval from below, the labor bureaucracy and the Democratic Party succeeded in channeling the movement into circulating referendum petitions to put Republic Governor John Kasich's even more draconian anti-union legislation on the ballot in November. In other states, too, the Democratic Party and union leaders saw this as an opportunity to rebuild their faltering fortunes and to reconstruct a base for President Barack Obama before the 2012 presidential elections.

Uncomfortable with the direct action of militant workers and students, with that roiling river of protest, Democrats worked to direct it into the calm canals that irrigate the Democratic Party's fields, a political countryside already well manured by the Republicans. While it was no doubt important to turn out the Republican legislators, the

strategy ignored the fact that around the country Democratic legislators are also working to cut public employee budgets and to reduce
public employee bargaining rights. The union officials hoped to go
back to the past of collective bargaining rights and Democratic Party
politicians in power, forgetting that it was just that past that delivered
them to Scott Walker.

Though the union officials and Democratic Party politicians may
hope to control the new American workers movement in this way, they
may inadvertently be setting in motion forces that will grow beyond
their grasp. Certainly in Wisconsin, there were thousands of activists
within the labor movement circulating those recall petitions who,
having experienced the Madison rebellion, know the power of the
strike, of direct action, of confrontation with authority, and of winning
over their friends and neighbors, of winning public opinion. In Ohio,
thousands of workers circulated referendum petitions and gathered an
astounding 1.3 million signatures—several times more than necessary—to put Kasich's anti-union law on the ballot. Though they circulated petitions in 2011, these workers will be looking in the future not
only to change the political balance of power in the narrow electoral
sense, but also to change the balance of power in the social and economic sense. If they succeed in recalling the Republicans and electing
Democrats, they will expect to do more than go back to the past. They
will be looking for a different future.

Meeting the Movement Where It's At

The fundamental axiom of all grassroots organizing is that organizers
and political activists must meet the movement where it's at. For those
of us on the labor left that means recognizing that we have a new level
of social and political consciousness among tens of thousands of
workers in Wisconsin, Ohio, and other states throughout the Midwest
and around the country. The right-wing attack on union and workers'
rights has created a solidarity consciousness and a defensive fight that
for now, under the control of the labor bureaucracy, is flowing into the

channels of the Democratic Party. What is important is that for the first time in forty years workers have been mobilized by their unions to resist and many of them want not only to resist but to fight back, regain old ground, and take new ground. The Wisconsin uprising, a genuine mass movement from below, whetted the appetite of thousands of workers for a fight against the right, and has opened the door to more radical developments.

This is not the first labor upheaval in American history. What does the history of the labor movement teach us about such events? First, we know that when masses of workers go into motion, as they have begun to do, political consciousness grows and changes rapidly. Workers who today simply fight to defend their union rights will, if they succeed in resisting the right's attempt to destroy them, go on to fight to expand not only their rights but to improve their working conditions and standard of living. Most important, workers will fight to expand their power. We are just at the beginning.

Second, when workers discover the strategy and tactics of their movement, those quickly spread to other groups of workers in society. When the rubber workers in Akron, Ohio, discovered the sit-down strike in 1936, it quickly spread to the auto industry leading to the great strikes of 1937 and '38. Remarkably, the sit-down also spread to such unlikely workers as the "shop girls" of department stores. During the 1950s and early 1960s, African American civil rights activists rediscovered the power of the sit-down, transforming it into the sit-in at lunch counters, bus stations, and other private and public places across the South.

The public workers of Wisconsin found strategies and tactics to defend their rights, such as the mass rallies and the campouts at the capitol. Having discovered such strategies and tactics they quickly spread like wildfire across the country. Within a year we had the Occupy Wall Street movement, then Occupy America, and by October 2011 a day of global action in support.

Third, real labor movements ignore the artificial separation between the economic and the political, taking up either or both as they follow the logic of the struggle. Industrial workers' struggles for higher wages in the 1930s were transformed into struggles for the employers' recognition of the unions and labor legislation granting workers the right to organize. Public employees in the 1960s on the other hand, fought for the right to unions and collective bargaining, which led in turn to more fights for higher wages and better conditions. What is today primarily a political fight in Wisconsin—that is, a fight to defend the right of public employees to have a labor union, bargain collectively, and strike—will inevitably become a struggle for better conditions, higher wages, and health and pension benefits.

Fourth, when a real labor movement arises, that is, a movement not merely of thousands or even tens of thousands but millions, it necessarily becomes transformative. Labor union officials who hesitate, who waver, or who knuckle under will soon find themselves challenged by new, younger leaders who will either force those officials to fight or push them aside. Such a movement will change the unions— often by changing the leadership first and sometime by changing the very institutions themselves. Such was the case with the rise of the industrial workers' movement in the 1930s, which broke the shell of the old AFL to create the new CIO.

A Political Alternative

Fifth, and finally, the labor movement has been repeatedly challenged over the decades to create a political expression, to create a party of working people. Soon a new American labor movement of millions will be forced to challenge the old political relationship between the unions and the Democratic Party. The unions will fight at first to force the Democratic Party to give up its own conservative budget, tax, and labor policies, and failing to do that will seek another vehicle. Unions may first attempt to change the Democrats by running union candidates in Democratic Party primaries, or they may attempt to take over the state party. Whether the new American labor movement will have the power to put forward a political alternative remains to be seen.

As already mentioned, Wisconsin has a long history of political groupings to the left of the Democratic Party, which, from time to time, have shown considerable influence: the Socialist Party held power in Milwaukee into the 1960s, the Farmer-Labor Party was once a power in the state, Progressive Dane (county) continues to thrive, and the Wisconsin Green Party has over a score of elected officials throughout the state. Though none of these had or has exactly what a workers' movement needs to achieve real political power, the presence of such political alternatives is indicative of a more tolerant and experimental attitude in that state. American workers have never in their history succeeded in creating a workers' party of any power, with the exception of the Socialist Party of the early twentieth century.

Today, with the Democrats lowering taxes on the rich, cutting budgets, and laying off public employees, we may be in for the kind of confrontation between workers and a pro-business Democratic Party that can produce a political alternative. Certainly the struggle over politics and government is directly built into this contest, as it seldom is in the private sector. We on the labor left should be involved in this fight at every level, from circulating the recall petitions in Wisconsin and the referendum petitions in Ohio, to rebuilding union consciousness in the workplace, to pointing out the opportunities for independent political action. The Wisconsin uprising has opened a path to rebuild the American labor movement, and now our goal must be to turn that path into a road forward.

5—The Wisconsin Uprising

FRANK EMSPAK

Describing the Wisconsin Uprising may be like the parable of the blind man and the elephant. There are many valid perspectives. Teasing them apart may diminish the whole, but to understand the extent and the depth of the uprising, we need to have some perspective to understand the actors. To continue the parable a bit further, the uprising was so unexpected that the blind man would have been trampled by the elephant had he arrived in Madison on Monday, February 14, 2011.

We look at the Madison Uprising from that of a news organization producing daily accounts of the events and from the perspective of a union activist. As producers of news, we at Workers' Independent News, a producer and broadcaster of news focused on the issues and concerns of working people, were driven by the day-to-day demands for coverage. From the labor point of view, we could see a growing institutional presence of organized labor, as more and more labor leaders came to speak, and especially as we saw certain infrastructural support: stages, sound systems, and the growing participation of national leaders. The uprising dwarfed any previous experience in Madison, Wisconsin, and in size and spirit rivaled anything since the march for Jobs and Freedom in Washington in 1963.

As the demonstrations grew in size, many characterized the labor movement as a sleeping giant awakened at last. (Revising this essay in July causes me to be less comfortable with that assessment than I was in May when I first composed this essay.) But is this really the case? Was the giant asleep, and if so, how long will it take for the giant to tone up for the fight? And what kind of fight will it be? Has the awakening giant decided to move beyond the usual, if reinvigorated, paths or is there a growing consensus among leaders that a new or additional path of shop floor resistance is in order? And if so, what intellectual and organizational resources are being mobilized to build that type of resistance?

Before trying to answer these questions, two points must be made. First, Wisconsin workers and, in fact, all public sector wage earners are on the spot, facing a fall in disposable income due to increases in pension and health care contributions and deteriorating working conditions. Pay increases (if any) are less than inflation and are often in the form of one-time bonuses, which are not added to base pay. Second, the state has now put in place measures that will worsen the circumstances of public employees. For example, at the time of this writing, the state has begun to issue employee handbooks. The handbook will specify how management will deal with workplace issues, but assuming it is consistent with the new restrictions on collective bargaining, it will not contain a meaningful and enforceable set of worker protections or dispute resolution procedures.

The Background

In November 2010, after a lackluster political campaign by Democrats, Wisconsin voters surprised the labor movement and the Democratic Party by awarding Republicans control of the state senate and assembly, the U.S. Senate, and the governor's office. There is much more to this story than can be discussed here, but Wisconsin voters did not so much choose a conservative agenda as vote on other issues—and in great numbers stay home. In the well-organized Republican gubernatorial campaign, candidate Walker emphasized budget problems and an attack on the federal government, especially funds for high-speed rail designated for Wisconsin. He did not focus on, hardly mentioned, employee or union rights. Voter turnout was far below that of 2008, especially among younger more progressive voters, many of whom had become de-energized or disenchanted by the national political scene. Closer to home, many did not see much of a difference between the Democratic gubernatorial candidate and the Republicans. To put it another way, there was not a convincing alternative narrative to job cuts and budget problems put forth by the Democrats. The task was made more difficult because Democratic candidate Tom Barrett had, as mayor of Milwaukee, pursued a similar strategy. So a combination of a stealth campaign, disillusionment, and lack of clear alternatives led to a Republican victory. The two-party system, which maximizes the impact of relatively small voter preferences, functioned as usual in this case. Small individual Republican victories in several state senatorial districts added up to overwhelming Republican control of both houses of the state legislature.

At the statewide level, in spite of poor campaigning by the Democratic candidate and the impediments mentioned above, Republican Scott Walker won by a relatively narrow margin— about 3 percent. To put that in perspective, Russ Feingold, running for the U.S. Senate, won every county except the conservative Waukesha county next to Milwaukee—thus losing the race. Organized labor backed all the losers. Its political eggs were all in one basket. On the other side, it became clear that the conservative wing of the Republican Party had energized its base. Now, the antiunion and anti-working-class bias was to be given free rein.

The Wisconsin legislature was deeply divided before the election, with the Democratic majority in the assembly shaky and the senate almost evenly divided (under Democratic control but only by one vote). So a minor political shift was magnified by the winner-take-all system and did not reflect a substantial political shift on the ground in Wisconsin.

These intricacies are crucial to public sector bargaining. The legislature acts as the decider of last resort, voting to accept or reject the tentative agreements that are the fruits of negotiations between the unions and the state. In Wisconsin, the Joint Finance Committee—composed of leaders of the assembly and senate—ultimately decide on the state budget and the financial portion of the collective bargaining agreements. This committee acts as the employer, and thus a small shift in control of the legislature can have drastic consequences for working people in negotiations conducted by the Office of State Employment Relations (OSER). Since the financial portions of the collective bargaining are ultimately decided by the legislature, the unions, in effect, become lobbying organizations. Of course, the state legislature determines the content of the State Employment Relations Act, the Municipal Employment Relations Act, and the various amendments that recognize union rights for Teaching Assistants at the University of Wisconsin (mid-1970s) and Faculty and Academic staff system-wide in 2009. Contracts covering the current biennium are not in place when the biennium begins, which in Wisconsin is July 1. The political year begins on January 1. The senate and assembly Joint Finance Committee usually determines the shape of the budget in May and June, and then the entire budget is voted on prior to the beginning of the biennium. This dual system has operated for years, even with administration changes. In October 2010, the contracts covering the 2009–11 biennium had not yet been approved by the senate and assembly. It was assumed by most observers that the negotiated agreements would soon be approved, prior to the election, or, failing that, immediately afterward but before the terms ended for the then current members of the assembly and senate, which prior to the elections had been controlled by Democrats.

However, the entire system was upended, not initially by Scott Walker but by senate Democratic leader Russ Decker.

Immediately after the election returns were announced, it became clear that the all branches of the government were in hostile Republican hands. Public sector labor leaders insisted that the senate act on the pending contracts—ratify them and send them on to outgoing Democratic Governor Doyle for signature. In other words, implement the usual system, now delayed for months. Getting the job done was more urgent than ever as it became clear that incoming Governor Walker was focusing his budget offensive on state workers.

All of a sudden, in late November, Russ Decker—the vote needed to keep control of the senate—announced that he would not support the contracts and resigned as the senate majority leader. With the senate tied, the vote to approve the new contracts failed. State workers continued to work under the old contracts, which had expired on June 30, 2009. No new contract was in place. Even if one was in place, it would expire on June 30, 2011. Negotiations for the 2011–13 contract needed to begin immediately if there was to be any chance of a timely agreement.

In effect, unless the governor decided to continue to extend the old contract, most state workers would in effect have no contract. Municipal and country workers had separate agreements and were not initially affected.

Democrats were embarrassed, and rank-and-file workers were disgruntled. But the enormity of the attack on working people was not yet clear. However, starting in mid-December 2010, Scott Walker began to clarify his political agenda. Even so, most labor leaders, though deeply concerned, believed that negotiations were still possible, albeit under hostile and difficult circumstances. To that end, state employee unions led by AFSCME and supported by AFT Wisconsin announced that they were prepared to make substantial concessions equal to the budget shortfall predicted by the governor. Thus, in theory, and based on past experience, this offer by the unions to match the $140 million shortfall would pave the way for a negotiated settlement and further negotiations for the coming biennium. Meanwhile, the Wisconsin Education Association Council, the largest public sector union, representing the greatest percentage of K-12 teachers and support staff, also announced that it was ready to encourage discussions, putting in play the issues identified by Walker, especially the organization of the Milwaukee public school system. On Monday February 7, Mary Bell, president of WEAC, made a dramatic appeal to this effect, surprising some of the local WEAC leadership with its scope and her determination to meet the Republican leadership halfway. The governor responded with a simple statement: "No negotiation." Even at this late date, many in leadership believed that negotiations and lobbying would work. Although the governor was clearly hostile to unions, he had not made public his desire to eliminate collective bargaining and destroy meaningful worker representation in the workplace and in the political system.

At the same time the governor was moving on his budget repair bill (a move to fix the budget shortfall), he had begun to target the University of Wisconsin system. He moved adroitly to split the system, with the elite Madison campus moved increasingly toward a privatized vision. In this, he was supported actively by the chancellor, Biddy Martin, and passively by many leading professors at UW in Madison. As it turned out, he had met privately with the chancellor at about the time of the election. Neither the president of the UW system nor the boards of regents were prepared to support the splitting of the system. The Teaching Assistants Association (TAA), the most politically mobilized of all the players, opposed the restructuring of the system and the proposed cuts in the budget. The TAA is affiliated with the AFT-Wisconsin and is a recognized national leader of graduate assistants' unions.

Valentine's Day 2011: A Wisconsin Massacre

The Teaching Assistants Association began its mobilization against budget cuts independently of the political maneuvering. Their contract was in place, but the key to it was the UW budget, as ultimately the number of teaching assistants, tuition remission, and other issues are directly impacted by the UW budget. The TAAs planned a Valentine's Day campaign titled "You Broke My Heart," referring to the proposed budget cuts and aimed at the governor. The TAA planned to deliver hundreds of Valentine's Day cards to the governor on Monday, February 14, but as Humphrey Bogart said in *Casablanca*, "It looks like fate took a hand."

On Thursday, February 10, news began to leak out that the governor planned major institutional changes as part of his so-called budget repair bill. Repair bills are a means of balancing the budget for the remainder of the fiscal year and, in theory, are not where major policy changes are proposed. In a radical move, the governor proposed the evisceration of public sector unions as the means to fix the budget.

While many in the labor union leadership had been expecting attacks on pensions, health care, and work rules, few, if any, expected an attack on the institution of collective bargaining itself, or on the idea of trade unionism itself. But the legislation proposed was designed to render unions ineffective at the workplace and eliminate them as major political players as well.

On Friday February 11, public sector union leadership began to reevaluate the situation. WEAC, which earlier in the week proffered an olive branch (some said the whole tree), to the governor, canceled its press briefings on their offer and met to reconsider.

The TAA, meanwhile, with its mobilization already planned, went ahead. Graduate assistants and their supporters made cards and posters and planned to deliver their cards to the governor at the capitol sometime on the Monday afternoon of Valentine's Day.

However, Valentine's Day turned out to be another thing altogether. Instead of a demonstration of a few hundred in support of the higher education budget, hundreds and then thousands began to gather at the capitol. Many were union members, but at least as many were there not as union members per se but because they were upset with what they saw as an assault on working people. The number of people coming to the capitol, primarily on their own initiative, was unprecedented.

The outpouring was completely unexpected. Just as state union leadership was surprised, so were all kinds of political experts. No one expected an attack on the system of collective bargaining or the existence of unions, and no one expected the response—an uprising of historic proportions.

But on this first day, the organized labor movement was not giving direction; it was seeking to figure out a legal and political response to the governor's steamroller tactics. People were mobilizing themselves, sparked by the TAA's decision to stay in the capitol rotunda and watch over the legislature. As Monday wore on, they were joined by hundreds and then thousands of people, and as the evening ended, it became clear that many had no intention of leaving the building. It became the people's house.

News reporters began to realize that something unprecedented was afoot. Monday afternoon, hundreds of high school students left their school, not in Madison, but in the working-class suburb of Stoughton, twenty miles away. They came to the capitol. These students and the thousands who joined them from high schools around the state were not simply protesting; they came to rally for a better society—a new vision. Many eloquently expressed this in interviews captured by Madison's community radio station, WORT, and by Workers Independent News. Together, both organizations provided a platform for the students, and thus their voices were heard all over the country and abroad. The students were joined by the teachers. Students had come in part to support their teachers, although they were not led by them.

By Tuesday afternoon, private sector trade unions had joined in. Building trades' workers were clearly in evidence—the crowd was sprinkled with them wearing their union jackets. They too came to the people's house. People came unbidden by anyone, perhaps because they felt that, at last, it was time to stand up. People wanted to stand up for something—union rights, decency, and better way of doing things. One sign said "Walk Like an Egyptian," referring to the then ongoing uprising in Egypt.

For the first time in at least a generation, the non-union people who came to the capitol saw the physical presence of unionized workers—their neighbors—standing up for union rights, proud and not talking about concessions. Throughout the first few days, as thousands were in the capitol building and additional thousands were marching around it, one saw ironworkers, sheet metal workers, plumbers, electrical union members, and teamsters with their big trailer trucks. The effect on the public was incredible, but it was soon dwarfed by the principled and outspoken leadership of the firefighters, who brought their bagpipes. The sound of the bagpipes meant the firefighters were there, and it gave those occupying the capitol a huge psychological lift. Most observers believe that the presence of the firefighters and the positive effect their presence had on the various police organizations prevented the governor from attacking the citizens rallying in the capitol and around it.

At this stage of the uprising, that is, during the first few days, saying that organized labor led the movement goes too far. The labor movement was supplying the infrastructure, platforms, sound equipment, and sleeping bags. As the state's challenge to the capitol occupiers became more vicious, the labor movement provided the funds for legal challenges and lawyers to fight for restraining orders, preventing the immediate eviction of the citizens from the capitol.[1] Once the governor succeeded in passing the legislation, the AFL-CIO and the NEA entered court on both state and federal levels to challenge the immediate implementation of the laws. Those legal challenges are still ongoing, and did, for a time, prevent implementation of the most onerous parts of the legislation—but that was all in the future.

Labor leaders at the state and national level increasingly made their presence felt. At the start of the week, many spoke in terms of lobbying the legislature. Others spoke about defending the middle-class standard of living. Few used the term "working class." The basic line was that Republicans were attacking the basis of American values—a stable middle class and the ability to govern via respect for the opposition, which implied the need to compromise. The Republicans would have none of this. They acted as one, making it clear there was no interest in compromise and that money was not the issue; it was the destruction of workers' rights.

During that first week, we saw and felt the power of working people. Workers had slowed the machine and for a moment disabled it. The presence of thousands of outraged citizens gave the senate Democrats the political support and space they needed to take direct action. On Thursday afternoon, February 17, senate Democrats left the state, thereby denying the senate the ability to have the two-thirds quorum necessary to pass fiscal legislation.

By the end of the first week, that is, by February 21, the giant was awake. Thousands had come to Madison, and rallies attended by 25,000 to 50,000 took place. Observers thought they would not see such big rallies again. But the question then, and now, is to what effect?

During that first weekend, after an appeal to members to gather at the capitol on Thursday and Friday, WEAC staff and volunteers called all 93,000 members, alerting them to the dangerous laws, telling them not to strike, and asking them to come to Madison the next weekend. Teachers belonging to Madison Teachers Inc. (the WEAC affiliate) had been out of school since Wednesday because the superintendent closed the schools. They did not return to work until Tuesday, due to a holiday. Later, when the union was challenged in court, the judge found that MTI had not called a strike in violation of state law. As the week came to a close, other unions began mobilizing, first for the immediate weekend and then for the second weekend. However, unions were careful not to advocate strikes or disruptions at the workplace.

Mass demonstrations and mobilizations are one thing. But what to do if the political leadership of the state determines that they are not interested in negotiations? What to do if it finally becomes clear that the governor and his political allies will use state power to crush you?

During the height of the rallies, more and more people, union and non-union, began to understand this challenge. On Thursday, February 17, after tumultuous hearings on the legislation, the Republicans gaveled them to a close. People refused to leave. Democrats continued the hearings until exhaustion set in at about 4 a.m. People attempted to testify and stayed all night.

Democratic legislators left the state to prevent a quorum, which was needed to pass the fiscal legislation with the anti-collective bargaining language. But they also left because they felt the Republican tactics of truncated hearings constituted a denial of legislative due process. This assessment was borne out as the year has progressed. Republicans have rushed through legislation designed by ALEC to limit voter rights, destroy environmental laws, and undermine civil service.

Many trade union leaders were still enraged by the Russ Decker incident and the continuing silence of former governor Doyle. Trade unionists were also increasingly dismayed by the silence from the Obama administration. When the senate Democrats left the state, this direct action demonstrated to them that Democrats were finally acting like Democrats. Thus, the basic political strategy of the trade union movement—alliance with the Democratic Party—was at last justified, at least on the state level.

After another week or so of futile attempts to get Republican state senators to peel away from the governor and vote against the bill, more and more citizens began talking about recall. Spurred on by independent citizens' actions to get a recall and the failure of the inside strategy, organized labor enthusiastically provided essential logistical and financial support for the recall efforts.

How much support labor provided is, as of this writing, increasingly clear. Labor and its allies spent approximately twenty million dollars to fund advertising plus untold hours of volunteer time. But working in a broad coalition, organized as a political action committee called "We Are Wisconsin," millions of dollars have been spent on media buys. According to the Wisconsin State Government Accounting Board, almost $7.9 million had been spent by We Are Wisconsin as of mid-July, a month before the recall elections. Thousands of hours were devoted to signature gathering and door knocking. While some of these tasks were done by paid staff on leave from other duties, the vast majority were done by union and community volunteers. For each Republican senator facing recall, at least 25,000 signatures had to be collected. This was achieved, and in most cases with thousands of signatures to spare. The large number of signatures for recall in what were Republican majority voting districts indicates the tremendous anger on the part of working people and their desire to get rid of the Republicans and, perhaps, Scott Walker. Judging from numerous interviews, signers are concerned by much more than the destruction of collective bargaining. There is a sense that the way the administration governs is not what is done here in Wisconsin. People expressed the view that the conduct of the governor and legislature was uncivil and insulting and thus not commensurate with the way Wisconsinites conduct business.

This type of concentrated and well-organized political work, though radical compared with politics as usual, was still completely within the normal two-party paradigm of political action. In a sense, it was a typical voter ID and registration effort, coming with challenging deadlines but on a scale commensurate with the level of presidential politics. In Wisconsin, presidential campaigns means hundreds of volunteers, financially resourced campaigns, and coordination often coming from paid consultants or Washington and not from the indigenous groups mobilized for the campaigns.

The support and concentration of the labor movement in the recall campaigns are also an indication of how invested organized labor is in the recall effort. All the political eggs are in this basket.

The goal was to win a net gain of three senate seats. A win of three seats would allow Democrats to control the senate. Then, they could block anti-working people bills. Control of the senate would, in and of itself, not change the laws already in effect. And in the meantime, the administration was working as fast as possible to pass legislation restricting voting, redistricting the assembly and senate seats, and limiting various green initiatives. The governor's goal was to enshrine institutional changes in legislation prior to the possible loss of the senate. So far, this successful offensive means that the Democrats will need to take back the assembly, the senate, and the governor's mansion, and maintain a high level of unity, just to repeal the legislation recently passed to return to the situation prior to Election Day 2010.

The results of the recalls on August 16, while impressive, did not accomplish all that was hoped. Two senators were recalled, one short of the number needed for Democrats to control the senate. However, newspaper comments the next day indicated that, given the slender majority, moderate Republicans would have more influence than before because they might need to cater to some Democrats.

For the state Democratic Party to accomplish this means that it will have to distinguish itself from the more pro-corporate, deficit-focused leadership of the national Democratic Party and mobilize working-class voters to vote Democratic when they are increasingly upset with the president.

There are many "ifs" in this scenario, which brings us back to what organized labor will do, in both the workplace and the political arena, now that the balance of power in the senate will remain Republican.

By the third week in February, it was clear to most rank-and-file participants and increasingly to labor leaders that massive demonstrations and legislative maneuvers could delay but probably not stop the passage of anti-union measures. However, the massive size of the demonstrations did send a message. More than 150,000 people came to Madison on two separate occasions. Such an outpouring of energy, anger, and a demand for change had never been experienced. Union members were clearly in evidence. No one could mistake the fact that thousands of union members had missed work and come to Madison, and though they came from all over the country, they came mostly from all corners of the state. For some, that meant a four- or five-hour drive in the Wisconsin winter. For example, on one day in question, when the temperature hit a high of about 20 degrees, a group of boilermakers came down from the northern tip of Wisconsin on Lake Michigan. Most of that day's demonstration was in the cold outdoors, across the street from the Koch brothers' new office in downtown Madison.

On the political maneuvering front, the Republicans dropped their claims that the anti-worker legislation was fiscally related, thus clearing the way for a quorum of 50 percent of the senate body. They tripped themselves up by violating the open records law, thus resulting in another restraining order and delay. The election of a pro-Walker state supreme court judge in a closely contested election in April gave the Walker people a majority on the court, which eventually vacated the restraining order. By mid-June, the laws were in effect. The increased worker contributions for benefits and cuts in these benefits will probably not be in the average person's pay until after the recall elections are over. In fact, the first pay cuts came at the end of August, two weeks after the recalls. Unions are already not able to collect dues. In some cases, dues income has fallen ninety percent.

In February, progressive activists succeeded in passing a resolution at the South Central Federation of Labor calling for education about a general strike. Although the media suggested that the federation had, in fact, asked for a strike, this was not the case. However, the fact that such an issue was even discussed, let alone received substantial interest, was an important milestone. In response, the federation authorized a committee to educate union members. The ad hoc committee devised a curriculum as to what a general strike is, the legal implications of a work stoppage, and the level of organizing that would be needed to even consider such an action. Over the next month, members of that committee met with several locals.

One consequence of that effort was the formation of Labor Forward. This group of activists, many of whom were part of the ad hoc education committee, carried on the education role after the federation declared the work of the committee over. The committee functions outside the federation but with its cooperation and support. To that end, the group organized a two-day "Troublemakers School." Well over a hundred unionists attended the school, held in mid-April. The group continued to meet, and a second mobilization school was held in mid-July, with more education efforts planned for the future.

A second consequence of the education and mobilization was the realization that working people had to organize. Concomitantly, a second group of activists put together an organizing committee. This committee functions independently of the South Central Federation of Labor.

In the meantime, the governor gradually succeeded in regaining control of the capitol, ousting the citizens and installing airport-like security. With the passage of the legislation, the demonstrations effectively ended. Increasingly, labor placed all its resources in the organization and implementation of a recall campaign aimed at vulnerable Republican senators. In one sense, the movement moved back into a more traditional role of political mobilization. Immense resources have been collected to support this effort. Union staff from around the country were brought to Wisconsin to help in the effort. Several million dollars' worth of advertising was purchased. Within the state, the public sector unions have devoted almost all of their efforts to the recalls.

However, the concentration on recalls meant that a clear means of organized resistance to management and rebuilding of the locals in the offices and work sites took second place. In general, local union officials have vigorously attempted to recoup union dues by arranging for members to have automatic deductions from checking accounts. Some unions, especially WEAC, have been conducting training for their local union leaders focused on member mobilization.

As the spring turned to summer, it became clearer that at the level of the workplace the Wisconsin trade union movement faced a much more difficult challenge. The challenge is ideological. The question for staff and members alike is this: What is a union? This challenge is especially severe since the culture and history of public sector unionism in Wisconsin has essentially been that of a lobbying organization combined with a legalistic contract enforcement system heavily dependent on arbitration. Now, for all practical purposes, the contract is gone. Arbitration is gone. So, many ex-members ask how the union can give me a helping hand, rather than asking for a handout. Almost all staff and union activists have grown up with the business union model. State public sector workers have not struck since a short strike over thirty years ago. In spite of talk in mid-February about a general strike, no organization embraced this as a real course of action.

The challenge is how to build union consciousness. How can those remaining unionists build their union within a state bureaucracy in the absence of a grievance procedure or enforceable work rules?

In many ways, what is happening in Wisconsin is a real back-to-the-future moment. The legal situation for public sector workers resembles 1929. The penalties for concerted action imposed on public sector workers are severe. Many types of actions are considered dischargeable offenses. There is no grievance and arbitration system for discharges anymore. A new absenteeism project that considers employees "resigned" if they are absent for more than three days without a supervisor's agreement is just one example of the harsh new world of public employment.

Workers in private sector workplaces responded to the dictatorial reign of management by eventually building shop floor organizations that could survive and take on management. But it was only with great militancy and sacrifice. Public policy followed actual changes on the ground—strikes and sit-downs. As with the labor movement of the 1930s and the civil rights movement of the 1960s, political change followed the social movements, and, in part, ratified their effectiveness. Where will this militancy come from now and who will lead it? As a practical matter, for the situation to change at the base, one would have to see an expenditure of resources similar to that in the political arena. The costs may not be as great, but a focus on building at the base is necessary to show disillusioned and angry workers that their organizations exist for them.

A final conundrum presents itself. Unlike the impoverished unions of old, many public sector unions have significant assets: buildings and pension plans, for example. They also have significant staff payroll costs that have to be met. The assets can become a target in the event of work actions that the state declares illegal, putting serious pressure on union finances. In other words, there is an institutional vulnerability that did not exist in the early days of union organization.

Public sector unions have taken a big hit in Wisconsin. However, not all public sector organizations are affected equally, especially in the short term. WEAC and AFSCME Council 40 and 48, with membership primarily at the municipal and county level, have kept a large part of their base and have signed contracts, so for now they are viable financial organizations. Unions such as AFSCME Council 24 and the AFT Wisconsin, with mostly state employees, are in a long-term untenable position unless they can organize their members to participate in individual dues collection programs. Though these public sector unions can survive short-term financial deficits, they cannot survive over the long haul except by the generosity of their internationals. So far, in mid-October, the results for individual sign-ups have not been too successful. Some larger AFSCME and AFT locals covering state workers have sign-up rates of only about 10 percent.

Much can be done in the typical state office to encourage management to recognize the strength of the employees. In order to change the social climate to make possible the legal resurrection of the trade unions in the public sector, the envelope must be expanded. What does this mean, practically speaking? One practical move that challenged the law has been a decision on the part of some of the public sector unions, such as AFSCME Council 24, not to bother with the yearly certification process. Union leaders said that it was simply not worth it to gain certification only for the purposes of truncated bargaining over wages. Compared with the past, this is a big step, since for years unions focused on gaining union recognition from the state as the prerequisite to conducting business.

At the office level, big changes are occurring. As a result of fear-mongering, budget cuts, and reductions in benefits, almost 6,000 public sector workers are retiring. Many of these jobs will be filled by incumbent workers. Who gets the job? As in the past, without a union, management favoritism will play a dominant role, and this will mean that race and sex discrimination will rear their ugly heads. However, employees can react—with petitions, demands that the senior qualified person get the job, public denunciations of discriminatory behavior, and the use of existing state and federal anti-discrimination laws. In many areas of the workplace, innovative use of current federal and state laws can be used to mobilize and unite one's fellow workers. In this regard, the unions can play an important role as trainers, advisers, mobilizers, and coordinators. The goal is to make life so uncomfortable for mid-level managers that they will want the union back. As such actions become widespread and successful, workers will gain more confidence.

What is the ground game of organized labor? Is there a ground game? All bets were placed on the recall efforts, which, while partially successful, did not result in the change needed. Between August of 2011 and January of 2012, when it will be possible to start the recall process against Governor Walker, there will be time to mobilize at the workplace. Will there be the will and leadership? It is not clear what is happening in the workplace. WEAC allowed each local to decide if it wished to go for certification. Well over two-thirds have decided to go that route, so in WEAC workplaces there are huge efforts being made to sign up members. The sign-up efforts are coupled with fierce struggles with some school boards over funding issues and regulations governing teachers. State employee unions have in the main not opted for certification and there the mobilizations are less visible. Unions seem to have adopted the vision that they should do what they can for their members, who in many places are only a small fraction of the workforce.

The massive demonstrations illustrated that organized working people had numerous allies. Many workers coming to the state capitol said that if they could they would be in a union. It was this sentiment that has fueled the development of the organizing committee mentioned earlier. Now more than ever, the union movement faces the issue of allies. Without alliances, it will be almost impossible to win community support for the economic demands of public sector workers. Often, organized labor wants and needs community support, especially in a budget-driven, legislative-driven environment. But now, what can unions give in return? What are unions able or prepared to do to make community-union relations a more equitable arrangement? Will public sector unions mobilize for increased public services, a fairer tax structure, or other changes in the political balance of power?

The attack on collective bargaining rights in Wisconsin and elsewhere tends to gnaw at the roots of American exceptionalism. This view holds that the United States is so different from Europe that U.S. workers do not need a class-based union movement, but rather one that accepts the class relations and seeks only the ability for workers to advance economically. Supporters argue that the workforce is so diverse, so prone to individual advancement to the middle class, that there is no need for a politicized rank-and-file-driven unionism. Underlying this ideology is the notion that, by and large, the capitalists are reasonable people, and that they will compromise balancing maximization of profit against social unrest. Or, to put it another way, U.S. corporate leadership needs a "middle class" with significant purchasing power. But what if the conclusion is that maximization of profit can come from lowering wages, eliminating benefits, and selling or producing goods elsewhere? Why does one need an effective civil service and good schools for a society whose leaders are looking elsewhere for profits?

Wisconsin's Republican political leadership continually linked the attack on the public sector to the need to have a business-friendly climate and compared the wages and benefits of public sector workers to the private sector. The leadership advocates a race to the bottom, not access to a decent life for working people. The Wisconsin Uprising demonstrates the limitations of the business unionism–political cooperative strategy. It was pushed to its limit. Demonstrations of 150,000 citizens are no small thing. However, the old union model has so far proven unable to protect the interests of either union members or the broader community. Yet, once again, all the efforts are being placed on a reinvigoration of that strategy. The sleeping giant is alive and awake now, but it is only fighting with one hand. Allowing the shop/office floor to wither makes it unlikely that progress will follow. Observers will be able to tell if the giant is fighting and mobilizing with all its faculties. One need only look at the efforts being made to train and involve members in member-driven shop level efforts to see.

It is too early to tell what will happen during the rest of the budget biennium. The mobilization to recall the governor is scheduled to begin on November 15, 2011. The early stages of the mobilization have begun. Undoubtedly, the recall effort will discourage many types of public or disruptive resistance. Some unions have decided that participation on the recertification system is a waste of time and money. Maybe this marks the first turning away from a restrictive rules-bound labor relations system. Two significant locals in AFT-Wisconsin decided to take public direct action when the implementation of the pay plan went into effect on August 25.

State workers wore black arm bands, but there was little visible mobilization beyond that. But one thing is clear. If workers are denied their rights on the job, sooner or later they will demand them back. They will want to "Walk Like an Egyptian," and if the current union structures are unable to meet this challenge, workers will replace them.

PART TWO

Moving Forward:

The Lessons of Wisconsin

• • •

It is always dangerous to try to define the meaning of events that have happened recently and may turn out to have been unique. If we thought that this always applied, however, we would not have written this book. The authors in this section have drawn remarkably complementary lessons from the Wisconsin uprising, given that each wrote without corresponding with the others. What this probably shows is that there are plenty of lessons to go around. The essays do have certain themes in common: grassroots, rank-and-file organization is critical to the success of any program of action; workers should always seize the moment and stay on the offensive as long as possible; compromise with capital is futile, given that capital wants the whole ball of wax and the working class is disorganized, confused, and insecure, easily manipulated and exploited; aggressive actions such as strikes are never outdated; traditional labor politics is a problem for and not a solution to the plight of workers; and workers always have power, whether they are in unions or not. A key lesson of Wisconsin is that a radically new labor movement will have to be built, from the ground up, if successful class struggle is to be waged.

6—Back to the Future: Union Survival Strategies in Open Shop America

RAND WILSON and STEVE EARLY

When the history of public sector deunionization in the Midwest is written, its sad chroniclers will begin their story in Indiana. That's where Governor Mitch Daniels paved the way, in 2005, for more recent attacks on workers' rights in Wisconsin, Ohio, and Michigan. A right-wing Republican, Daniels was elected in 2004. Immediately after taking office, he began cutting jobs and, via executive order, revoked bargaining rights granted by his Democratic predecessor, Evan Bayh. Over the next six years, the number of state employees dropped from 35,000 to 28,700. In 2005, 16,408 of them were paying union dues; today, only 1,490 still belong.[1]

For state workers in Indiana, the end of collective bargaining led to a pay freeze in 2009 and 2010, introduction of a new merit pay system, loss of seniority rights, and health care cost shifting. Several workers interviewed by the *New York Times* in February 2011 reported paying $5,200 a year for their insurance premiums—$3,400 more than when Daniels took over. According to *Times* reporter Steven Greenhouse, the resulting drop in union membership was due "to workers deciding it was no longer worth paying dues to newly toothless unions." Jim Mills, a welfare worker in New Castle, Indiana, offered a different explanation of why his union branch shrunk from 260 to twelve members. Workers were afraid that management would retaliate against them for union activity once they were no longer protected by union contracts.[2]

Republican governors elected in the fall of 2010—like Scott Walker in Wisconsin, John Kasich in Ohio, and Rick Snyder in Michigan—all looked to Indiana as their model. For unions like SEIU; the American Federation of State, County, and Municipal Employees; the two national teacher organizations, NEA and AFT; unionized firefighters and police, the Mitch Daniels scenario is a formula for union marginalization, if not total extinction. As soon as they took office in early 2011, Snyder and Kasich used executive orders to rescind bargaining rights for 40,000 state-funded home day care providers and health care aides that had never been incorporated into legislation. (These workers had only recently been organized by the United Auto Workers and SEIU; none of their bargaining units were covered by the costlier medical and retirement plans enjoyed by other state workers, with a longer history of collective bargaining.)[3]

Broader anti-union measures introduced by Walker in Wisconsin (and Kasich in Ohio) were adopted by state legislators not long afterward, triggering the mass community-labor protests in Madison described and analyzed elsewhere in this book. In Wisconsin, these demonstrations reached truly unusual and inspiring proportions before the focus of organized labor's counter-campaign became a recall effort aimed at Republican legislators and a legal challenge that delayed implementation of the law for several months. Union campaigners gathered enough signatures to force votes in six districts, while Republicans organized to unseat three incumbent Democrats. After winning five of the nine recall elections, the anti-Walker campaign forces announced they would begin gathering signatures to recall the governor.[4]

University of Wisconsin labor historian Stephen Meyer has described Walker's legislation as being worse than the state right-to-work laws spawned by the 1947 Taft-Hartley Act "because it requires that unions get re-certified by their members yearly, at the same time that the unions are prevented from accomplishing anything for them."[5] Weighing its impact on 360,000 public employees in the Buckeye State, others have argued that "Ohio's Anti-Union Law Is Tougher than Wisconsin's" because uniformed public safety employees are stripped of their rights along with everyone else.[6] In Ohio, labor opponents of SB-5 collected enough signatures to force a referendum vote, scheduled for November 2011, on whether Kasich's curbs on collective bargaining should be overturned.

If repeal efforts in either state fall short, more than half a million public employees will be working under the same open shop conditions as their pubic sector counterparts in Indiana and private sector workers in the twenty-two states with right-to-work laws. Most of the 1.6 million workers in America who are not union members but are covered by union contracts can be found in those states. Unions are barred from negotiating contract provisions that require automatic deduction of dues or fees for the representation they remain legally obligated to provide to everyone, regardless of membership status, in their bargaining units. (In New Hampshire in 2011, it took a Democratic governor's veto, which the Republican-dominated legislature was unable to override, to prevent the open shop from being imposed, for the first time, in both the private and public sector in New England.)[7]

Dues Deduction Dependence

Wherever legally sanctioned, negotiated provisions for automatic payroll deduction of dues have long produced a guaranteed income stream for labor organizations. With the revenue from dues and "agency fees"—payments required by workers who chose not to join—unions have paid for their lawyers, lobbyists, full-time negotiators and field staff, not to mention funded state, local, and national election campaign activity (which is also financed by voluntary membership contributions to union political action funds).

Some commentators on the left have argued that "dues checkoff" has made unions less responsive to workers, because the latter can't withhold financial support to get the leadership's attention. One such critic, a longtime organizer for the ILGWU, believes that labor's reliance on government certification and automatic dues deduction in a system in which unions win exclusive representation rights "precludes any meaningful internal democracy—a precondition to a militant mass organization."[8]

Now, for better or worse (depending on your point of view), national and local labor organizations face the specter of hundreds, if not thousands, of workplaces in which union membership will be voluntary again, just as it was before passage of the Wagner Act in 1935 and later public sector bargaining laws based on the NLRA model.

According to editors of the *New York Times*, Republican sponsors of recent anti-union legislation are mistaken in their belief that "public sector unions will simply fade away" when they have "no ability to raise funds." Says the *Times*, optimistically: "As much as unions may struggle with these new shackles, their members—and their motivation—are not going away."[9] However, any combination of rank-and-file fear, anger, or dissatisfaction over past union representation (including recent concession bargaining about wages and benefits) could easily send dues receipts plummeting to Indiana levels.

The most dramatic example of this phenomenon occurred in a longtime bastion of union militancy and strength, Local 100 of the Transport Workers Union (TWU) in New York City. In 2005, after a citywide bus and subway system strike, 35,000 transit workers were punished under the terms of New York State's draconian Taylor law which prohibits walkouts by public employees. Local 100 members were forced to pay fines ranging from $650 to $750 (the equivalent of three days' pay for most strikers). The local was fined $2.5 million, its president briefly jailed, and automatic dues deduction suspended. The contract settlement, which included benefit give-backs, was rejected narrowly but later imposed by an arbitrator.

The punitive suspension of TWU's dues check-off deal with the Metropolitan Transportation Authority resulted in the local's paid-up membership sinking to nearly 50 percent in the bargaining unit involved in the strike. Local 100's weak and demoralized steward structure made systematic hand collection of dues impossible in many workplaces. Members were very bitter and angry about being fined for striking against concessions they were forced to accept anyway, after a work stoppage that many felt was poorly organized by the union.

Dues deduction was eventually restored but, as recently as late 2009—when a reform slate took over the union—about 17,000 former strikers were not eligible to vote because they still owed as much as $900 in back dues and couldn't or wouldn't pay that amount. Members of the Take Back Our Union slate, headed by current Local 100 president John Samuelsen, were faced with the monumental challenge of restoring rank-and-file confidence in the TWU and gradually coaxing as many lapsed members as possible back into the fold. In late 2010, when Local 100 began preparing for its next round of contract negotiations, stewards, officers, and staffers were still trying to get 14,000 bus and subway workers back into good membership standing.

In this essay, we examine the unfolding debate within labor about how best to respond to such daunting open shop conditions, whether they arise in atypical Local 100 fashion or as the result of legislation and executive orders that fundamentally weaken union financing, administration, and day-to-day functioning. Clearly, conducting "business as usual" is not a viable option in new open shop states. If government employee unions remain what Stanley Aronowitz calls "insurance companies and grievance machines," the soft underbelly of mainstream unionism (public sector division) will soon be exposed for all to see.

Are there ways that these organizations can operate "outside the protection of the law"?[10] Can they function with membership consent, more active participation, and voluntary financial buy-in that were unnecessary, to the same degree, in the past? Can they develop internal organizing game plans based on worker-to-worker relationship building, rank-and-file leadership development, and collective action on the job when they lose the ability to engage in formal collective bargaining?

Lessons of Southern Organizing

Public sector unionists with long experience in open shop states like Tennessee, Mississippi, North Carolina, or Texas argue that all is not lost for their brothers and sisters north of the Mason-Dixon Line. In North Carolina, notes United Electrical Workers (UE) organizer Leah Fried, "collective bargaining rights were stripped from public employees in 1959 by an all-white state legislature [which] made it illegal for state and local governments to enter into collective bargaining agreements with workers." For more than fifteen years, the UE has "helped public workers across North Carolina, Virginia, and West Virginia form non-majority unions that organize and fight to improve workers' lives on the job without a contract."[11]

UE Local 150, the North Carolina Public Service Workers Union initially concentrated on gaining strength within the state university system, which includes sixteen campuses and over 19,000 workers. The union's primary base and leadership came from parts of the workforce that were majority African American and female—like housekeeping, grounds-keeping, and other blue-collar jobs. As UE organizer Steve Bader reported in *Labor Notes*:

> When UNC refused to meet with the union, UE 150 organized Martin Luther King Day leafleting, Black History Month black arm-band days, and meetings with legislators [that] culminated in a meeting between UNC System president Molly Broad's office and 18 rank-and-file workers. The meeting pressured the president into issuing an official memo that recognized workers' rights to join and build their union without retaliation, changed the grievance policy to allow a co-worker grievance assistant, and established "meet and confer" bodies between employees and top management.[12]

Later, the UE expanded to other UNC campuses and the Department of Health and Human Services, where members hold union meetings during lunch or break time to decide on issues and strategies. An independent union of city workers in Durham voted to affiliate with UE Local 150 and has even conducted several strikes. Whether they are state or municipal employees, rank-and-file activists are trained to represent co-workers in grievance meetings with management and serve as elected stewards and officers. According to Bader:

> Victories in this area include winning formal grievances over unfair discipline. In at least three cases, racist managers and supervisors have been forced to leave the job due to pressure from the union. At almost every institution, union chapters have had direct meetings with management regarding workplace issues. In several instances they have won concrete changes, such as improved equipment, respect for or changed policy, and internally granted raises of $1,500–$3,000 for individual workers.

UE Local 150 also gathers, organizes, and distributes information regarding wages, benefits, personnel practices, and employment-related legislative initiatives that may be publicly available but difficult for workers to obtain. The union has established a regular presence in the capital when the legislature is in session and regularly contacts lawmakers about issues affecting public workers. Workers are organized and encouraged to speak directly to elected officials rather than rely on professional lobbyists. UE legislative priorities or accomplishments in the past include winning flat rather than percentage raises (to aid the lowest-paid), passage of bills to improve the grievance procedure, and stronger family and medical leave rights and protection against discrimination based on disability. The UE has also generated much publicity for its creative challenge to North Carolina's ban on public sector bargaining as a violation of international labor standards.

Tom Smith is an organizer for and former president of Communications Workers of America Local 3865, which focuses on higher education in neighboring Tennessee. His local is a "non-majority union" of state university workers that has grown from two-dozen members on one campus to more than 1,200 in eight cities in the last ten years. "While having dues checkoff helps, not having it isn't fatal," says Smith, although he notes that "we struggle with self-sustainability every day." According to Smith, in the early years of Local 3865

> elements of our leadership argued that having to hand-collect dues kept the local's leaders and organizers honest. This attitude meant attending weekly meetings to make plans to collect dues. Quickly we realized that spending the majority of our time playing bill collector was not part and parcel of union democracy, nor did it help build the kind of political relationships we're aiming for on the job.[13]

Instead, stewards started to spend more of their time "listening to co-workers, gathering opinions about how to build the union, organizing meetings, and working to save jobs from budget cuts." Local 3865 switched from hand collection of cash or checks to a bank draft system that enables the deduction of dues straight from members' accounts. But that requires new members filling out a form providing their bank routing and account numbers, which creates "a new layer of difficulty in signing up members."

> Bank drafts are complicated. We have a number of different drafts depending on pay periods. As anyone who has lived from paycheck to paycheck knows, automatic withdrawals need to be timed so that enough "available funds" are left behind to ensure groceries and gas don't overdraw the account. When possible we deduct dues from the check that does not contain the health insurance premium.

According to Smith, "Very few people sign on first contact" because "a longer relationship must be built" first. The amount of work required for dues collection via bank drafts is still "very large." Local 3865 staff devote dozens of hours each month to adding new members to the system, dealing with transaction fees, returns that slam the union with an additional fee, and costly "drops" when workers drop out of the union. "We now know all the local bank routing numbers," he says, "so new members signing up can simply put their bank's name on a dues form that specifies savings or checking account, to prevent expensive returns.[14]

In Texas, the CWA-backed counterpart of Local 3865 is the Texas State Employees Union (TSEU), CWA Local 6188, a group launched as a "non-majority union" organizing project in the early 1980s. Although heavily subsidized by the national union for many years, TSEU has built up a dues-paying membership base, now numbering about 12,000, in the same fashion as higher-ed union organizers at CWA Local 3865 in Tennessee. (Texas has more than 120,000 state employees.) Both white-collar and blue-collar state workers can join, in any state department, agency, or university system campus. As TSEU lead organizer Jim Branson explains: "The union can represent workers in grievance hearings, which means that individual workers don't have to be on their own when faced with some kind of adverse personnel action."[15] But individual worker representation in grievance proceedings is just "a small part of what TSEU does," Branson says.

> We have a voice on the job because we are an active and growing movement that puts a lot of emphasis on organizing. We have agency caucuses, made up of union activists, who meet regularly to formulate goals and plan actions for winning those goals. From time to time, members of the caucus will meet with agency heads to discuss our goals, and when the legislature is in session, caucus members will speak directly to lawmakers. . . . If a united group of workers act like a union, they can have a voice on the job. It's not easy, but it can be done.

TSEU activist William Rogers says his union "has managed to win some victories even though it has very few legal rights." In 2007, for example, TSEU led a campaign that saved thousands of government jobs by preventing further expansion of privatization of the state's health and human services. "That was a fight of organized workers, even though we weren't a majority in the health and human services agency and we didn't have a collective bargaining contract," Branson said. "But members mobilized like crazy. Their mobilization turned public opinion against the privatization plan, and when the contractor screwed up, the state had no choice but to fire it."

TSEU members throughout Texas lobbied elected officials and succeeded in getting about a hundred counties and municipalities to pass resolutions against the governor's privatization plan. They also visited state legislators, marched, rallied, demonstrated, held press conferences, and spoke out at public hearings. In the process, reports Branson, "We got workers, who had been sitting on the fence, to join the union. We were able to maintain our presence in the agency—even though a lot of workers were quitting in anticipation of being laid off— because we never stopped organizing."

Rethinking the Union Idea in Wisconsin

From the early 1930s until 1959, Wisconsin's public workers practiced "informal bargaining" and worked to secure collective bargaining rights. Their efforts began during the great union wave of the 1930s when many public employees, like private sector workers, asserted their rights to organize and negotiate with their employers, wherever they could. It was through organizing, demanding voluntary recognition, and working to expand these bargaining relationships that Wisconsin public sector unions were finally able to win a legal mechanism for formal certification and dues checkoff. Before that, union members hand-collected dues to pay for their organizational activity.

Unions already or soon-to-be deprived of automatic dues deduction in Wisconsin are reeducating their present-day activists about union functioning under these new conditions. "We have had a huge discussion of the old-school style of unionism with our rank-and-file members that we haven't had in the past," says Edward A. Sadlowski, a staff member of AFSCME Council 40, which represents 32,000 public workers. Already, Sadlowski notes, some workers in the state highway department have utilized various forms of direct action over safety issues that might not have been necessary before. While the fifty-year-old statute repealed by Republican legislators and Governor Walker granted collective bargaining rights, it was also designed "to promote labor peace and keep people complacent." Sadlowski observes:

> Due to the [new] law, we simply can't return to the model of having a staff representative do everything for workers and expect to survive as a union. Now, we actually have to involve people in their unions and make them feel like they run the unions, not their staff representatives. This is going to have amazing results for the labor movement over the long run.[16]

Jack Bernfeld, associate director of AFSCME Council 40, agrees with Sadlowski that union staff must shift from servicing workers to "mobilizing people to show up at city council meetings, school board meetings, protests, influencing the public and elected officials to do the right thing." As Jane Slaughter reported in *Labor Notes*, however, Bernfeld's union was reluctant to provide the kind of "dues relief" that would make signing up members for bank draft (or credit card) deduction easier.

AFSCME university locals asked the district council to lower dues, since members were facing a big pay cut due to the concessions negotiated with the Walker administration. But they got just a few dollars knocked off average dues payments of $39 a month. Both rank-and-filers and officials agree that paying dues voluntarily will be a "hard sell." As one statewide union officer told Slaughter: "People have different perspectives on whether the union will still be what it was or should be and that may affect whether they're willing to pay dues." If members are asked to pay for a statewide organization and "they don't understand what they get for it," Anne Habel of AFSCME Local 171 believes that some of her co-workers may be less likely to join.[17]

As reported in the *Milwaukee Journal-Sentinel* in May 2011, the Wisconsin State Employees Union (WSEU) was also considering how it might function as a voluntary membership organization instead of trying to retain formal bargaining rights via the annual "re-certification" election now required in Wisconsin. "There has been a discussion about not recertifying because of the fact there would be little or no benefit," said WSEU president Bob McLinn, referring to the limited scope of bargaining under Walker's new law.[18] Even if state worker unions abandon their status as bargaining representatives and no longer have the ability to take contract grievances to binding arbitration, they can still help civil service employees defend themselves against unfair discipline in cases before the state labor relations commission.

The American Federation of Teachers-Wisconsin, which represents white-collar state workers, is also weighing alternative strategies for representation, issue-oriented advocacy, and membership recruitment. "We may just continue to be a membership organization that advocates for all sorts of things," AFT president Brian Kennedy told the *Journal-Sentinel*. "We're still in discussions about what we want to do."

The AFT in Wisconsin has set up an easy way to sign up for voluntary dues collection on its website.[19] The AFT site boldly proclaims, "Walker thinks he can cripple our union by making payroll deduction for union dues illegal. By recommitting to our union and continuing membership, we are standing strong and sending a message: Walker can't legislate away our union, he can't decide that we don't have power, he doesn't decide—we do. To join in building our union, click the button below and continue your union membership and our ability to fight Walker, his agenda and the stripping of our rights."

In Milwaukee, leaders of the Milwaukee Teachers Education Association predicted that their union would now have to pressure the school board directly about issues once subject to bargaining like class size. "We would continue to pursue all avenues to be a voice for our students and our members in Milwaukee," said Mike Langyel, president of the association.[20]

Conclusion

Longtime union activist and sociology professor Stanley Aronowitz has written extensively about the unhealthy synergy between membership expectations and public sector union functioning as it has evolved since the rank-and-file upsurge that won collective bargaining rights for teachers and other civil servants in the 1960s and '70s. Over time, members came to "view their unions as service providers, rather than as instruments of mobilization." As Aronowitz notes:

> The unions may fight individual grievances and negotiate decent contracts, but to call upon their members to conduct collective polit- ical fights—including direct actions that might disturb the comfort- able relationship that the leadership enjoys with the employer—is well beyond the perspective, and therefore, the capacity, of the union. In short, the member is now generally a client of the union rather than its owner.[21]

The rupture of labor-management relationships that may have been "comfortable" in the past, plus the accompanying loss of legal rights in a growing number of states, has triggered membership mobi- lization activity reminiscent of the original struggles for collective bargaining. In Madison and elsewhere, labor's recent defensive bat- tles demonstrate that a new model of union functioning is not only possible but necessary for survival. As a first step in this process of union transformation under duress, workers must definitely shed their past role as "clients" or passive consumers of union services. In workplaces without a union (or agency) shop and collective bar- gaining as it was practiced for decades, they must take ownership of their own organizations and return them to their workplace roots, drawing on the experiences of public workers in the South whose practice of public sector unionism has, by necessity, been very dif- ferent for the last half-century.

7—In the Wake of Wisconsin, What Next?

JANE SLAUGHTER and MARK BRENNER

The revolt in Wisconsin is the most impressive response of American workers to the employer offensive that began three decades ago—remarkable for its numbers, for its sustained nature, for the labor-community-student coalition that spontaneously arose.

The stunning support from non-union workers distinguishes it from most other labor struggles. In insisting on the right of workers to have something to say about their conditions of employment, it expressed the bedrock basis of unionism.

The national spring 2006 walkouts and demonstrations for immigrant rights were larger in numbers, but the Wisconsin actions were more long-lasting: four weeks of intense action.

The Wisconsin revolt is filled with lessons and will be analyzed by labor activists and historians for years to come. We focus here both on what we can learn from the Wisconsin struggle and what unions elsewhere should do in its wake.

The lessons:

1. THE STRIKE IS STILL A POWERFUL WEAPON. The decision by Madison teachers to walk off the job, soon joined by the statewide

teachers' union, was the linchpin in the Wisconsin struggle. The strike raised the bar at the outset. It set an example of anger, militancy, and sacrifice (Madison teachers lost four days' pay) and swelled the ranks at the capitol. The capitol occupation, together with the big street demonstrations, were crucial parts of the struggle. But absent the teachers' strikes, the rebellion wouldn't have been the same.

By the same token, it was a missed opportunity for the labor movement not to call all public employees out of work immediately after the legislature rammed through the budget repair bill on March 9.

The teachers' union had already shown, early on, that its members would heed the call to come to the capitol instead of the classroom. If union leaders had met March 10 and called a one-day strike for Friday, March 11, or Monday, March 13, that action would not have made Governor Scott Walker back down. But it would have put the depth of workers' anger and determination on vivid display, using what everyone knows to be labor's strongest weapon. A short strike would have sent a message to everyone across the state: "We are organized. We can do this. We are not defeated." It also would have added job actions to the collective toolbox needed for later springtime actions.

The leaders of Wisconsin unions were in no way prepared to take such a bold step, if they considered the idea at all. No doubt they worried that a strike could spark a backlash and feared squandering the public backing they had garnered through the weeks of occupation and protest. But given the heightened emotions throughout Wisconsin, the shock at Walker's disregard for state law in forcing the bill through, and the widespread support the unions had experienced from unexpected quarters, it is unlikely that a one-day general strike of public workers would have turned hearts and minds against the labor movement, although it certainly would have cemented the views of those already opposed to "Big Labor."

The advantage would have been not only the strong collective nose-thumbing of Walker but also, for public employees, the personal experience of defying authority by taking the strike step. The shift in mindset that occurs when a worker dares to strike—breaking the law to do so—should not be minimized.

An argument could, of course, be made for not just a one-day strike but an open-ended one. There was much talk of a general strike in some quarters in Madison, especially after the South Central Federation of Labor passed a resolution February 21 "endors[ing] a general strike, possibly for the day Walker signs his budget repair bill." The Wobblies in town made agitating for a general strike the focus of their activism. The chant was sometimes taken up at rallies. Firefighters' union president Joe Conway echoed the theme the night Republican legislators bullied their bill through.

An open-ended strike, general or not, was unfortunately so far beyond the capacities of the Wisconsin unions as they existed that it doesn't seem worthwhile to spill ink on that subject here. Moreover, it is hard to imagine winning such a strike. Walker and the Republican legislative leadership had already shown their willingness to bulldoze their opposition, despite the nearly two-week occupation of the capitol and the flight of fourteen Democratic senators that shut down the senate. Drastic retaliation would have been a real possibility. The likelihood of retaliation for a one-day display of anger, especially after Walker had just gotten his way, was far lower.

Political strikes (against or for legislation or public policy) have been rare in the United States in recent decades. The 1969 strike by West Virginia miners for black lung legislation, the April and May 2006 one-day strikes and marches by immigrant workers and their allies against the odious Sensenbrenner bill, and the West Coast longshore union's one-day coastwide shutdown against the Iraq war in 2008 stand out for their rarity.

Now that city councils and state legislatures across the country have joined corporations in their attack on working-class living standards, public sector unions will need to learn, over time, how to redeploy the strike tool. To be sure, this will be difficult. Thirty-eight states prohibit strikes by public sector workers (another eleven allow no collective bargaining rights at all), and as the 2005 transit strike in New York City demonstrated, officials will use fines and even jail time to blunt workers' most powerful weapon.

But the Wisconsin events show the necessity—when the labor movement is capable of pulling it off—of not merely demonstrating opposition to injustice but actually throwing sand in the system's gears. Scott Walker looked out the window of the capitol and dismissed more than 100,000 protesters as outside agitators and "a small minority." Similarly, governments in Europe have grown accustomed to orderly one-day general strikes, finding it quite easy to pass neoliberal measures the next day.

Ultimately, in order to win, unions must disrupt the workings of business as usual, either by striking or by direct action, or both. A strike must either hurt some corporation's profits or provoke a political crisis severe enough to compel those in power to end it. The civil rights movement emptied the buses and filled the jails. The strikers of the 1930s filled the factories with sit-downers and surrounded them with supporters. In Egypt protesters closed factories and government offices and filled Tahrir Square. In Madison, workers filled their public square, too, but in order to go all the way we will also need to empty the workplaces.

2. THE WAY FOR UNIONS TO WIN PUBLIC SUPPORT IS TO STAND UP. A Bloomberg poll of March 4–7 found 64 percent nationally saying public employees should have the right to bargain collectively, and 72 percent that had a favorable opinion of public employees. It was clear that many were inspired by the idea of backing a winner, or at least a fighter.

Outrage over their own economic insecurity and the gloomy landscape of home foreclosures and high unemployment fed people's support for the unions. Walker's tax cuts for his corporate backers and wealthy donors only sharpened the "which side are you on" character of the protests. Those already angry at the banks and the super-rich found this fight a flash point for those frustrations. It seemed that after decades of wage cuts, layoffs, and service cuts, for union and non-union alike, culminating most recently in what looks like creation of a permanent second-class tier of low-paid workers, many were glad to finally see someone fighting back.

Public support was likely enhanced by the fact that the workers seen at the forefront were sympathetic figures—teachers, police, and firefighters.

3. UNIONS NEED TO EDUCATE THE PUBLIC ABOUT THE REASONS FOR DEFICITS INSTEAD OF ACCEPTING BLAME.

Many in Wisconsin argue that one reason support was high was that union leaders immediately offered to take all the economic concessions contained in Walker's bill—an 8 to 10 percent pay cut—if he would only permit them to retain collective bargaining rights. Both Mary Bell of the Wisconsin Education Association Council (WEAC), the statewide NEA affiliate, and Marty Beil of AFSCME Council 24 made this generous offer, without consulting members. (WEAC, as a council of member unions, does not actually negotiate any contracts, so Bell was offering concessions she was not empowered to make.)

Thus leaders could present unionists as willing to "do their share" to mend the state budget—heading off the ire of any citizens jealous of the relatively good salaries and benefits of public employees. Their willingness to compromise allowed them to appear as the reasonable ones, while Walker looked intransigent. Dave Poklinkoski, president of an Electrical Workers (IBEW) local in Madison, said, "[Offering concessions] smoked out what Walker's true intentions were. That might not have gotten through to the general public otherwise."

Appearing reasonable did not, of course, soften Walker's stand. He moved not an inch. But union leaders maintained their generous offering of concessions even after the budget repair bill was declared valid by the state supreme court in June. The state AFL-CIO, when announcing unions' federal discrimination lawsuit against the budget repair bill, said, "Significantly, the unions do not seek to enjoin the pension and health insurance contribution requirements imposed by the Budget Repair Bill. Public sector unions have made it clear from day one that Wisconsin workers would do their part to share in the sacrifice and keep our state moving forward."

Whatever the tactical reasons for offering concessions, doing so reinforced the notion that state employees were overpaid and to blame for the deficit. By leading with concessions, the unions lost an opportunity to forcefully point out, from the outset, the real cause of the state's red ink: a tax system designed to let corporations and the very rich off the hook. Instead they reinforced the belief that the state really did face an insurmountable deficit, that public workers were part of the problem, and that concessions were therefore justified.

This stance raised some dissent within Wisconsin unions. As the struggle wore on, the notion that banks, not workers, should pay for the recession they caused became more prominent, as did negative publicity for Walker's tax cuts. A meeting called by National Nurses United under the banner of "no concessions" planned a March 3 "jazz funeral" that drew 7,000 protesters. Rapidly evolving coalitions used the names "Kill the Whole Bill" (that is, the wage cuts, too) and "No Cuts, No Concessions." Colette Brown, a state employee, summed up the thinking of this wing of the labor movement: "Blame should be placed on Wall Street for the country's economic woes, not on workers. The solution to budget challenges lies in taxing the rich and closing loopholes—not in Walker's budget cuts. Gains for workers must be considered as much a priority as saving collective bargaining rights."

This message resonated but did not spark a groundswell of action, and almost every labor leader in the state retained the stance that workers had to "do their part."

In any case, for purposes of pure bargaining strategy, all seasoned unionists know that you don't lead with your bottom line. You aim high, to pull the process in your direction. Republicans know this, too. Look no further than Wisconsin Congressman Paul Ryan's federal budget proposal, where he asked for $61 billion in cuts in 2011 and got $38 billion.

4. UNIONS NEED TO BECOME DEFENDERS OF THE PUBLIC GOOD RATHER THAN PRACTITIONERS OF THE INSIDE GAME. It was certainly more comfortable, as a public employee union member or leader, to tell the world you were fighting for the right and dignity of collective bargaining rather than against paying more for your health insurance and pension.

But part of what has fed public resentment, and made public sector unions such a target for conservatives in the first place, is their very real participation in the "inside game" of state and local politics—an often dysfunctional political process that excludes most ordinary people from decision making and leaves broad swaths of the population cynical and suspicious. After years of avoiding the public spotlight and relying on political connections and "a seat at the table," most public sector unions were ill prepared to take their case to the people—that their work was essential and their pay and benefits justified.

To effectively make that case—and win the battle of public opinion—would have required unions to be visible and vocal defenders of the public good long before the current budget squeeze, a position quite at odds with the go-along-get-along game of insider politics that labor has grown so comfortable with.

A reputation as the watchdogs and whistleblowers, as a check on the system that so many people see as shutting them out, could have been the starting point for a very different fight, one where unions were forming coalitions with clients to maintain services; relentlessly hammering on the real causes of the deficit; making the unions a known quantity with a human face, rather than a shadowy special interest. With that groundwork not laid, it is not surprising leaders would seek the path of least resistance.

The situation is complicated. On the one hand, public employee unions can argue truthfully that their members are the people who teach our kids, care for us in hospitals, keep the roads in repair, drive the buses, and cut the grass in the parks. A society without their work is unimaginable.

On the other hand, in a macro sense, the state has, in fact, been completely captured by the top 1 percent of the population and pressed into service for corporations and the super-rich. As such, ordinary citizens are justified in feeling "the government" is not ours in any way, shape, or form. It is no wonder that disillusionment with government is taken out on its most visible representatives, public employees.

But it is also true that people still believe in and can be mobilized around the idea of "democracy" and the "will of the people"—note the many chants of "This is what democracy looks like!" as protesters filled the capitol.

In order for unions to work *with* as well as *for* the public, they need to acknowledge government's many shortcomings (from underfunded schools to potholes), tying these limitations to the way corporate donors and other monied interests drive what the government does and does not do. Unions need to convince taxpayers they are not willing participants in the dysfunction, but rather part of the cure.

5. THE WAY TO GET DEMOCRATIC OFFICEHOLDERS TO SUPPORT YOU IS TO FIGHT ON YOUR OWN BEHALF. The role played by the fourteen Democratic senators who boycotted the legislature for more than three weeks was crucial to keeping the bill at bay and thus keeping the struggle alive. But the "Fab 14" left the state *after* teachers began their strike and tens of thousands of protesters had descended on the capitol. It is difficult to imagine that they would have fled, or stayed away, without the heartfelt backing of voters or without tens of thousands of activists in the streets.

In their Illinois exile, the senators' resolve was kept up by the constant pressure of their constituents on the homefront. They did not call the shots of the movement as it developed—rather, they purposely remained at arm's length.

6. DON'T WAIT FOR PERMISSION. When members of the Teaching Assistants Association decided to spend the night in the capitol, they didn't call their national AFT president, Randi Weingarten, to get her OK. When the Madison teachers' Faculty Rep Council voted to ask members to come to the capitol instead of to work, they didn't wait to see if their parent body, WEAC, would agree. (The tail wagged the dog, and WEAC followed suit.)

Nor did these unions consult with legislators about what constituted an effective course of action. If they talked to lawyers, they apparently took the view that it is not a lawyer's job to tell you what you can't do but simply to help you deal with the consequences. They decided to be bold, and lo and behold, they inspired others to be bold alongside them.

The boldness and the enthusiastic response from inside and outside labor led to an unusual situation: high-level union leaders did not try to derail the momentum but instead encouraged it. They paid for the big rallies. They sent in staff. It is true, as Wisconsin insiders vividly recount, that the dynamic changed somewhat once the struggle grabbed national attention and staff and leaders from outside the state arrived in full force. But as Rich Trumka famously said, "The members are way ahead of the leaders here." And to some degree leaders were willing to try to catch up.

7. WORKERS WILL FIGHT FOR EVEN A BORING BUSINESS UNION. We have argued for years that unless a union is a real presence in the workplace, workers won't be moved to organize others into it or to follow its leaders' political guidance. But Wisconsin public employees came out in numbers to defend unions that, in the main, were not strong on the shop floor, particularly among the state employees.

Activists told us that even if contract enforcement was poor and members were alienated from officers who seemed far away, they still wanted the protection of a contract and a grievance procedure. They knew what conditions are like for non-union workers, subject to management's every whim and under constant risk of termination. Workers wanted a counterweight to management's never-ending push to chop their benefits and to surveil, speed up, and micromanage their work.

In fact, the majority of workers stuck in the legalistic mindset may place more weight on the contract than it deserves, crediting the contract with giving them their rights, rather than their own collective action, banding together and having one another's backs.

So without a contract the union will lose, in the minds of most members, its reason for being and their reason for paying dues. Six years earlier in Indiana, membership plummeted after the governor killed bargaining there. Therefore . . .

8. BOTTOM-UP UNIONS ARE NEEDED NOW MORE THAN EVER. Unions that lose their contracts, dues checkoff, and eventually most of their paid staff must replace "servicing" by paid reps and outside staff with members who will take responsibility for the daily work of pushing back against management. There is nothing to stop members from organizing themselves at work—except a lifetime of inactivity and, perhaps, blowback from higher-ups.

Since the first boss hired the first workers, people have been using their informal networks on the job to lay the basis for action. Organizing today, after Walker's restrictions on collective bargaining, is no different. Union supporters can stay active. They can organize small workplace actions to resist supervisors' bullying. They can elect a plethora of stewards, as many as they want. They can construct more formal organizations such as stewards committees that meet across unions. They can organize everything from button days to brown-bag educationals. They can take direct action, such as group visits to supervisors' offices.

For example, in one state office building in Madison, an informal cross-union committee of stewards from four locals has existed for years, jointly working on bulletins, group grievances, petitions, and the like. Besides the nuts and bolts of unifying members around enforcing their rights, the committee puts on creative actions like a union orientation for kids on "Take Your Kids to Work Day." "We showed a slide show about child labor," said state employee Barbara Smith, "and did a participatory play called 'Trouble in the Henhouse' about organizing chickens. The kids seemed to enjoy the story, wearing the chicken masks and clucking in the right places."

After Scott Walker was elected but before he took office, this group put out two newsletters warning fellow workers and providing facts on the real situation of state employees and the state budget. When Walker released his plans February 11, they immediately set up a building meeting. All the committee's work—which is continuing— is done without the benefit of paid staff time or formal backing from the respective unions. (Later, when Walker, with a straight face, decreed a State Employee Recognition Day in early May, they pro-

claimed their own State Employee Depreciation Day, with a ceremony on the capitol steps in which Wisconsin corporations received
spoof awards.)

The open shops that Wisconsin public sector workers are now
facing requires this kind of DIY unionism, which can come only with
an exponential increase in the number of people with the skills, confidence, and authority to act on behalf of the union. But those skills
don't necessarily come naturally. Training is needed.

Mostly, public employee local leaders were way behind the curve
on the need to rethink and rebuild their unions. Their first impulse
was to campaign for members to pay dues through credit card
pledges—without giving a clear argument as to what "the union"
would be in the new circumstances. A group of local leaders hoped to
counter with training on the basics of organizing. "Our biggest
problem in February and March," said Dave Poklinkoski, "was the
lack of internal ability of unions to mobilize to do more. So we are
working to fix that, through a series of Solidarity Schools."

Despite these brave efforts, the balance of power has undeniably
changed. Republicans won this round and the landscape for public
sector workers in Wisconsin will be much bleaker for a while.

9. SEIZE THE MOMENT. By the time this book appears, the
"moment" will be long over. But late last winter, Wisconsin inspired
tens of thousands to take action, such as those who came to the
Indiana and Ohio statehouses. Copycat Indiana legislators even left
the state. And the ferment aroused unionists across the country, both
to come to Madison and to hold support rallies at home.

The April 4 demonstrations across the country, under the banner
"We Are One," were a well-intentioned attempt to seize the
moment—within limited parameters. Communications Workers
president Larry Cohen was the one who proposed nationally coordinated worksite actions to the AFL-CIO Executive Council. The goal
was both to commemorate Martin Luther King's assassination in
Memphis and to lend support to the embattled unions in Wisconsin,
Ohio, and Indiana.

The AFL-CIO said more than 1,000 mobilizations happened under the "We Are One" umbrella, with more than a million workers—both figures are doubtful—joining rallies, participating in T-shirt days, and the like. The most impressive was the West Coast long-shore workers' shutdown of the Port of Oakland, leaving ships waiting in the San Francisco Bay. When some ILWU members joined other union activists to stage a sit-in at Oakland Wells Fargo offices, the bank shut down for the day.

The initial call for a workplace focus was right. But most actions didn't feel powerful or effective precisely because they did not do what the longshore workers or the bank sit-downers did. The day's events demonstrated the limits of symbolic activity, especially when orchestrated from the top, as well as the degree to which a culture of solidarity and struggle must be rebuilt for the current generation of union members and activists.

Despite the inspiration that stirred even the most bureaucratic hearts, leaders still showed no stomach for breaking rules or even for admitting that that's what will be required. And decades of passivity had bred bad habits among lower-level leaders as well. At the United Auto Workers convention in March, for example, president Bob King gamely tried to get delegates to brainstorm how members could carry out the We Are One actions. The discussion fell flat, as delegates—unused to having their ideas solicited—instead used the session to compete in bombastic praise of their respective regional directors.

Big gains for labor have never come about through steady accretion but in tremendous bursts, and it is hard to know what will carry the spark from one event to others. The Wisconsin rebellion was one such opening and now has become a missed opportunity.

In the gallery of the Michigan capitol February 22, for example, as hundreds of unionists let security guards tell them where they could sit and where they could not, it was achingly clear that leadership willing to seize the moment could have made a difference. But union members let their officials set the parameters of polite opposition and were brushed aside by Rick Snyder, Michigan's version of Scott Walker.

While the Wisconsin uprising didn't stop Walker's anti-union leg-islation or put much of a damper on union-busting politicians in other states, it was a tremendous eye-opener for everyone in the crosshairs across the country. Mostly, since the financial collapse of 2008, public resistance had been sporadic and stayed well within the lines (the Republic Windows and Doors workers of Chicago being a notable and inspirational exception). As banks got away with murder and employers followed suit with concession demands, workers seemed too dazed to do more than take it on the chin.

But the Wisconsin revolt, taking everyone, including its own par-ticipants, by surprise, showed discouraged activists around the country that workers *will* fight for themselves. It taught non-union observers that lesson, too, revising their stereotypes of union mem-bers. In some cases, it even inspired new unions to form: at the University of Wisconsin, faculty at five campuses voted by big margins to unionize *after* Walker introduced his bill.

Among both the most jaded and the newly involved, Wisconsin seems to have changed the mindset of union activists to one more hopeful. Miya Williamson, a Michigan public employee who cara-vanned to join the joyous throngs at the capitol in Madison, declared, "I will never be the same."

10. DON'T WAIT FOR ELECTIONS TO PUNISH THE POLITICOS. After Walker rammed through his anti-union legisla-tion, labor's primary focus became the recall of six Republican sena-tors. Promoting recalls was a natural impulse for public sector union leaders—all too prone to see labor's power emanating from its cam-paign contributions and get-out-the-vote machinery. But after the Republicans' shock-and-awe tactics, "throw the bums out" had real appeal among rank-and-file members, too, as well as the general public. Promoting recalls gave people a way to be involved after the fight with Walker was cordoned off into the courts. And a ballot-box reckoning could put the fear of God into some godawful senators.

Reducing the struggle to a single strategy was a mistake, though. The sole focus on recalls changed the message to: "The solution to our problems is getting rid of these six senators and having Democrats control one branch of the legislature. That will let us block Walker until we can get rid of him via recall, too."

A better statement of the problem would be, "Politicians of all stripes are carrying water for corporations and the super-rich, leading to a completely screwed-up set of priorities for government and an upside-down tax system. The only way we're going to fix that is to build our power outside the electoral system, that is, in the streets and on the job. The best laws working people ever won came after we stormed the halls of power, not when we were waiting outside for someone to let us in."

With an orientation like this, Wisconsin unionists could have used a vast array of creative tactics to bird-dog the baddies, keep the juices flowing, and educate the public. The idea would be to turn up the heat on the deep pockets funding Walker's anti-union agenda and to target its prime beneficiaries, like corporate welfare recipients, placing the blame on them for the state's budget woes.

Actions like this were visible during the rebellion and afterward, but much more is needed. Walker campaign contributor and active home forecloser M&I Bank was an early target of pickets. When the corporate backers of the Tea Party organized an April 16 demonstration at the capitol, they were surrounded by 5,000 counter-protesters. More than 1,000 teachers and other public employees came to a state budget hearing in Milwaukee April 11—and chanted "Shame!" as Republicans walked out on them. In early June, unionists allied with other activists to set up a tent encampment, "Walkerville," in the Capitol Square to protest Walker's budget. A militant faction of 1,000 led by the fire-fighters' union tried to blockade the square, but were outflanked by police. Through the spring and summer, unionists continued to dog Scott Walker's heels whenever he spoke in public, even sending placard-waving flotillas out on a Wisconsin lake. Others tried to bring the multiple strands together through a "people's budget," drawn up by allies and advocates of the victims of Walker's draconian budget cuts.

In the end, of course, elections make a difference only if workers have candidates to vote for who are committed to true democracy:

working people in the driver's seat. The Wisconsin Democrats lined up to challenge the Republican senators in the summer of 2011 were not in that category.

11. THE WAY TO SOLVE THE BUDGET CRISES IS TO FIX OUR UPSIDE-DOWN TAX SYSTEM. Unions, both public and private, need a coordinated and intense education campaign, for members and for the public, to show that the country is not "broke."

The message is simple and already being promulgated by many unions: Wall Street caused the crisis; it recovered with the help of our tax dollars; the banks are doing fine, we're not, make them pay. The notion that "we" all have to sacrifice together should be addressed specifically, to attack the notion of a "we" that turns out to mean working people.

While insisting on who should foot the bill for cleaning up the fallout from the 2008 financial crisis, labor can link these problems to the changes in our tax code over the past generation. When corporate giants like General Electric, Boeing, and Verizon are paying less taxes proportionately than most working people, it is not a difficult argument to make. But detailing how, at every turn, our tax system has been tilted in favor of corporations and the very wealthy is necessary to break through the conservative strategy of lumping all taxes together, tarring them as job killers that hurt ordinary people.

Campaigns can be tailored to the conditions in each state, with as much specificity as needed about who and what could be taxed to balance our budgets. Ideally, such campaigns would go beyond simply how to cover deficits to engage a more ambitious goal: imagining what public services our communities deserve. In the richest country in human history, there is no reason to accept the case for austerity.

Labor should take a page from the conservative playbook and start stumping for a vision of the world we want to live in—with programs like health care for all, free public higher education, and environmentally sound mass transportation as cornerstones. Such ideas don't become common sense overnight, but as the right wing has proven, with enough focus and time a different worldview can work its way into the debate and shift the political center of gravity.

Such an education campaign won't do it all, of course. Substantial shifts in public opinion don't happen through TV ads or Twitter. Eyes are opened—as Wisconsin shows—when people are in the streets.

8—What Can We Learn from Wisconsin?

STEPHANIE LUCE

Like many people, I was glued to the news in early February 2011, watching as the Egyptian people filled Tahir Square, demanding that Hosni Mubarak step down. By Thursday, February 10, the world watched anxiously to see if the story would end in bloodshed or victory.

Meanwhile, on the other side of the world, the governor of Wisconsin announced his "Budget Repair Bill," which would command major cuts to social programs, and remove almost all collective bargaining rights for public sector workers in the state. The next day, as Mubarak was resigning in Egypt and handing over power to the military, Governor Walker announced he was planning to mobilize the state's National Guard to do the work of any state worker who protested his law.

According to journalist John Nichols, most statewide union leaders assumed they were defeated. After all, public sector workers are under attack across the country, and many states do not even allow them the right to collective bargaining at all. A similar bill had passed in Indiana only a few years ago. But graduate students and undergraduate Student Labor Action Coalition members were paying attention and ready to fight back. On Monday, the Teaching Assistants Association (TAA) at UW-Madison organized a small march from the campus to the capitol to oppose the bill. Protesters stayed at the capitol building, and the next day they began lining up to testify against the bill at a hearing. Their numbers grew quickly as other protesters joined them. Teachers began calling in sick and showing up at the capitol. Soon, students from Madison high schools walked out of class and marched to the capitol to support their teachers. Later that day Madison schools announced they would be closed on Wednesday since 40 percent of teachers had called in sick.

The protests grew, with tens of thousands outside the capitol, and hundreds more inside, occupying the statehouse around-the-clock. People around the country (and even some in other countries) rallied in support of the Wisconsin protesters. Much has already been written about the next few weeks, including discussion of the fourteen Democratic senators leaving the state, life inside the capitol, and the resolution passed by the South Central Federation of Labor's resolution regarding a general strike.

I will not go over the details of those months here but instead discuss lessons for organizing. Though Wisconsin has captured our attention, the struggle there is going on around the country. Some of it has been going on for a while, such as in North Carolina, where the Black Workers for Justice and United Electrical Workers have been fighting for collective bargaining rights for public sector workers for many years. Some of it is more recent—including large rallies in support of Wisconsin and protests against other state budget cuts and attacks on workers' rights. Many activists report the unprecedented turnout and spirit of these protest and solidarity events. People are also scared about attacks in their own state, and are also eager to be part of a movement that finally wakes up to resist the attacks.

Here are five lessons I think we can learn from Wisconsin:

1. MOBILIZING A FIGHTBACK TAKES ORGANIZATION. Why is it that the protests in Wisconsin grew so quickly, and so large? Social

movement research tells us that we cannot really predict when an "upsurge" will happen. In fact, as political scientist Eve Weinbaum argues, all social movements begin with a lot of blips—many of which are failures. But what makes for a "successful failure" that helps lay the ground for a larger movement? As with Mohamed Bouazizi setting himself on fire in Tunisia on December 17, 2010, there is no magic answer about what will eventually set off a much larger wave of protest.

But despite some claims to the contrary, the upsurges are not built from scratch on Facebook and Twitter. No doubt these are tools that organizers can use, but whether it's Egypt or Wisconsin, the large-scale protests were built upon existing movement infrastructure and organization.

Madison is well known as a center of antiwar and student organizing in the 1960s and 1970s, and the city and state had a progressive tradition long before that. In the 1990s, Wisconsin unions and community groups built Progressive Wisconsin, a statewide independent third party connected to the national New Party. The national public sector union AFSCME began in Madison, back in 1932. Madison is also home to Union Cab, a worker-owned cooperative founded in 1979; the city also has a community radio station and an extensive food and housing cooperative system. The University of Wisconsin-Madison is also home to the first graduate student union in the country—the Teaching Assistants Association, which won its first contract in 1970. In Milwaukee, *Voces de la Frontera*, a workers' center, began in 2001 and played a major role in the 2006 immigrant rights protests across the Midwest. The Welfare Warriors has been organizing mothers and children in Milwaukee since the mid-1980s, producing a regular newsletter and fighting attacks on the poor.

The key point is that the structures of organizations were in place. Though they are not all strong, they have access to resources, including politicians and staff in the legislature, steward systems in the unions, long lists of contacts, and some independent media. Facebook is only useful if you have a lot of "friends"—and if your friends have friends. And if you and your friends have some history and trust around organizing. No one wants to show up at a protest and be the only person, so you need to have some faith that your networks will be there, too.

This is an important point because activists sometimes want to find some kind of technical solution or magic bullet to organizing, and though the Internet and blogs can be useful, they cannot take the place of good old-fashioned person-to-person outreach and organizational structures.

2. THE RIGHT WING IS MAKING THIS THE FIGHT OF A LIFETIME. We have seen some outrageous maneuvering from the Republican Party and their allies to get this bill passed. This should not come as a surprise, but it is still shocking.

Most notably, the Republicans were furtive in their attempt to pass the bill. State Representative Gordon Hintz (D., Oshkosh) first heard about the Budget Repair Bill from a radio ad from a Washington lobby group on Friday, February 11, and found out he was expected to vote on it only a few days later without public debate. When the senate finally passed the modified bill they gave less than two hours' notice.

After the Republicans passed the bill, a Dane County judge issued a restraining order on the bill, based on grounds that a conference committee had violated the state's Open Meetings Law. Despite the judge's ruling, Walker went forward and published the law a week later and announced plans to implement it, including stripping dues checkoff and other unilateral measures.

The Republicans have employed a number of other outrageous tactics. I am not saying this to suggest Democrats don't also pull dirty tricks. I am simply pointing it out to remind us that the opposition may stop at nothing to push their agenda. Just as organizers do during a unionization campaign, we need to be prepared to inoculate potential supporters—warning them of the range of tricks the opposition will likely try, including ones that are illegal. We need to be armed with our facts to counter their claims, but we must also anticipate their moves.

3. WE HAVE TO BE BOLD. Because the right has been so powerful, the left has often been timid, afraid of alienating "the middle" and losing everything. We temper our demands to sound "reasonable" but usually end up just ceding all ground. The protests in Madison did not start from a position of "reasonable." Graduate students and public school teachers marched to the capitol to demand "Kill the Bill." They did not wait to see what focus groups or polls said about their message. The head of the state's largest police union defied orders to kick out the protesters at one point, saying that despite what the legislature told them, they knew the difference between right and wrong.

The solidarity was not just between unions. The protests against the bill were from workers angry about cuts in their health care and attacks on their unions, but also from thousands of people worried about the impact of the bill on public services overall. The repair bill, along with Walker's proposed budget, includes a wide range of cuts, including on the state low-income health care program (Badgercare), school budgets, recycling programs, and more.

Political analysts claimed that the November 2010 election results proved the popularity of the Tea Party in Wisconsin; they said it could be seen as a mandate for the Tea Party platform of smaller government. But those who marched on the capitol building did not let that stop them. Instead, many signs and banners immediately framed the issue as one of basic rights and a defense of the public good. Protesters did not just oppose Walker's plan, but asserted that "We are Wisconsin"— that public employees themselves, along with their allies, were the heart and soul of the state. In this way they did not start by ceding ground to the Tea Party/Republican mantra of smaller or no government. Public employees and their democratic rights were fundamental to the quality of life of all Wisconsinites.

Of course, not all participants took such a bold stand. Leaders of the large statewide unions immediately and unilaterally agreed to the fiscal concessions in Walker's proposal, against the wishes of local leaders and members. Some national labor representatives came into town with a "script" to follow, and I heard stories that they were using polling numbers to guide their decisions. Some Democratic Party officials tried to get the protesters occupying the capitol to leave so that others could negotiate a settlement. Later, some of the same Democrats tried to convince protesters to leave things in the hands of the lawyers pursuing legal challenges.

But the message here is that taking a bold stand can often build more support than pragmatic leaders might have you believe. If you base all your decisions on current attitudes, you don't allow for the possibility of people changing their mind. The realm of what is possible can change quickly. When the Egyptian people used peaceful protest to topple a dictator one Al-Jazeera reporter said in tears that suddenly it seemed as if anything was possible, from women's rights to freedom for Palestine. If we believe that the white voters of Wisconsin are truly Tea Party supporters at heart, we close ourselves to trusting that they can learn and grow by struggling for their own rights, alongside their neighbors.

There is also a lesson for political leaders, and this is that you sometimes need to step out of the way of the members. The Wisconsin teachers' unions urged members to go to the capitol *after* the teachers themselves had started to do so in large numbers. Jim Cavanaugh, president of the South Central Federation of Labor, agreed that members were out in front. He said even AFL-CIO president Rich Trumka saw this when he came to Madison. John Nichols says that the TAA led the protests because they did not let anyone tell them they could not fight back, unlike the rest of the unions in the state who believed the fight was lost.

The status quo is against us, and many of the rules are not in our favor. Building a fightback movement will require us to disrupt the status quo, to break the rules, and to take risks.

4. HOLD POLITICIANS ACCOUNTABLE FROM THE LEFT. While Wisconsin, Michigan, and Ohio are all dealing with Republican governors, plenty of Democrats elsewhere are attacking public sector workers. Notably, Andrew Cuomo ran for governor of New York based on the promise to rein in the unions. And on the national level, even with Democrats in the White House and controlling both

houses, there were few gains for labor. President Obama gave only tepid support for the Wisconsin workers. The attacks from Republicans are more extreme in that they are explicitly trying to eliminate the right of workers to join unions, and they are proving that they are not even willing to negotiate. The Democrats have stepped up in places to defend workers' rights to organize. However, few Democrats are willing to take the necessary steps to fix state budgets or influence the national agenda in a way that protects jobs, wages, and benefits.

This highlights the question of accountability. One thing we learned in third-party work in Wisconsin and which the Tea Party seems to highlight is the need for a left pole: social movements and organizations that steadfastly make demands for what is necessary, and not just what is possible. The work of politics is about negotiation, and even when we do not want to compromise, the reality of politics involves compromise on a daily basis. When negotiating, you want as many tools as possible to strengthen your hand. Having a mobilized left pole that is ready to take to the streets is a tool that Democrats theoretically should want if they were serious about their promises. The other pole is big money and big corporations, ever hovering about with the threat of withdrawal. The left has no way to counter that pole other than with people power.

Right after Obama was elected, the network of over 13 million volunteers that got him elected was converted into "Organizing for America" and put under the auspices of the Democratic National Committee. Nonprofits, labor unions, and activists in Washington were given "access" to the White House through coordinated regular meetings, but under unilateral terms set by Obama's people. The rules were clear: if you want to maintain access you need to stay on message.

When the attacks against ACORN ratcheted up, the White House remained silent—as did most of the left, and one of the largest organizations of people of color was quickly dismantled. Although ACORN had problems, it demonstrated throughout its history that it was not afraid to take direct action and pose challenges to those in power, even if they were supposed to be allies.

Obama was never going to be a left-wing president, but even under his own agenda, he and his administration quickly benched one of their greatest strengths: a large movement of people that could mobilize for issues they cared about and that would demonstrate popular support for progressive reform.

It is not just Obama and the Democrats who missed this point. Many on the left worried too much about arguing with others on the left, trying to convince them of a particular point of view. Instead, we need to see the multiple perspectives as a strength.

When I was at the University of Massachusetts-Amherst, students and faculty formed a group called the UMass Anti-War Coalition. We were opposed to the wars in Afghanistan and Iraq, and we had a general critique of U.S. foreign policy and neoliberalism. Soon another group formed, called Students Against the War. This group was not necessarily opposed to wars other than the one in Iraq. There were some students new to politics, and even some who had been in the military. They were not sure how they felt about Afghanistan. At first there was tension between the groups, but we soon realized that we could both be stronger due to the presence of the other group. We could both set up literature tables in the Campus Center and attract different people. We could promote some of the same events and sometimes do our own thing.

I am not saying that the differences in positions do not matter, because they do. And I am not suggesting that we do not engage in debate about politics and strategy on the left. But instead of focusing so much energy on trying to persuade one another, we need to spend a lot more time talking to the millions of people who do not usually engage in political organizations and actions. Instead of spending hours crafting statements about why Obama supporters were delusional, or setting up panels to debate Obama supporters, left groups with a critical perspective could have spent more of their time building networks of people who were ready to mobilize about the particular issues they cared about (such as stopping the war or getting single-payer health care). Instead of trying to keep left voices and critics out, or denounce those who did not support Obama as sectarians or racists, Obama supporters should have recognized that they might need some of these critical voices down the line to keep Obama accountable to his promises.

To take the fight national, we need to accept the range of voices in the fightback. This will include Democrats, such as the Wisconsin 14 who left the state to block a vote. It will include left organizations that call for general strikes and direct action. It will also include activists who press for immediate reforms. This range is a strength, not just in the sense of diversifying our base but also because we build in mechanisms of accountability. This range lets us focus on the pragmatic goals of defense, but keeps alive the longer-term vision of alternatives.

It would be a serious mistake to put all our hopes on the Democratic Party as a way out of the budget crisis and undermining of labor rights. No doubt many on the left will focus heavily on the 2012 elections, but it is crucial that we get serious about accountability. Even where Democratic candidates may have the best intentions, they will not be effective in office without large, vocal, and independent social movements in the streets.

5. OUR MOVEMENTS HAVE TO BE INCLUSIVE. One of the reasons the Wisconsin fightback was inspirational is because it was so broad. Whereas the trigger point for many was the attack on collective bargaining, the protests were about more than that. The protesters at the capitol did not just talk about their unions, but about a whole way of life in Wisconsin. Teachers' rights were connected to students learning. Public sector bargaining was attached to the bigger vision of democratic rule.

Unfortunately, too many of our unions have become narrowly focused on the immediate needs of their members. This makes sense, as no one else is looking out for most workers. But we need to see our labor struggles as community struggles, and vice versa. This is so because workers are residents and consumers and parents; it is also true because our ability to get affordable housing or child care affects our ability to go to work and do our jobs. At the same time, unions are the largest democratic working-class organizations in the country, with the most resources. Most people have very little power in most aspects of their life except for potential power in the workplace, united with co-workers. This kind of power can help us win improvements in the workplace but also, possibly, in the broader society.

The campaign by Memphis sanitation workers was about the right to form a union and engage in collective bargaining, but it was also about civil and human rights. Workers asserted that their work mattered, and that they mattered, to their community. Many in the community supported them, agreeing that workers' rights were necessary for creating a just society. (Anyone who hasn't done so needs to read *Going Down Jericho Road* by Michael Honey, and to see the documentary *At the River I Stand*.)

Our unions need to think boldly, about their demands and their organizations. They need to find ways to allow members to lead. They need to use their power to push for greater changes that will affect whole communities. Specifically, this could include unions uniting to push for increased corporate taxes, closing corporate loopholes, or re-regulating financial markets. These are the kinds of demands that can address budget deficit problems over time, improving conditions for public sector workers and public programs.

In addition to a broader vision from unions, we need to make our movements inclusive in other ways. Wisconsin is 89 percent white. It is clear that the Wisconsin protests were overwhelmingly white compared to the U.S. population overall, and many of the videos and recall commercials seem to highlight the "average white American." I remember when I was active in Progressive Wisconsin that I would sometimes be challenged at meetings around the country by people who asked, "Why are you organizing in a predominantly white state?" My answer was: "That is where I live, and that is where a lot of white people live." If I was working for a national organization trying to decide where to send organizers and resources I would not choose Wisconsin. But when people already live in a place, why shouldn't they be organized? And shouldn't white people try to organize other white people into a progressive movement rather than see them in a right-wing one?

But it is also true that Milwaukee is ranked the most segregated city in the country, and the history of Wisconsin politics is heavily laden with racialized attacks on people of color. The national welfare reform laws got their start in Wisconsin under Governor Tommy Thompson. People often talked about the "generous" social programs in Wisconsin that attracted "people from Chicago" (meaning, black people). As an African American airline employee said to me when I was recently in the Milwaukee airport, "There is a certain racial undertone to these attacks on public services—and the people of this state voted for that when they voted for Walker."

While I am happy to see white people organizing around a progressive fightback, we will do this potential movement harm by not acknowledging the racial dynamics at play in the formation of the policies and the impact of attacks on the public sector. African Americans are disproportionately employed in the public sector, and people of color are more likely to use a range of public services. Nationally, we need to be clear that people of color need to be in leadership positions within this movement if it is to grow.

Similarly, the Wisconsin protests have been framed by some as "middle class," or an effort to save the middle class. This framing is antithetical to many of us on the left who realize that to have a middle class presupposes there is a lower class—a working class, the unemployed, the disenfranchised. "Middle class" terminology suggests an accepted and acceptable position in the ladder of a capitalist economy. This is a problem we have in a number of our movements that frame their demand for rights for certain groups because they are "deserving"—such as "hardworking immigrants," "working families," or even "full-time workers who deserve a living wage." This language can be exclusionary and create divisions between those who work for pay and those without employment; those who have "done everything right" versus those who "messed up." It also restricts us to defending the status quo rather than building something different. I think the moment is here to expand our message and demands. We are fighting to defend the notion of the public good, full labor and civil rights for all, and a world where work is fulfilling and rewarding.

We are fighting for a democratic society in all aspects, and where our economy is centered around human need. We are for fighting collective problems with collective solutions.

We cannot accept the lure of framing our demands to play best with focus groups or highlighting only the most "respectable" parts of our movement. This will only serve to divide us and then weaken us, and to limit our dreams.

.

PART THREE

Broadening and Deepening
the Class Struggle

. . .

The events in Madison and throughout Wisconsin have, as we have seen, a specific history, although workers there faced problems that workers everywhere in the nation face as well. It is this latter fact that allows us to draw a more general meaning from what happened. However, it must also be recognized that certain aspects of Wisconsin are perhaps not suitable for making generalizations. For example, the state is overwhelmingly white, and most of the protesters in Madison were white. It is not possible to build a labor movement without the active participation and leadership of people of color. The problem of race has been critical to the failure of the U.S. labor movement to organize workers and to create democratic labor unions. One very positive impact of Wisconsin has been the encouragement given to the organization of immigrant communities, which have been fighting against the devastating assaults on their rights by the immigration authorities.

Another barrier to the reconstitution of the U. S. labor movement is the strength of blind devotion to the nation. No meaningful solidarity with workers in the rest of the world is possible if we support the U.S. war machine, which is the main enemy of our best potential allies throughout the globe. As capital penetrates every corner of the earth, no labor movement can survive unless it has an international perspective. By the same token, here at home, the labor movement cannot survive if is built solely inside workplaces or if it excludes any group of workers.

The essays in this section confront these issues and offer hope that they can be addressed and that the problems they create can be overcome.

9—Potholes and Roadblocks on "The Roads Not Taken"

ELLY LEARY

My essay, "The Roads Not Taken," published in the June 2005 issue of *Monthly Review*, grew out of a presentation/training session at the Massachusetts Jobs with Justice Solidarity School in November 2004. The school, an outgrowth of strategic planning schools initiated by the New Directions Movement, the progressive caucus of the UAW, gave grassroots activists from the workplace and the community a space to reflect, develop a worldview, strategically plan, and most important, learn from one another and grow together. This talk was the opening in a longer program on how to move forward in the political climate of a consolidated second-term Bush presidency. My sense at the time was that resolving internal contradictions—like those detailed in "The Roads Not Taken"—was the key link to any labor resurgence, despite the external political conditions.

The situation has only worsened since then: unemployment is hovering around 10 percent, much of it seemingly permanent, especially for nonwhite youth; unionization in the private sector is now below 7 percent and most union members are now from the public sector; war and empire-building are galloping along; in 2010 executive pay grew 27 percent, with that for workers in private industry increasing a measly 2.1 percent; and a persistent and growing racial wealth gap, unrelieved by post-secondary education, for African Americans. More significant, however, is the full-out attack by the right wing of capitalism. Guided by think tanks like the Heritage Foundation and the Koch-funded Cato Institute, the right has adopted a long-range, all-encompassing strategy on par with the deepest Marxist and socialist thinkers. These folks are not limiting their thinking to third-quarter profits or immediate pragmatic solutions. Beginning in the mid-1960s, the hard-line right has slowly and painstakingly organized at the base, while investing heavily at the policy level. For example, when asked in a mid-1990s interview on how the "Contract with America" succeeded, Newt Gingrich unabashedly said he used CIO tactics and strategy from the 1930s. The right-wing assault, reaching fruition with the 2010 midterm elections, rests on three pillars: ideology (government is the problem; only the private sector creates jobs; if I don't have it neither should you); governance (removing all "red tape" that stands in the way of business—from taxes to OSHA, to environmental safety); and decimating the institutions of those who stand in the way (ACORN, unions, and Planned Parenthood).

Now, five-and-a-half years later, I see that labor renewal will not come primarily from resolving the persistent internal contradictions articulated in "The Road Not Taken." The script is now flipped. Renewal must take place in the context of dealing with the external conditions. As Marta Harnecker and Michael Lebowitz have argued, the working class and all those oppressed by capitalism must begin to create spaces for an alternative form of society inside the current capitalist one. It will be centered on developing human potential, full democracy, and "protagonism"—or "agency" to use a more familiar American term. To quote Harnecker, "Using that same state, we [must] begin laying the foundations of new institutions and a new political system, creating spaces from the bottom up where popular protagonism can be exercised; spaces where popular sectors learn to exercise power from the simplest level up to the most complex."

Let's be honest. This is an extremely difficult organizing task, undertaken in extremely trying circumstances. As self-financed institutions of the working class, unions must take the lead. It means reaching down to the local level and building back up to the top, a strategic shift back in time to the era of the Knights of Labor. It will require dealing with the intersecting oppressions of race, class, and gender, as well as the ferocious grip of white supremacy. It will certainly require taking on capitalism in all its forms. It will require redefining what constitutes progress and the good life. Here I am talking about moving directly away from capitalist and socialist notions of continuous growth—the profit motive in the former and the theory of productive forces in the latter—as the key to progress. It will require rethinking organization building and development. In short, this process must take on the internal contradictions articulated in "The Roads Not Taken," reprinted below.

The fight-back in Wisconsin showed some glimmerings of this new direction, as teachers, firefighters, students, nurses, small business, farmers, women's rights advocates, and laid-off and downsized private sector workers coalesced in the capitol building. The fight, as it should, took on the larger question of what kind of society we want to live in, the values we stand for, the collective steps we need to get there. We need to thing big and long term, taking a page out of the right-wing playbook (whose signal callers took it from us!). If resistance is limited to recall petitions, unions fighting for union rights, building separate/sector movements which are tangentially connected to each other, or a left celebrating small but important victories like Rite-Aid and Republic Window workers, we'll never really fill those potholes or remove those road blocks.

THE ROADS NOT TAKEN

EDITOR'S NOTE: As stated above, the essay below was published in 2005. We have not updated the data, but it is safe to say that economic conditions for workers are worse now than then.

There is no disputing that these are tough times for the working class and its allies (all those oppressed by capitalism). The working class lacks a political party; social services to assist us with the inevitable problems we face have been eroded; and even our few precious institutions, especially unions, seem overwhelmed by the relentless attacks.

Consider these few facts: The federal minimum wage of $5.15 has not changed in seven years; it is now 61 percent of poverty level. Forty-five million people lack health insurance; for those who have it, premiums have risen 33 percent and out-of-pocket expenses 49 percent, more than eating up most pay raises. Twenty-two of the thirty-one "red states" (those that voted for George Bush in the 2004 election) have right-to-work laws. Manufacturing jobs have declined 12 percent in the last several years, but unionized manufacturing jobs in the same period have declined 66 percent. Union membership is barely 13 percent. In the private sector it accounts for a smaller percentage of the workforce than in the 1920s, the period that has usually been identified as the low-water mark.

As the debate rages about what to do, it is useful to step back and see how it got to this point. As Ella Baker persuasively put it, "I am saying as you must say, too, that in order to see where we are going, we not only must *remember* where we have been, but we must *understand* where we've been."

Many labor analysts place the onset of the crisis in the early 1970s. After the Vietnam War things really began to blow apart. That's when the post–Second World War "consensus" came unraveled. At the heart of that consensus was the tacit agreement that if labor signed on to the Cold War empire-building agenda, the capitalists would lay off. This consensus, of course, barely existed for nonwhite workers.

The 1970s were when white workers, who more than anyone else had made great gains after the Second World War, saw their way of life under attack. Only those folks of color, principally blacks of African descent, who were working in manufacturing, and unionized, benefited from the consensus.

But placing the crisis at the collapse of the consensus misreads history and is, I would argue, too simplistic. This isn't the first time labor has been at the crossroads. All along the labor movement has faced choices about what to do in times of crisis and difficulty. I want to point out how these different choices, and more important, the roads not taken, have led to where we are today. These choices revolve around three critical and interconnected issues. For this discussion they have been separated, but in real life each one builds and intersects with the other, so that the result is something different than merely the sum of its parts.

For example, take the first issue, white supremacy. In this country it was built on the platform of patriarchy. Furthermore, no conversation about white supremacy can be separated from issues of class. So while we may talk about white supremacy, we know its contours and dynamics are determined by the additional interplay of patriarchy and class. As historian Robin Kelley says, "Racism is gendered, sexism is racialized, and class differences are reproduced by capitalism." What I point out are just a few major markers of a more complex situation that requires a deeper analysis that pulls together the interconnectedness of issues and oppressions.

Issue 1: Not Confronting White Supremacy

At the start of the modern-day labor movement after the Civil War when the first national unions formed, in particular the National Labor Union (NLU), choices were made about who could belong. After some angry debate, the NLU decided to exclude former slaves. Indeed, the majority forces inside the NLU were "Copperheads," pro-Confederate northern Democrats, who attracted northern workers over the 1863 draft law, passed by a Republican Congress, which allowed the rich to buy their way out of military service.

The 1870s saw the birth of a number of labor unions, some local or regional in influence, others national in scope. Most of these unions were skill or trade based—printers, ironworkers, and the like. Many of these unions had members and leaders who were part of socialist or anti-capitalist parties. Even so, uniformly these unions and parties were racist and sexist. In the East and South, blacks were the main target; in the West, there was a virulent anti-Chinese racism. Most labor activists in this country know the racist origins of the union label—a scheme by the cigar makers union, wholeheartedly supported by the socialist Workingmen's Party, to show their product was not made by Chinese immigrant labor that they had barred from union membership.

Both the Knights of Labor, which was a major player from the early 1870s through the early 1890s, and the Industrial Workers of the World (IWW), whose star shone from 1905 through 1918, had better records on confronting white supremacy (and patriarchy). However, by the time the American Federation of Labor (AFL) assumed the driver's seat of the labor movement during the First World War, efforts to build a more inclusive labor movement were dead in the water. The AFL vigorously enforced a policy of black and Asian exclusion. A little known but telling example is the case of the Japanese Mexican Labor Union, born in the beet fields of California in the early years of the twentieth century. Initially, sugar farmers used Mexican and Chinese contract labor, but that ended with the Chinese Exclusion Act of 1902.

Japanese workers were then aggressively recruited through an ethnically based subcontract system. The Sugar Beet Association, afraid of the growing power of the subcontractors to improve wages and working conditions, refused to hire through subcontractors, cut wages, and tightened their grip on purchases through the company stores.

Unexpectedly, the Japanese and Mexican workers and subcontractors formed a labor association, went on strike, crippling the industry and eventually winning all their demands. Soon after, the Japanese Mexican Labor Association (JMLA) applied to the AFL for a charter. Samuel Gompers, then president of the AFL, granted the union a charter on the condition that Asians could not become members. The JMLA was furious and rejected the charter saying, "We would be false to them and to ourselves and to the cause of unionism if we accepted privileges for ourselves which are not accorded to them."

Until the 1930s, when the first national labor laws were passed (the famous Wagner Act), unions were not legally recognized. Workers trying to organize could be tried for conspiracy. In order to get the necessary votes in Congress, President Franklin Roosevelt had to make a deal with the "Dixiecrats," the significant number of Southern Democrats, many of whom were wealthy farm owners descended from slaveholding planters (thus their other name, "plantocracy").

The Dixiecrats agreed to vote to legalize labor unions if the law excluded agricultural and domestic workers. This compromise eliminated most of the black working class in the South from legal union coverage. This compromise was originally intended to keep former slaves and their descendants in a state of poverty and dependence; today immigrant farmworkers from Mexico, Guatemala, El Salvador, and Haiti feel its consequences.

And of course there was the failure of Operation Dixie, the post–Second World War effort by the Congress of Industrial Organizations (CIO) to organize the South. Operation Dixie failed because of three essential mistakes:

1. Transplanting the northern strategy that successfully organized automobile plants and steel mills onto the South without any regard for southern culture and usually at the hands of northern organizers.

2. The refusal to confront white supremacy because it was thought that it would be too difficult and no white workers would join the union. We should be clear. A frank reckoning with white supremacy was a task of extreme difficulty. It meant taking on the complex and volatile mix of class, gender, and religion that was the foundation of, as southern author Lillian Smith so clearly put it, the "drug of white supremacy." Instead, the CIO focused exclusively on economic issues, avoiding discussion of race, white consciousness, or what role nonwhites would play inside the union.

    The dread of confronting this core issue was part of the reason that Operation Dixie targeted textile mills. That workforce was almost entirely white. Textiles were chosen even though the bitter memories of repression from the strike wave of 1934 were still fresh and the mill owners' iron grip on southern mill towns made General Motors' role in Flint, Michigan, seem benign.

Demonstrating the lengths the CIO went to avoid the issue was the failure to organize in tobacco—the South's other main industry—where organizing drives had been very successful during the early 1940s. Tobacco's workforce was multiracial. Up to December 1946, the Food, Tobacco, Agricultural and Allied Workers of America-CIO (FTA) had been involved in sixty-two Operation Dixie drives, winning fifty-two of them for a gain of more than 12,500 workers.

3. Purging or banning any organizer or shop activist who was "left" or "red." One of the first to go was the FTA, whose leadership and organizing staff in the South were dominated by women and men of color, many of whom had joined the Communist Party. This left Operation Dixie in the hands of racially conservative, anticommunist white males, many of whom had little experience in southern ways of organizing. None of them were about to challenge the economic, social, and political hegemony of the Dixiecrat-controlled system of white supremacy, nor the patriarchal foundation it rested upon.

Issue 2: The Defeat of Community Unionism

The Knights of Labor organized not just by sector but also geographically. In cities across the country the Knights formed "lodges" that included everyone in the community, regardless of their job, or no job. Women, African Americans, and Mexicans were part of the Knights and served in leadership roles. At their 1886 national convention in Richmond, Virginia, the Knights successfully demanded that African American delegates be admitted to all hotels and theaters. The Knights did, however, exclude the Chinese.

The Knights were popular because they emphasized land reform, education, and mutual aid societies, held social functions, and urged workers to form cooperatives. In many places, they were the hub of all working-class and progressive activity. For example, the New Mexican Knights, under Mexicano leadership, helped form the People's Party, which dominated local politics for several years.

The demise of the Knights allowed the AFL to consolidate its position as the "legitimate" trade union movement. Their policy of "bread and butter" unionism limited to workers' wages and working conditions at a specific work site became the predominant paradigm.

The formation of the CIO was a much-needed counterweight. Because most CIO organizing was centered in mass production industries which had a large immigrant workforce (Eastern Europe predominantly) as well as some African Americans, CIO organizers relied heavily on ethnic community organizations like social clubs, burial societies, churches, and the like. Many CIO organizers were recruited from these organizations.

CIO organizing efforts in the South prior to Operation Dixie similarly relied on organizing both in the community and the workplace. An excellent example of how this strengthened both the movements in the workplace and in the communities is FTA Local 22 in Winston-Salem, North Carolina. In early 1947 the local campaigned vigorously for three candidates for city alderman. All three won, and the top vote-getter, Kenneth Williams, received the largest vote for any alderman in the history of Winston-Salem. Moreover, he was the first black alderman since Reconstruction.

It is little known that in 1946 the CIO's plan was not limited to organized workers. Their program of class demands, accompanied by the largest strike wave in U.S. history, covered both union and non-union workers: thirty hours work for forty hours' pay—a program designed to help integrate tens of thousands of returning soldiers while still allowing women and minorities, who had taken their jobs, to retain some much needed, well-paid (union) employment; national health insurance; 25 cents-an-hour pay raise for every worker, roughly a $3.25-an-hour raise today. That CIO front was broken by Walter

Reuther of the United Auto Workers (UAW) in the fall of 1946 when he signed an agreement with General Motors, locking into place our society's pattern of company-sponsored health insurance and ending any discussion about national health insurance for decades.

Issue 3: Not Challenging Capitalism (the "C" Word) and Empire

As mentioned, the consolidation of the second industrial revolution—and the financial meltdown in the 1870s—set the stage for the rise of the Knights. Not only were they grounded in the community, they were anti-capitalist. Part of their program was to return to a simpler way of life, before the industrial age of robber barons. They wanted a "cooperative commonwealth." The Zapatista program of cooperatives and niche economics is very similar to the Knights' cooperative commonwealth.

Once the Knights of Labor had been crushed, two other labor federations rose to prominence. One was the AFL, the other the IWW. The IWW was avowedly anti-capitalist. The preamble to the IWW's founding convention boldly states, "The working class and the employing class have nothing in common....It is the historic mission of the working class to do away with capitalism." This was not mere rhetoric. For example, they opposed union contracts as compromising with capital.

The IWW believed the way to settle scores, both at work and in the community, was through direct action. But it was their stand against the First World War as a war of the bosses in which the working class worldwide would lose that doomed them. They faced outright repression from the government—jailings, beatings, deportations, and endless trials. The AFL rode to preeminence on its pro-war stand and frankly aided and abetted governmental repression efforts of the Wobblies.

Another significant fork in the road came after the Second World War. There were massive Cold War purges inside the union movement of those who challenged capitalism. Not coincidentally, most of these were the same forces that were challenging white supremacy (and did the most to cultivate and develop woman leaders). This took place at the same time as Operation Dixie and compounded its mistakes. The purges led rather quickly to the merger of CIO and AFL and signing on to the Cold War agenda.

For years, international relations of the AFL-CIO were squarely in line with the ruling Cold War consensus. Through its international department, the American Institute for Free Labor Development (AIFLD), founded in 1962 in response to the Cuban Revolution, actively promoted only "free trade unions" and crushed indigenous union movements around the world, many of them anti-capitalist.

Even though the AFL-CIO under John Sweeney backed off from many of these abuses, the record is still poor. For example, we heard a lot about supporting the oil workers' union in Venezuela, a union that proclaimed Chávez a threat to democracy and the unions. It was never mentioned that the union the AFL-CIO supported was the union of bosses and supervisors, not the union of the workers, who actually went to work and manned the oil facilities.

Overall, labor's official "international relations" are mired in U.S.-centric arrogance and begin and end with rhetoric about mutual aid and support, or "labor solidarity." Real analysis of forces, context, and conditions rooted in an anti-neoliberal framework are not part of the current dialogue.

Finally, there is the steadfast allegiance of the dominant trend within the union movement to the Democratic Party, even when that party has carried out over the last dozen years a pro-neoliberal, anti-worker agenda.

But capitalism isn't only about foreign relations, politics, and economics. Capitalism is also about culture, and consequently, social control. The more powerful the dominant system, in this case capitalism, the more dominant its culture and the less it needs to rely on force for social control. Culture is way more than "good" art and music or popular culture. It encompasses how people view and interpret the world around them, what passes for "common sense," "normal," "moral values," and right and wrong. Culture gives meaning to ideas like "democracy," "equality," and "freedom." It even extends to ideas about what makes a good organization, something quite central to the current debate inside the union movement.

Most of the time everyone in this country, including our institutions like unions, is constrained by U.S. capitalist culture. For example, much of the language of the current union debate is about capturing "market share." The organizational suggestions have much in common with capitalist business practices—mergers and consolidations for efficiency; power shifting to the top for accountability; and a tremendous reliance on charismatic individuals (in this case all white men!) at the national level to exemplify the program and mobilize the base around what the top leadership has developed for them. None of the major proposals questions this dominant organizational model of top-down, leader-centered groups in the context of capitalist cultural hegemony.

But in times of strong social movements, countercultural ideas can gain, at least temporarily, a foothold. These organizations are characteristically bottom-up, with developed grassroots leaders who are group-centered. Additionally, they have strong ties to the community and larger social and political issues and movements. It is no coincidence that this countercultural model deals with the intersectionality of issues and oppressions.

Put another way, if the issue of organization for working-class power revolves around the axis of class (capitalist social relations), it is also true that the solution must simultaneously include, and solve, issues around white supremacy and patriarchy. As I've tried to show throughout, issues of race, class, and gender are inextricably woven together. Situations determine which one holds the key to solve the others.

In any event, organizations that successfully combine all these elements and deal with all the intersecting issues hold the promise of merging disciplined action, which members collectively plan and control, and a place where individuals can develop their full potential as critical thinkers and well-rounded human beings. These organizations I call "liberatory organizations." Time after time, though, they have become the roads not taken. But when such organizations have become part of the labor movement the results have been stunning.

One of the most famous IWW actions was the ten-week strike of 23,000 against the American Woolen Company in Lawrence, Massachusetts, in January 1912. Lawrence was a typical mill town. The official U.S. government investigation into the strike estimated that 60,000 of the 85,000 residents were dependent upon the textile industry, the largest employer being American Woolen.

Most remember the strike because of the leading role women strikers played. Polish women led the walkout. Erroneously thinking that the police would not beat or jail women, they were central to organizing the picket lines. Women strikers coined the famous strike slogan, "We want bread but we want roses too." Less is known about their unique methods, usually not shared with male leaders, of dealing with scabs. What also stands out is the innovative organizational solution to build unity among twenty-four ethnic groups with twenty-two different languages—a bargaining committee of nearly 300, with delegates from each language and ethnic group.

Another example is graphically replayed for us in the movie *Salt of the Earth* where issues of race, class, and gender collide in the building and maintenance of a member-run local. Here Mexicano/Chicano miners of the International Union of Mine, Mill and Smelter Workers struck Empire Zinc from October 1950 to January 1952. The strike, as well as the movie's filming, is set in the context of McCarthyism and a company town ruthlessly ruled by an Anglo minority. As the strike grinds on it escalates into a community strike because of mass evictions and assorted corporate/law enforcement evil doings that are chock full of white supremacy and sexism. Women get involved in a big way, altering their role and consciousness. And workers from surrounding mines arrive to lend support.

The underlying internal contradictions among the strikers are rolled out on film for everyone to see. There is the racism of the white organizer sent from the international even though he is part of a "Communist dominated" union (to use the phrase of the day). Front and center is the issue of the patriarchy of Mexicano and Anglo men. As Debby Rosenfeld's brilliant 1976 review says, "These struggles— against racism, sexism, the unchecked power of the ruling class—converge and coalesce. At times they conflict (or seem to conflict) with one another. Where they conflict, the mining community becomes divided against itself. Where they converge, there is unity."

Fortunately, these liberatory organizations do exist today as well, even inside the labor movement. Some local unions do operate in this way and can be found in the most unlikely places—like the International Union of Electrical Workers (IUE, now merged with the Communications Workers of America) and GE aircraft engine local in Lynn, Massachusetts, which has transcended its anticommunist past and come full circle. A number of Jobs with Justice chapters are trying to create these kinds of organizations. But they are far from being the dominating model that the Knights and IWW were in their time.

However, inside the other sections of the labor movement—worker centers in particular—this model has gained a strong foothold. That is why we need to ask them to play a part in the conversation about the crisis in the labor movement. We need to be painfully aware that the answers for labor renewal may not lie in the 13 percent that are organized.

So as we debate where to go from here we need to keep our history in mind. I would also offer five questions for us to answer as we evaluate some of the plans and strategies put to us as part of the solution.

- How does any strategy for labor renewal engage and build on the strengths and leadership of the grassroots/rank and file, in particular women and people of color?
- How does a strategy for labor renewal address the challenges of empire in all its forms?
- How does a strategy for labor renewal confront the historic obstacles (white supremacy, sexism, and heterosexism) to building real working-class unity?
- How does a strategy for labor renewal build liberatory organizations for the long haul?
- How can a strategy for labor renewal link labor and community in seamless and reinforcing ways?

10—The Assault on Public Services: Will Unions Lament the Attacks or Fight Back?

MICHAEL HURLEY and SAM GINDIN

We are living in one of those historic moments that cry out for rallying the working class to build new capacities, new solidarities, and concrete hope. The crucial question is not how far the attacks on the public sector will go. The question is how far we will let them go. How will working-class activists inside and outside the unions respond? Do we have a counterplan? Are we preparing one? Can we act as decisively as those attacking us?

What's at stake is not just a new round of concessions. The aftermath of the deepest capitalist crisis since the Great Depression has provided political and economic elites, here in Canada and around the world, with an opportunity to lock in two longer-term changes: a reduction and privatization of public services on a scale not seen before and, with private sector unions devastated by job loss and unable to significantly expand unionization, a weakening of the remaining stronghold of unionism—public sector workers.

The attack on public services is commonly posed in terms of "cut-backs," but it is crucial to link it to privatization. For some time now corporations have been chomping at the bit to profit from what are now public services. Governments have been moving to accommodate this by restructuring how these services are organized and delivered so that they can—piecemeal if necessary—be privatized. The crisis in government finances is being used to accelerate this trend. The end result will be losing services that aren't privately profitable and sacrificing quality and access while paying more for health care, garbage collection, utilities, mail, and all the other services left that we will then need to buy (or still finance through taxes).

An effective response requires a social movement much stronger than we currently have; and this raises the issue of the attack on unions. We obviously need to fight back; we know from experience that if we don't, it only invites the other side to be even more aggressive. But given what we are up against—a state determined to change the rules—it's also clear that "business as usual," even if more militant, won't be enough. We need to engage this struggle in new ways, and this means reevaluating everything about our own union structures, processes, and strategies.

Strategic Choices:
Leading the Fight for Public Services

Unions emerged as sectional, not class, organizations: they united workers in a particular workplace or sector and focused on making gains for those particular members. In an earlier time, this achieved important benefits that were subsequently spread to others beyond the unionized sector. But when circumstances changed and corporations and governments concluded that working-class gains had to be reversed to preserve profits, we were ill prepared to address this new aggressiveness. That former legacy of concentrating on our own compensation and conditions left us fragmented and vulnerable to the latest attacks.

Governments have been exploiting that weakness for some time and are now more aggressively trying to use fiscal deficits to isolate public sector workers: choices are framed as lower payments to workers or lower levels of services. This involves framing the choice as being between the level of worker compensation and the level of public services. With the rest of the working class taking it on the chin, the fact that the public sector remains relatively well-off aggravates the danger of its separation from the rest of the class. The retreats in the private sector, the cutbacks in employment insurance and increase in precarious work, the continuously falling rates of social assistance (now 55 percent lower in real terms than in the mid-1990s as neoliberalism consolidated as the prevailing policy framework)—all this leaves public sector workers open to resentment.

To argue that we've always supported better social services, we must point to our progressive union conference resolutions, and insist that the rich should be taxed to pay for decent services and that fair compensation is valid. But that won't convince those we need to reach. Our commitment must be proven in practice, through the priorities we set and carry out. This means making a strategic choice: we must reset our focus from traditional collective bargaining to the defense of public services as a primary priority and take on—in bargaining, in our relationships to service recipients, and on the streets—the leadership of the fight for adequate, high-quality, and responsive social services.

It is important to be clear about what such a reorientation means. It will require radical changes to *all* our strategies, tactics, and structures. It implies reallocating union resources, building new local and sectoral as well as national capacities, a profound deepening of membership participation, rethinking how we relate to the community, daring to publicly expose poor services while speaking to how they could be improved, and developing the confidence and vision to move beyond fighting on "their" terrain—a terrain on which competitiveness and keeping bankers solvent and happy dominates all other values. It essentially involves, to put it bluntly, a revolution inside our unions.

Many activists and leaders will be nervous about such a transformation in union life. Given the union culture they've grown up in, they may view this as "trading off" their entitlements for a worthy but secondary cause. The reality, however, is that the level and quality of public services is hardly a "secondary" issue; it represents the crucial contribution public sector workers make to the rest of society. Second, improving the level and quality of services is inseparable from improving our workloads and working conditions. And third, we need to come to grips with the fact that as things stand, though we need to continue to defend our past gains and may win some short-term battles, we can't win the war—no matter how legitimate our demands are—unless we broaden our struggle.

Trade unionism as usual will only lead to public sector workers becoming even more cut off and vulnerable. Developing the strength to defend our jobs and conditions can only come from getting a key part of the public on our side. If we can't find ways to develop this kind of public support—especially from other sections of the working class, be they unionized or non-unionized, fully employed or precariously employed, unemployed or the poor—we won't get very far in sustaining our wage demands and benefits, raising the standards of lower-paid members, or defending working conditions.

Moreover, whereas the primary focus of unions has been on bargaining collective agreements and resolving workplace grievances, the attack is now coming directly from the state, and it will come on many fronts—from attacking seniority rights of teachers to privatizing health care services, to limiting the right to strike. This reinforces the limits of struggles confined to our own particular workplaces, sectors, and unions. Those struggles can only have a chance of widespread success if taken on as a class, alongside the rest of labor and new allies.

Facing Austerity: The Ontario Tories

The social cuts and attacks on union rights that we've already seen in Canada from politicians of all stripes are clearly going to get worse. The more aggressive cuts in the States can be expected to bring mounting pressures for the same here and we of course already have our own home-grown politicians and economic elites ready to lead that charge. With Rob Ford as mayor of Canada's largest city, Toronto; Stephen Harper's majority in Parliament; and the Ontario Tories of Tim Hudak now leading in the polls against the Liberal government of Dalton McGuinty it would be foolish to underestimate what we are about to face.

The Ontario Tories' platform includes compulsory tendering of support services across the public sector—everything will be up for sale. Legislation would presumably be introduced to override collective agreement provisions that would otherwise obstruct such tendering (since the constitution blocks this being done unilaterally, it would most likely follow a period of so-called consultation with public sector unions to protect against a legal challenge).

Should this tendering become a reality, support workers such as cleaners and food service staff would be "allowed" (encouraged) to bid against corporations for their jobs—which could only be done by agreeing to significantly cut labor costs to compete in this new market, including not just wages but benefits and defined benefit contribution plans. Those who don't compete will lose their jobs under this proposal. Because the proposed tendering policy targets support workers while at the same time protecting teachers and nurses (for now!), the Conservatives' platform also threatens to divide the unions.

Unions may simply ignore or downplay the threat. Based on responses to date, a good many public sector union leaders seem complacent after a decade of growth in membership and members' incomes and are distracted by day-to-day responsibilities. The loss of 600,000 public sector jobs in Britain to austerity, or the layoff of 60,000 Texas nursing home workers thanks to U.S. federal budget cuts, are seen as unique, distant, and unfortunate events rather than a systematic pattern of attacks on the working class that will also play out here.

Another response will be to look to political parties to save us, and unions will spend millions to affect the outcome of the election. Teachers, registered nurses, and the construction trades, identifying the Liberals as the lesser of two evils, will support the Liberal Party while some private and public sector unions, emphasizing their traditional ties, will support the New Democratic Party (NDP).

The problem here goes beyond the electoral divisions in the labor movement. There is a history of the labor movement's electoral involvement, and even where we have been united around social democratic parties, the results—not only in Ontario but in other provinces, and not only in Canada but elsewhere—are sobering.

The issue is not whether elections matter—they obviously do—but rather that we need to be frank about the limits of even "sympathetic" political parties as they now stand. No party is committed to a fundamental challenge to financial and corporate power. No party is arguing that in a society so much richer than it was a generation ago that workers should be raising not lowering their expectations. No party is looking to develop the working class into a powerful social force. No existing political party will save us.

The point is that "politics" needs to be redefined as building the kind of working-class organizations and capacities that can ensure that our needs are taken seriously. This means public sector unions using their significant resources to advance a political agenda that includes the entire working class. To the extent that this includes electoral politics, it means a number of things.

1. Our support must not be given automatically but conditionally to a party endorsing specific policies that defend all working people.

2. We need to be wary of political alignments and deals in which professional, trade, or craft interests are delivered legislative improvements in return for supporting, or at least not criticizing, other government policies. This transactional relationship between unions and governments tends to turn what should be a class-based politics into a class-divisive politics (e.g., the Ontario government providing special union certification procedures for the construction trades while denying them to other sections of labor).

3. Beyond policies, we must fight against the stultifying identification of politics solely with parliament and insist on the use of party resources, structures, and authority to escape the narrow confines

of Ottawa and actively mobilize in the community. (This is especially important in Quebec, where a number of union and movement activists have been elected to the NDP.)

4. We should expect progressive parties to be ideological leaders in
   challenging and reversing orientations that have worsened
   inequality, made insecurity an increasingly permanent feature of
   our lives, narrowed social values, and left us with a democracy constrained by the "reality of global competitiveness."

5. Unions' electoral activity must not come at the expense of ade-
   quately supporting the infrastructure and campaigns of movements that are addressing, on a relative shoestring, crucial issues
   like universal childcare and fighting poverty.

6. Most important, we cannot allow electoral activity to replace the
   independent mobilizations of the trade union movement. Without
   any substantive independent weight, our demands could be set
   aside and our support simply taken for granted (a past lesson we
   learned the hard way). The last thing we need is to put all our eggs
   in the election basket and wake up one morning with the Tories in
   office. The Tories will move rapidly to freeze wages, limit political
   involvement by unions, restrict bargaining, and introduce tendering while also significantly cutting transfers for public services—and we'd be left scrambling to make up for the preparations
   that should have long been going on.

Building a Labor Movement
Up to the Task

If the only thing that will prevent Ontario's public sector workers from
being defeated in the coming battle will be our resolve to engage in
militant action, intelligently and creatively deployed to build public
support, then how do we build that kind of movement?

A starting point is to acknowledge the weaknesses within our own organizations—weaknesses that predate the present attacks. (There are of course pockets of impressive strength in our movement, but it seems fair to say that these are exceptions.) Our weaknesses range from debilitating cultures of bureaucratization to thin and ineffective democracy, inadequate expressions of class solidarity, and little strategic sense of how to respond to the great changes that have occurred over the past three decades.

Weaknesses are what workers and worker activists should be discussing *now*. How do we move into motion to fight the most immediate battles but do so in a way that builds the capacities we'll need to expand our options and fight the larger battles? How do we get this on the agenda of our unions and push them to come up with concrete implementation plans and timetables? Among the specific issues that beg addressing:

1. Union leadership needs to relinquish mechanisms that were used to maintain political control through the period of relative prosperity for the public sector. The very characteristics that some leaders find threatening—creativity and militancy—are the strengths now needed from leaders at all levels of the union. Dissent needs to be seen as strength, because debate makes us look at issues more deeply.

2. An effective democracy includes building the capacities of local unions by passing on a significant share of national resources and a doubling or trebling of union activists that have the ability to mobilize the memberships. Local leaders, whose training currently emphasizes workplace and legislative issues, need to be trained and supported so they can also lead larger campaigns in defense of their members and services.

3. Although many public sector unions have established intermediate structures across locals in the same sector, they rarely include the accountability mechanisms or full-time officers, assigned staff, and

necessary funds to do real mobilizing and campaigning. They consequently often offer only the mirage of sector coordination. Such sectoral organizations also need to be democratized—that is, they should be led by elected members and provided the resources to coordinate fights beyond locals. (And where such sectoral arms of labor do not exist, they should be established.)

4. In too many public sector unions, corporate cultures are making staff activists cynical. Activism drains away in hierarchical environments where creativity is frowned upon, honest criticism is punished, and staff are reduced to being technicians rather than allowed to be activists. The thousands of staff in full-time positions are a major resource for organizing and mobilizing our members and communities into the coming fight, but only if they are given the space and encouragement to lead and rediscover the enthusiasm and optimism that first brought them into the movement.

5. If unions (including public sector unions) follow through in commitments to increase the rate of private sector unionization, this comes up against limits on staff times. If they are to be redeployed to organizing and campaigns, members in local elected positions will have to be trained to handle some functions currently done by staff, and new activists will have to be recruited and trained to carry through the expanded demands on the union.

6. We must be absolutely adamant about not compromising the defense of services for promises of "labor adjustment." It is, unfortunately, natural for unions to accept trading off jobs for redundancy payments—that exchange follows the nature of collective bargaining and its legalism—but it is a dangerous trap. It further legitimates drastic downsizing and cuts to services and thus turns our back on the public while casting the laid-off workers into an economy where they will likely never earn as much again.

7. The struggles of private sector unions to defend their pensions or to fight concessions have often been fought as local struggles. But as their standards fall this is quickly translated into pressures for public sector workers to also lower their standards. As a matter of both solidarity and self-defense those private sector fights need much greater support from the public sector.

8. A neglected dimension of mobilizing our potential strength, especially in the private sector but now also in the public sector, is retaining contact with those who are laid off. Unions should be providing not only services but opening their union halls to the unemployed as a space for discussion and education as well as music and films—all part of easing their social isolation and mobilizing their frustrations. (Absent such support, it's hardly surprising that a good number of newly unemployed workers see unions as only being there when they paid dues, and so they turn against unions.)

9. Public sector unions need to invest in activist anti-poverty organizations and organizations of precarious workers (workers stuck in part-time, temporary, contract work with no union and little legal protections) that can rally communities behind demands for living rates of social assistance, public housing, free and accessible transit, and minimum enforceable labor standards. Where we directly interact with the people who receive services our members provide, we need to find ways to collectively address how to overcome or at least limit the tensions that often exist because of the nature of the relationship. This includes being frank in exposing weaknesses in the services provided by the public sector and using our direct experience and knowledge to lead the discussions on how they can be improved.

Examples of Creative Class Interventions

As we struggle with renewing our unions, a number of past and present trade union experiences and examples are worth reviewing. In the mid-1990s, the Ontario Days of Action introduced an internationally unique form of protest. Confronted with massive cuts to social programs and the erosion of labor legislation, unions and social movements worked together in an imaginative and disciplined spirit to hold a series of one-day general strikes moving into different communities over a 30-month period.

With workers asked to lose a day's pay and risk employer retaliation, unions were pushed to explain the importance of issues beyond their members' immediate bargaining interests. And with the press warning of hordes of union organizers coming to their community, local debates intensified over the Mike Harris cuts. One limit was that, after building new labor-community structures in various cities, we didn't keep them in place after moving on to the next shutdown. It would be worthwhile returning to that experience to more generally ask what—both positive and negative—it can teach us about becoming more successful next time.

CUPE, Canada's largest union, funded the Ontario Council of Hospital Unions (OCHU) to sponsor a joint forum last fall with the Ontario Coalition Against Poverty (OCAP), under the auspices of the Greater Toronto Workers' Assembly, on the relationship between cutbacks in the special diet and poverty and health care service privatization, and an expanded forum is planned this summer, this time in conjunction with other health care providers, on the relationship between poverty and health outcomes.

More recently, CUPE Ontario, using resources from its national union, hired an organizer to work full-time, in cooperation with OCAP, on the education and mobilization of CUPE members around poverty issues. As well, OCAP has been invited to speak to CUPE's front-line workers about mutual interests and also about tensions. This kind of tangible engagement, moving beyond well-meaning rhetoric, holds out the hope of convincing others that unions do in fact speak to a larger interest.

In response to Toronto's drive to garbage privatization, CUPE's Local 416 didn't simply threaten a strike that it likely couldn't sustain, but put together analysis and information that a trained cadre of rank-and-file workers used for door-to-door canvassing of support from the households they service. And both the Toronto Hydro workers and the Amalgamated Transit Union have experimented with public forums where the union—not management—invites the public in to discuss the quality of services and how they can be defended and improved.

In the educational sector, CUPE's janitorial and educational support workers (Local 4400) have hired eight full-time organizers to mobilize at the community level against threatened school closures. Though an important defensive battle, it also raises larger issues about public spaces—if there is no reasonable reason to keep a particular school open, why can't it be converted into a community space for public meetings, adult education, childcare, workshops on videos or photography, recreation, or even a space where supervised tools and computers and arts and crafts can be collectively shared by the whole community?

In the early 1990s, when the government tightened unemployment insurance (UI—as it was then called) and pushed its employees to cut more people off from qualifying, the union—the Public Service Alliance of Canada—found a way of expressing meaningful solidarity. It put together pamphlets on how to answer questions so it was harder to block people from being disqualified and, since the frontline workers couldn't distribute them at risk of discipline, the union had other members as well as staff distribute the pamphlets outside the UI offices.

Also in the early 1990s, the Canadian Union of Postal Workers, on strike against their employer, delivered pension checks without pay during that strike to emphasize that they didn't consider retirees the enemy. When the government stopped this and forced pensioners to line up at a warehouse to get their checks, the postal workers came down not to picket but to hand out water and offer lawn chairs to pensioners standing in long lines in the heat. (Currently involved in another dispute with the post office over working conditions, CUPW has creatively used rotating strikes to limit public resentment and focus the attention on providing better services without denying respect to the workers providing the service.)

Other examples, and crucial challenges for public sector production and work, are emerging out of the current crisis of public services in Canada as the turn to austerity sets in. Could transit workers who are engaged in a dispute show their support for free and accessible transit by not collecting fares before withdrawing their services and refusing to police the paying of fares if they are denied the right to strike? Could garbage workers defending the public provision of the essential service they provide take the lead in redirecting garbage bags to the financial district when service is interrupted rather than (as in the summer 2010 strike) to our parks ?

It is also worth asking, as the attacks on public sector work escalates, whether it makes sense to leave it to each union in the public sector to go on strike according to their own schedule and strength. In most cases, such strikes will quickly be made illegal or ended through public pressures, but even where an occasional union holds its own, it will become the target for isolation and more intensive pressures for rollbacks later. Wouldn't a union be better off, in the strategic spirit raised above, coordinating a larger response of rotating strikes across sectors and creative disruptions in each sector?

One idea discussed within CUPE goes further. Its Ontario hospital division, OCHU, has been conducting provincial demonstrations and many community fights against hospital service cuts but understands that more pressure is essential to defend the hospitals from closure and privatization. Withdrawing labor to defend hospital services seems contradictory, so the question is how to act in a way that avoids or limits negative impacts on patient care and the consequent loss of public support. Union activists are now discussing the possibility of experimenting with a new tactic: a work-in rather than a walkout—a counter-strike. Members who are off work would come in to work at a specific time to highlight the crushing workloads and the large cuts to staff and beds in Ontario (19,000 over the last twenty years in Ontario while needs were growing). This approach would demonstrate the kind of services that could be provided if these services were in fact a social priority. The actions could be rotated across communities, concretely demonstrating the reluctance of workers to withdraw their services and their commitment to their clients, while putting management on the spot publicly. In placing the level of services on the bargaining table, the union would be both challenging management rights and politicizing bargaining in the sense of challenging the state's pressure for cutbacks.

The work-in seems to pit the members' traditional entitlements against the defense of the service. But that is also its strength, because it can only be discussed in the context of the austerity agenda and the need for approaches that build alliances with the public. That activists remain skeptical about this tactic is understandable. Some see it as a betrayal of the basic principle that union strength is about withdrawing labor, not working for free; to others, the contrast with past tactics raises new complexities and uncertainties; and others are uncomfortable with the added pressures this would bring to educate and mobilize the members.

The work-in therefore requires the union to convince activists that it will both provide central coordination and also resources for local mobilization, as members will have to be won over to the tactic in unit and department meetings. In any case, just raising this issue has forced the need for broader membership involvement in the debate over strategy. It will go forward, but as an experiment in one community, which will be followed by analysis and more discussion.

One of the key ongoing questions facing the union movement—all the more so as private services expand at the expense of publicly organized services—is that of unionization. In the United States unionization in the private sector is now under 7 percent, and even including the public sector it has fallen below 12 percent. Though Canadian union density remains much higher than that of the United States, the American figures are an uncomfortable warning about our future. Because unionization is approached as a matter of gaining members rather than building the working class, unions increasingly compete for those members rather than cooperating to bring some organizational strength to groups of workers. This wastes resources and often also leads to unions undermining one another's drives. Consider, for example, Ontario's homecare system. There are approximately 20,000 unorganized homecare workers in Ontario. After the Conservative government introduced compulsory tendering for homecare services in the 1990s, non-union multinational corporations with much lower labor costs largely displaced the not-for-profit unionized agencies. Unions that successfully organized homecare workers found that their new units were lost the next time the contract was tendered because of their higher costs, and this generally discouraged unionization.

The compensation of private homecare workers—$12.50 an hour, no guaranteed hours of work, no pensions or benefits—is accelerating the movement of work away from the unionized hospital and long-term care sectors. It's an example of an organizing dilemma that likely can only be solved through cooperative organizing by multiple unions with a sector-wide focus. The point would be to pool our resources, organize all of the unorganized agencies at once, bargain as a council of trade unions, bring the state rather than the individual corporations to the bargaining table, and use militant action to move these workers to compensation comparable with the public sector. But that kind of strategy is conditional on first going much further toward changing our unions.

Conclusion: Concrete Hope

In the 1930s, in the midst of the Great Depression and unemployment rates over 20 percent, workers invented an industrial unionism that overcame divisions between skilled and unskilled workers, introduced the tactic of sit-down strikes, initiated their own democratic structures via elected stewards and generated industry-wide pattern bargaining. Those breakthroughs were largely responsible for later bringing us many of our social services and benefits and, in the 1960s, organizing by workers in the public sector who were tired of government paternalism. That public sector breakthrough also created vitally significant new opportunities for women and revived the trade union movement.

In that earlier period, capitalism legitimated itself by offering steady material gains, the promise of greater equality, a more meaningful democracy, and a quality of life that went beyond the pressures of economic survival. That era is over. Today, the message is that if you don't like the way things are, tough—you have no alternative. The real lesson of course is that if the present economic system can't offer us a better life, then it is that system, not our expectations, that needs changing.

Previous generations of workers came up with creative responses to the challenges they faced. It's now our turn—the turn of the great number of committed activists in the labor movement—to truly start taking on these issues within their unions, build networks of support across unions and across communities, and convert widespread frustrations into concrete hopes.

11—Marching Away from the Cold War

DAVID BACON

One sign carried in almost every May Day march of the last few years in the United States says it all: "We Are Workers, Not Criminals!" Often it was held in the calloused hands of men and women who looked as though they'd just come from work in a factory, cleaning an office building, or picking grapes.

The sign stated an obvious truth. Millions of people have come to the United States to work, not to break its laws. Some have come with visas, and others without them. But they are all contributors to the society they've found here.

In the largest U.S. May Day event in 2011, marchers were joined by the public workers who had protested in the state capital of Madison, Wisconsin, who have become symbols of the fight for labor rights in the United States. Their message was the same: we all work, we all contribute to our communities, and we all have the right to a job, a union, and a decent life.

May Day marches and demonstrations over the last five years have provided a vehicle in which immigrants protest their lack of human rights and unions call for greater solidarity among workers facing the same corporate system. The marches are usually organized by grassroots immigrant rights groups, which have been increasingly cooperating with labor unions and the AFL-CIO. This year the attacks on public workers provided an additional push to unions to use May Day as a vehicle for protest.

AFL-CIO president Richard Trumka spoke at the largest of those marches, in Milwaukee, where national attention has focused on the attacks on public workers and their mass resistance. Trumka's presence marked two important political changes in labor. May Day is no longer a red-baited holiday in the U.S. labor movement but one used to promote a defense of workers' rights, as it is in the rest of the world. And unions are slowly adopting a tradition of May Day demonstrations calling for immigrant rights, a tradition begun by immigrant communities themselves in 2006.

For the last five years, May Day protests have responded to a wave of draconian proposals to criminalize immigration status, and work itself, for undocumented people. The defenders of these proposals have used a brutal logic: if people cannot legally work, they will leave. But undocumented people are part of the communities they live in. They seek the same goals of equality and opportunity that working people in the United States historically have fought to achieve. In addition, for most immigrants, there are no jobs to return to in the countries from which they've come.

Instead of recognizing this reality, the U.S. government has attempted to make holding a job a criminal act. Thousands of workers have already been fired. Some have been sent to prison for inventing a Social Security number just to get a job. Yet they stole nothing and the money they've paid into Social Security funds now subsidizes every pension or disability payment.

Undocumented workers deserve legal status because of that labor—their inherent contribution to society. Past years' marches have supported legalization for the 12 million undocumented people in the United States. In addition, immigrants, unions, and community groups have called for repealing the law making work a crime, ending guest worker programs, and guaranteeing human rights in communities along the U.S.-Mexico border.

Undocumented workers and public workers in Wisconsin have a lot in common. With unemployment at almost 9 percent nationally, and higher in many states, all working families need the federal government to set up jobs programs, like those Roosevelt pushed through Congress in the 1930s. If General Electric alone paid its fair share of taxes, and if the troops came home from Iraq and Afghanistan, every person wanting a job could find work building roads, schools, and hospitals. All communities would benefit.

Immigrants and public workers need strong unions that can push wages up, and guarantee pensions for seniors and health care for the sick and disabled. A street cleaner whose job is outsourced and an undocumented worker fired from a fast-food restaurant both need protection for their right to work and support their families.

Instead, some states like Arizona, and now Georgia, have passed measures allowing police to stop any "foreign-looking" person on the street, and question their immigration status. Arizona passed a law requiring employers to fire workers whose names are flagged by Social Security. In Mississippi an undocumented worker accused of holding a job can get jail time of one to five years, and fines of up to $10,000.

The states and politicians that go after immigrants are the same ones calling for firing public workers and eliminating their union rights. Now a teacher educating children has no more secure future in her job than an immigrant cleaning an office building at night.

In Milwaukee Trumka told marchers, "It's the same fight. It's the same people that are attacking immigrants' rights, workers' rights, student rights, voting rights." He paid tribute to the role immigrants have played in resurrecting May Day as a day for worker demonstrations in the United States.

"Your voices have been heard across this nation," Trumka said, "inspiring an uprising of America's working people, standing together and saying 'No!' to divide-and-conquer politics. 'No!' to tearing working families down, rather than building us up. 'No!' to corporate-backed politicians trying to turn us into a low-wage, no-rights workforce as payback to their CEO friends. And what is this America we want? It's a land of equal opportunity, a land of fairness in the workplace and society."

While May Day marches this year were smaller than the millions-strong turnout of five years ago, they had a more organized participation from unions themselves. That marks a fundamental shift in the attitude of U.S. labor toward May Day. Although May Day was born in the fight for the 8-hour day in Chicago more than a century ago, during the Cold War U.S. unions stopped celebrating it. In 1949 nine left-wing unions were expelled from the Congress of Industrial Organizations and a witch hunt then purged activists, including Communists, socialists, and anarchists from leadership in most unions. The U.S. labor movement grew more conservative, enshrining a "business unionism" model, which negotiated increases in wages and benefits while defending the corporate system.

Eventually, some of the highest elements of U.S. labor leadership collaborated with U.S. intelligence services in supporting right-wing coups in other countries, in which labor and political militants were murdered. At the same time, unionists in the United States who advocated celebrating May Day as a symbol of international labor solidarity were attacked and red-baited.

In the late 1970s and 1980s, however, large corporations, assisted by the government, intensified their attacks on unions and workers. The percentage of workers belonging to unions fell drastically, causing an internal crisis in the labor movement. Many Cold War–era leaders were challenged, and at the AFL-CIO convention in New York in 1995 a contest over leadership brought John Sweeney to power as president. Richard Trumka, who'd led a critical battle of coal miners against the Pittston Corporation, was elected secretary-treasurer.

At that time, Trumka proposed a new model for internationalism in U.S. labor. "The cold war has gone," he declared. "It's over. We want to be able to confront multinationals as multinationals ourselves now. If a corporation does business in fifteen countries, we'd like to be able to confront them as labor in fifteen countries. It's not that we need less international involvement, but it should be focused toward building solidarity, helping workers achieve their needs and their goals here at home."

Jack Henning, past executive secretary of the California Labor Federation, one of the most vocal critics of the old AFL-CIO Department of International Affairs, admitted, "We were associated with some of the very worst elements . . . all in the name of anti-communism. But I think there's an opportunity now to review our foreign activities, to stop the global competition for jobs among the trade unions of the world."

Their ideas embodied a pragmatic view of solidarity, a first step away from that Cold War past. But it was not radical enough to confront the new challenges of globalization—the huge displacement and migration of millions of people, the enormous gulf in the standard of living dividing developed from developing countries, and the wars fought to impose this system of global economic inequality.

Slowly, Cold War barriers began to come down. In Colombia, the United Steel Workers became a bastion of support for the embattled unionists of the left-wing labor federation. In Mexico, the USW supported striking copper miners in Cananea, and gave refuge to their exiled union president in Canada. Under pressure from US Labor Against the War, the AFL-CIO publicly rejected U.S. military intervention in Iraq. But progress was uneven. The Democratic Party's support for war in Afghanistan and for Israel's attack on Gaza was greeted with silence. In Venezuela, U.S. labor even supported coup plotters against the radical regime of Hugo Chávez.

Among U.S. union members at home, the key issues were jobs and trade policy, and their corollaries, displacement and immigration. The implementation of the North American Free Trade Agreement in 1994 (supported by both U.S. political parties) and the battle in Seattle at the World Trade Organization meeting of 1999 profoundly affected workers' thinking about their own future. Many were educated by the fight against corporate trade policy, and began to understand the way neoliberal reforms displaced workers and farmers in Mexico, leading to migration across the U.S.-Mexico border. That understanding created a base for solidarity with Mexican workers in the United States that did not exist during the Cold War era.

During the years after 1994, when NAFTA took effect, over six million people from Mexico migrated to the States in search of jobs. The number of people living in the United States without legal immigration status climbed to over 12 million. Those workers, as they faced threats of being imprisoned as criminals because of their immigration status, began using May Day marches to call for human, political, and labor rights. People migrating to the United States came with a tradition of using May Day celebrations to call for labor rights. May Day became their vehicle to challenge anti-immigrant hysteria.

This wave of increasingly assertive workers was hardly the first to challenge U.S. unions, many of which were organized by earlier immigrants and their children. But U.S. unions organized in a working class deeply divided by race and nationality. Some unions saw (and still see) immigrants as unwelcome job competitors, and sought to exclude and even deport them. But other unions fought racism and anti-immigrant hysteria and argued for organizing all workers together.

Today, undocumented immigrants wonder, "Will my union defend me when the government tells my boss to fire me because I don't have papers?" It's not an abstract question. Thousands of workers have already been fired in the Obama administration's program to enforce immigration law in the workplace. Last year alone, almost 400,000 people were deported, almost all ordinary workers.

The debate over immigration policy puts critical questions before U.S. unions. Are unions going to defend all workers, including the undocumented? Should unions support immigration enforcement designed to force millions of workers from their jobs? How can labor achieve the unity and solidarity it needs to successfully confront transnational corporations, both internally within the United States and externally with workers in countries like Mexico?

The White House website says, "President Obama will remove incentives to enter the country illegally by preventing employers from hiring undocumented workers and enforcing the law." A few months after taking office he told Congress that the government was "cracking down on employers who are using illegal workers in order to drive down wages—and oftentimes mistreat those workers."

The law Obama is enforcing is the 1986 Immigration Reform and Control Act, which requires employers to keep records of workers' immigration status, and prohibits them from hiring those who have no legal documents, or "work authorization." In effect, the law made it a crime for undocumented immigrants to work. This provision, employer sanctions, is the legal basis for all the workplace immigration raids and enforcement of the last twenty-three years. "Sanctions pretend to punish employers," says Bill Ong Hing, law professor at the University of California at Davis. "In reality, they punish workers."

The history of workplace immigration enforcement is filled with examples of employers who use audits and discrepancies as pretexts to discharge union militants or discourage worker organization. The sixteen-year union drive at the Smithfield pork plant in North Carolina, for instance, saw two raids, and the firing of three hundred workers for bad Social Security numbers.

Whether motivated by economic gain or anti-union animus, the firings highlight larger questions of immigration enforcement policy. "These workers have not only done nothing wrong, they've spent years making the company rich. No one ever called company profits illegal, or says they should give them back to the workers. So why are the workers called illegal?" asks Nativo Lopez, director of the Hermandad Mexicana Latinoamericana. "Any immigration policy that says these workers have no right to work and feed their families is wrong and needs to be changed."

President Obama said sanctions enforcement targets employers who hire illegal workers, pay them low wages, and treat them badly. This restates a common Bush administration rationale for workplace raids. Former U.S. Immigration and Customs Enforment (ICE) director Julie Meyers asserted that she was targeting "unscrupulous criminals who use illegal workers to cut costs and gain a competitive advantage." An ICE Worksite Enforcement Advisory claims "unscrupulous employers are likely to pay illegal workers substandard wages or force them to endure intolerable working conditions."

Curing intolerable conditions by firing or deporting workers who endure them doesn't help the workers or change the conditions, however. And that's not who ICE targets anyway. Workers at Smithfield were trying to organize a union to improve conditions. In Minneapolis, 1,200 fired janitors at ABM belonged to SEIU Local 26, got a higher wage than non-union workers, and had to strike to win it. And despite President Obama's notion that sanctions enforcement will punish those employers who exploit immigrants, employers are rewarded for cooperation by being immunized from prosecution. This policy only hurts workers.

The justification is implicit in the policy's description on the White House website: "Remove incentives to enter the country illegally." This was the original justification for employer sanctions in 1986—if migrants can't work, they won't come. Of course people did come, because at the same time Congress passed the Immigration Reform and Control Act, it also began debate on the North American Free Trade Agreement. That virtually guaranteed future migration. "The real questions we need to ask are what uproots people in Mexico, and why U.S. employers rely so heavily on low-wage workers," says law professor Bill Ong Hing.

No one in the Obama administration wants to stop migration to the United States or imagines that this could be done without catastrophic consequences. The very industries it targets for enforcement are so dependent on migrant labor they would collapse without it. Immigration policy consigns those migrants to an "illegal" status, and undermines the price of their labor. Enforcement then becomes a means for managing the flow of these migrants, and making their labor available to employers at a price they want to pay.

Managing the flow is the object not just of current policy but also of the proposals for immigration reform that have been supported by the Obama, Bush, and Clinton administrations. Bush's Secretary of Homeland Security, Michael Chertoff, explained the purpose of these proposals clearly: "There's an obvious solution to the problem of illegal work," he said, "which is you open the front door and you shut the back door." "Opening the front door" allows employers to recruit "guest" workers to come to the United States, giving them visas that tie their ability to stay to their employment. And to force workers to come through this system, "closing the back door" criminalizes migrants who work without "work authorization." When she was Arizona governor, current DHS Secretary Janet Napolitano supported this arrangement, signing the state's own draconian employer sanctions bill, while supporting guest worker programs.

The comprehensive reform bills died in Congress over the last several years. But Bush and Obama both began implementing their key provisions through administrative action. The use of guest worker programs, especially for farmworkers, has grown rapidly. And enforcement through deportations, detention, and firings has mushroomed.

This growing wave of firings is provoking sharp debate in unions, especially those with large immigrant memberships. ABM's janitors, for instance, were dues-paying members for years. They expect the union to defend them when the company fires them for lack of status. At American Apparel, where 2,000 sewing machine operators were fired in 2009, there was no union, but some workers had actively tried to organize one. "I worked with the International Ladies' Garment Workers and the Garment Workers Center," recalls Jose Covarrubias. "When I got to American Apparel I joined right away. I debated with the non-union workers, trying to convince them the union would defend us." Covarrubias was fired with the rest, and unions in Los Angeles did very little to help them.

The 12 million undocumented people in the U.S., spread in factories, fields and construction sites throughout the country, include lots of workers like Covarrubias. Many are aware of their rights and anxious to improve their lives. National union organizing campaigns, like Justice for Janitors and Hotel Workers Rising, depend on their determination and activism. That reality convinced the AFL-CIO in 1999 to reject the federation's former support for employer sanctions and call for repeal. Unions recognized that sanctions enforcement has made it much more difficult for workers to defend their rights, organize unions, and raise wages.

Opposing sanctions, however, put labor in opposition to the Obama administration, which it helped elect. Some Washington lobbying groups now support sanctions enforcement instead. One group,

Reform Immigration for America, says, "Any employment verification system should determine employment authorization accurately and efficiently." The AFL-CIO and the Change to Win labor federation in 2009 also agreed on a new immigration position that supports a "secure and effective worker authorization mechanism . . . one that determines employment authorization accurately while providing maximum protection for workers." Verification of authorization is exactly what happened at American Apparel and ABM. When workers couldn't provide authorization, they were fired.

With a few exceptions, U.S. unions have been mostly silent in the face of the firings. That undermines their growing criticism of the way corporate trade policies produce undocumented migration.

Before he retired and was succeeded by Richard Trumka, John Sweeney, former president of the AFL-CIO, wrote to President Obama and Canadian prime minister Harper. He reminded them that "the failure of neoliberal policies to create decent jobs in the Mexican economy under NAFTA has meant that many displaced workers and new entrants have been forced into a desperate search to find employment elsewhere." The joint immigration position of the AFL-CIO and Change to Win federations recognized that "an essential component of the long-term solution [to immigration reform] is a fair trade and globalization model that uplifts all workers."

Continued support for work authorization and employer sanctions contradicts this understanding. Even with a legalization program, millions of people will remain without papers, as more come every year. For them, work without "authorization" will still be a crime. And whereas employer sanctions will not stop migration, they will make those workers vulnerable to employer pressure.

In a speech in Cleveland in 2010 AFL-CIO president Trumka challenged "working people who should know better, some in my own family, [who say] that those immigrants are taking our jobs, ruining our country. . . . When I hear that kind of talk, I want to say, did an immigrant move your plant overseas? Did an immigrant take away your pension? Or cut your health care? Did an immigrant destroy American workers' right to organize? Or crash the financial system? Did immigrant workers write the trade laws that have done so much harm?"

Trumka accurately described the class exploitation that underlies U.S. immigration policy. "Too many U.S. employers actually like the current state of the immigration system—a system where immigrants are both plentiful and undocumented—afraid and available," he explained. "Too many employers like a system where our borders are closed and open at the same time—closed enough to turn immigrants into second-class citizens, open enough to ensure an endless supply of socially and legally powerless cheap labor."

Trumka concluded by declaring "We are for ending our two-tiered workforce and our two-tiered society. . . . We need to restore workers' fundamental human right to organize and bargain with their employers. And we need to make sure every worker in America—documented or undocumented—is protected by our labor laws."

When he called for "a land of fairness in the workplace and society" in Milwaukee a year later on May Day, immigrant workers in the audience at that march, and those who read his words later, hoped this would mean a sharper challenge to the Obama enforcement policy.

Across the country, tens of thousands marched and rallied to call for national immigration reform and to support all workers' rights. Marchers often bore placards declaring: "Somos Unos—Respeten Nuestros Derechos" or "We Are One—Respect Our Rights." In addition to the 100,000 in Milwaukee, ten thousand marched in Los Angeles, five thousand in San Jose (in the heart of California's Silicon Valley), and thousands more in New York, Atlanta, Houston, Buffalo, Chicago, and other major cities. Smaller towns with a large immigrant population, like Fresno, in the heart of California's agricultural complex, also turned out large demonstrations. In Boston, marchers demanded, "From Cairo to Wisconsin to Massachusetts—Defend All Workers' Rights."

In Milwaukee, Jose Salazar, a volunteer with Equality Wisconsin, joined Trumka on the stage. "Issues relating to immigration and labor law affect us all," he told the crowd. "That is why the lesbian and gay community is joining today's May Day March for Immigrant and Worker Rights. We march to protest Governor Scott Walker's budget cuts that hurt our families and children. And we march to support the union between immigrant and worker communities."

EDITOR'S NOTE: David Bacon has published an essay in which he discusses the immigrant labor rights' movement and the Occupy Wall Street uprising. See http://www.truth-out.org/unions-and-immigrants-join-occupy-movements/1323183717.

12—"No, No, No,
the People Have the Power"

DAVE ZIRIN

1968 was a revolutionary year, one when the established order was shaken to its foundations. In Vietnam, the Tet Offensive showed that the U.S. military could be challenged by a popular uprising. In France, there was the largest general strike in the history of the world. In Czechoslovakia, Prague Spring stood up to Stalinist tanks. Revolution was in the air, and the United States was not immune. The assassination of Dr. Martin Luther King and the mass revolts that followed shook every city in the country. The growth of the Black Panther Party inspired millions and terrified J. Edgar Hoover's FBI. This wave of radicalization ricocheted with electric fashion into the world of sports. The year 1968 saw Muhammad Ali—banned from boxing, and out on appeal after receiving a five-year prison sentence for avoiding the draft—giving two hundred speeches on college campuses and saying to his audiences, "Keep asking me how long on Vietnam I sing this song, I ain't got no quarrel with them Viet Cong." It saw the greatest stars like Bill Russell, Jim Brown, and Lew Alcindor embrace politics without shame. And if there was one moment that crystallized not only 1968 but this entire era of resistance against war and racism, it was on October 2 when Tommie Smith and John Carlos raised their black-gloved fists to the sky and brought the revolt to the most unlikely of places: the Olympic Games.

Just as in 1968, the spirit of radical change has defined 2011, a year that revolutions and revolts have been felt from the Middle East to the Midwest. From Mubarak to Madison, nothing is the same as it was a year ago. And just as in 1968, this has been felt in the world of sports. We have seen soccer players and soccer clubs in the Middle East play critical roles in the struggles, particularly in Egypt and Bahrain. In the United States, we have seen players like Steve Nash, Sean Avery, and Michael Strachan lend their voice to Marriage Equality in New York. We've seen the lockouts in the NFL and NBA have a radicalizing effect on players. Troy Polamalu, the All-Pro safety for the Pittsburgh Steelers, said:

> I think what the players are fighting for *is something bigger*. A lot of people think it's millionaires versus billionaires and that's the huge argument. The fact is it's people fighting against big business. The big business argument is "I got the money and I got the power therefore I can tell you what to do." That's life everywhere. I think this is a time when the football players are standing up and saying, "No, no, no, the people have the power."

That statement was so great I had to ask: "Does that mean I have to like the Steelers?"

Demaurice Smith, head of the NFL Players Association, found strength in his lockout in the struggles of the Middle East, saying:

> There are some socially and politically significant things occurring in the world that don't have anything to do with the final score. . . . I've just been glued to what's been going on in Egypt and the way in which ordinary people are taking a stand against what they feel is oppression. And let's get it clear, those folks are risking everything to

take ownership of what their lives are going to look like. It's the least we can do.

It was also seen in Madison, Wisconsin. The groundwork was laid for sports and politics to intersect when the Green Bay Packers won the 2011 Super Bowl. The production around the game was the typical bombastic mess of militarism and sexism.

And yet somewhere amid the noise, the smoke, the tributes to Ronald Reagan and the Black Eyed Peas, a football game actually broke out and it was a dandy. In every previous Super Bowl, no team had ever come back from more than a 10-point deficit and before you could blink the Steelers were down eighteen, 21–3. This was thanks to two costly interceptions by Pittsburgh quarterback Ben Roethlisberger. But Pittsburgh is a team with two-dozen players who were part of their Super Bowl championship team two years ago and they refused to quit. The game wound down with Green Bay leading 31–25 and Pittsburgh having the ball with just two minutes to play. Green Bay's defense held, and a fantastic game ended as the Pack came away with the win. Packer quarterback Aaron Rodgers was absolutely brilliant, completing 24 of 39 passes for 304 yards, three touchdowns, no interceptions and winning the MVP.

Yet for all the celebration of the Packers and their history, there was one brazen decision made by the show's producers, and announcers Joe Buck and Troy Aikman, that was an insult to everything the team stands for. Often, the Super Bowl includes numerous shots of the two teams' owners fretting in their luxury boxes like neurotic Julius Caesars. But the Packers are a team without an owner. They're a community-run nonprofit owned by 112,000 fans. Rather than celebrate that fact, Fox didn't mention the Pack's unique ownership structure once. They also did not include shots of the Rooney family, the most celebrated ownership family in the NFL.

After the game, during the traditional passing of the Lombardi Trophy to the winning team's owner, the award was handed to the Packers' "CEO and Chief Executive Officer," Mark Murphy, who barely looks old enough to shave. NFL Commissioner Roger Goodell, amid threats to lock the players out, clearly wanted to hide the truth that the Packers have no single billionaire owner. They want it hidden because the team from Green Bay stands as a living, breathing example that if you take the profit motive out of sports, you can get more than a team to be proud of: you get a Super Bowl Champion. It ain't Tahrir Square, but it was something in our overcorporatized, hyper-commercialized sports world to cheer.

If the broadcast did not mention Green Bay's unique ownership structure, the people of Wisconsin celebrated it. When Coach Mike McCarthy rallied in front of thousands of cheeseheads, Lombardi Trophy in hand, he said, "We're a community-owned football team, so you can see all the fingerprints on our trophy." When Governor Scott Walker took the stage, the boos came raining down on the recently elected and still unknown entity at the statehouse. Walker, after the Super Bowl victory, bathed himself sensuously in the team's triumph, declaring at a public ceremony that February was now Packers Month. He oozed praise for the franchise. But just days later, the governor offered cutbacks, contempt, and even the threat of violence for state workers. Walker unveiled plans to strip all public workers of collective bargaining rights and dramatically slash the wages and health benefits of every nurse, teacher, and state employee. Then, Walker proclaimed that resistance to these moves would be met with a response from the Wisconsin National Guard. Seriously.

Yes, in advance of any debate over his proposal, Governor Walker put the National Guard on alert by saying that the guard is "prepared" for "whatever the governor, their commander-in-chief, might call for." Considering that the state of Wisconsin has not called in the National Guard since 1886, these bizarre threats did more than raise eyebrows. They provoked rage.

Robin Eckstein, a former Wisconsin National Guard member, told the *Huffington Post*, "Maybe the new governor doesn't understand yet—but the National Guard is not his own personal intimidation force to be mobilized to quash political dissent. The Guard is to be used in case of true emergencies and disasters, to help the people of Wisconsin, not to bully political opponents."

The marches then began, with hundreds of thousands of people sporting signs like, "If Egypt Can Have Democracy, Why Can't Wisconsin?" "We Want Governors Not Dictators," and the pithy "Hosni Walker."

But also intriguing is the intervention from past and present members of the Super Bowl Champs. Current players Brady Poppinga and Jason Spitz and former Packers Curtis Fuller, Chris Jacke, Charles Jordan, Bob Long, and Steve Okoniewski issued the following statement:

> We know that it is teamwork on and off the field that makes the Packers and Wisconsin great. As a publicly owned team we wouldn't have been able to win the Super Bowl without the support of our fans. It is the same dedication of our public workers every day that makes Wisconsin run. They are the teachers, nurses, and child care workers who take care of us and our families. But now in an unprecedented political attack Governor Walker is trying to take away their right to have a voice and bargain at work. The right to negotiate wages and benefits is a fundamental underpinning of our middle class. When workers join together it serves as a check on corporate power and helps ALL workers by raising community standards. Wisconsin's long-standing tradition of allowing public sector workers to have a voice on the job has worked for the state since the 1930s. It has created greater consistency in the relationship between labor and management and a shared approach to public work. These public workers are Wisconsin's champions every single day and we urge the Governor and the State Legislature to not take away their rights.

The players who signed on did not have quite as high a profile as Aaron Rodgers. But Rodgers is one of the Packers' union representative in negotiations with the NFL, and people carried signs that read, "Aaron Rodgers reps his union and I rep mine!" On Tuesday, February 15, the players' union issued their own statement in support of state workers, writing, "The NFL Players Association will always support efforts protecting a worker's right to join a union and collectively bargain. Today, the NFLPA stands in solidarity with its organized labor brothers and sisters in Wisconsin."

Then, the following week, the only Packers player with the profile, respect, and cultural currency to rival Rodgers went public. His name is Charles Woodson. Woodson is the team's defensive captain, and in many ways its icon. Because he is a former Heisman Trophy winner at the University of Michigan, an NFL defensive player of the year, and a perennial pro-bowler, news that this voice had been lent to the struggle evoked cheers in the capital and shockwaves in the governor's office. The great Woodson is also the acknowledged emotional leader of the team, charged with pumping them up at halftime and making speeches after the game. He was the person who said during the playoffs, "The President [a Chicago Bears fan] doesn't want to watch us in the Super Bowl? We'll go see him! Say White House on three!" This much watched YouTube moment certainly takes on a different meaning right now.

Woodson is also one of the team's union reps. As the state wondered if Chris Jacke was going to be the most high-profile Packer to speak out, Woodson said the following:

> Last week I was proud when many of my current and former teammates announced their support for the working families fighting for their rights in Wisconsin. Today I am honored to join with them. Thousands of dedicated Wisconsin public workers provide vital services for Wisconsin citizens. They are the teachers, nurses and child care workers who take care of us and our families. These hardworking people are under an unprecedented attack to take away their basic rights to have a voice and collectively bargain at work.
>
> It is an honor for me to play for the Super Bowl Champion Green Bay Packers and be a part of the Green Bay and Wisconsin communities. I am also honored as a member of the NFL Players Association to stand together with working families of Wisconsin and organized labor in their fight against this attempt to hurt them by targeting unions. I hope those leading the attack will sit down with Wisconsin's public workers and discuss the problems Wisconsin faces, so that together they can truly move Wisconsin forward.

The support of the Packers players was not lost on those marching in the streets. Aisha Robertson, a public school teacher from Madison, told me, "It's great to see Packers join the fight against Walker. Their statement of support shows they stand with us. It gives us inspiration and courage to go and fight peacefully for our most basic rights."

Walker no doubt envisioned conflict when he rolled out his plan to roll over the workers of Wisconsin. But I do not think he foresaw having to go toe-to-toe with the Green Bay Packers. I also do not think he foresaw the other sports union involved in a labor conflict stepping up as well—the National Basketball Players' Association. The NBA players have been threatened with layoffs, contraction, and steep cuts in pay and benefits in their current collective bargaining negotiations with NBA commissioner David Stern and the assorted team owners. Considering that no one ever bought a ticket to look at Mark Cuban, a Maloof brother, or (shudder) Donald Sterling, theirs is a struggle worthy of support. Well, solidarity is a two-way street, and it was another media moment when NBAPA executive director Billy Hunter and Milwaukee Buck Keyon Dooling—an NBAPA VP—spoke out on behalf of Wisconsin's workers. When the Wisconsin political bosses convened a late-night vote in the state assembly to strip the public sector employees of their very rights to collectively bargain, that was, for Hunter and Dooling, a bridge too far. "Last night's vote by the Wisconsin Assembly was an attempt to undermine organized labor and the men and women across the country who depend on their unions for a voice in the workplace," said Hunter. "The NBPA proudly supports our brothers and sisters in Wisconsin and their stand for unequivocal collective bargaining rights."

Hunter, who earned his law degree from Berkeley while playing in the National Football League, has been part of the struggle for workers' rights for many years. Keyon Dooling's voice, as a player in Wisconsin and a leader in the union, is perhaps even more welcome. "Wisconsin public sector workers tirelessly deliver services on a daily basis to millions of Wisconsin residents," said Dooling. "The right of these hardworking men and women to organize and bargain collectively is fundamental. Wisconsin's workers deserve better than last night's vote. Today, our union stands proudly with our fellow union members throughout the state as they continue their fight."

Dooling, it is worth noting, has now officially taken a stronger stand than his team's owner, Wisconsin Democratic Senator Herb Kohl. It is a stand, at this critical moment, worth taking and worth defending. The EMTs, teachers, and child care workers of Wisconsin deserve nothing less.

When dealing with periods of profound protest, it always makes sense to get the point of view of those who have been there before. I spoke to Dr. John Carlos, the 1968 Olympian who, along with Tommie Smith, raised a black gloved fist at the Mexico City Olympics. This is perhaps the most famous image in sports history. It also made Dr. Carlos an avatar of resistance for an era that shook the foundations of this country. John Carlos knows intimately the price that must be paid to speak truth to power. And as you'll read, he thinks that the actions of the resistance fighters of the Midwest are more than appropriate: they're righteous. Here is what Dr. Carlos said to me:

> I don't think Governor Walker realizes that workers are the people who built this country and workers are the people who keep the fabric of our communities together. Workers are the people of the grassroots. For him or any political figure to try and cut their wages, take their health care, crush their unions, or subjugate them in any way is just a travesty. And if he really, like I heard on that prank phone call, was thinking of sending disrupters and plants into the protesters, which could have caused people and even children serious harm… well, that would be simply despicable. I read that the police might be investigating Scott Walker for those statements and I hope that this is in fact the case. I commend what the workers, students, and all protesters are doing to stand up for their rights and I am with them 1,000 percent. Every person from the world of sports with a heart or sense of humanity would say the same.

These pro athletes, past and present, made a conscious choice to link arms with the tens of thousands of nurses, teachers, and firefighters standing as one against Governor Walker's efforts to destroy their unions and drive them into poverty. The fact that a steady stream of players from the only nonprofit, fan-owned team in American sports lent their voices to this fight makes the struggle all the more remarkable.

As we learned from Egypt, envisioning unforeseen consequences is never an autocrat's strong suit. As we have learned in Wisconsin, fighting austerity is not an Egyptian issue or a Middle Eastern issue. It is a political reality of the twenty-first-century world. And as Scott Walker is learning, messing with cheeseheads can be hazardous to your political health.

13—Fighting Wage Cuts in Upstate New York Teaches Chemical Workers the Value of Mobilization

In 2006, General Electric sold its Waterford, New York, silicone products plant to Apollo Management, a private equity firm. For many years, the only news most people heard about this plant was about its occasional spills into the Hudson River, which some riverside communities in the area use for their drinking water. Workers at this plant are exposed to and work with dangerous chemicals, eight of which, according to a company website, are regulated under the EPA's Risk Management Program rule (RPM).

The Momentive workforce in the Waterford plant, which sprawls along the Hudson in about 800 acres a dozen miles north of Albany, inherited the almost $30-an-hour wages and decent working conditions that had been fought for by generations of union families, going back to the great days of the CIO in the 1930s, when the original United Electrical Workers (UE) was organized. Like GE's mothership plant in nearby Schenectady, the Waterford GE local went with the International

Union of Electrical Workers (IUE) in the Cold War split of the UE. Declining IUE membership led to a merger with the Comnunication Workers of America (CWA), resulting in the union local at the plant, IUE-CWA 81359, getting an eight added to its local number.

Local labor activists were apprehensive about what might be in store for the 600-plus workers after the Apollo Management takeover. Headed by Leon Black, a notorious graduate of the infamous 1980s Drexel Burnham Lambert school of leveraged buyouts, Apollo has a background of buying up "distressed" properties and "restructuring" them, which usually means workers take the hit in wages and pensions.

Things under the new boss started out without incident. The company, whose silicone products are caulks, adhesives, foams, cosmetics, and tires, was rebranded as Momentive Performance Materials. It negotiated a new three-year contract in 2007 with the chemical, maintenance, and warehouse workers represented by IUE-CWA Local 81359 that locked in gains in pay and pensions and retained key job security provisions.

On Nov 7, 2007, Apollo Management founder Leon Black announced that Apollo Management had sold 9 percent of itself to the Abu Dhabi Investment Authority. ADIA is among the largest government investment authorities in the world and is responsible for investing all of Abu Dhabi's state oil revenues and assets.

Also in 2007, the government of Abu Dhabi took a major stake in the semiconductor firm GlobalFoundries, as the computer chip maker Advanced Micro Devices spun off its chip-making capacity in its quest to be another "fabless" chip company, which is one that contracts out manufacturing to concentrate on the design of computer chips.

GlobalFoundries was in the process of building a plant just north of the Momentive factory. The influx of money from Abu Dhabi helped underwrite the chip fab plant for upstate New York, which is also being subsidized by the taxpayers of that state to the tune of $1.2 billion.

The IUE/CWA union jobs at Momentive were paid far more than the chip fab standard, which is $15 an hour in non-union semiconductor plants in the United States. Now the owners of GlobalFoundries were also part owners of the Momentive plant.

Not long after the Abu Dhabi sale, the hammer fell. With the contract signed and in place, Momentive executives approached the union in early 2008 saying they needed to transform the business. Months before the economy crashed, they sought wage cuts and outsourcing of warehouse work, plant labor, and heavy equipment operation, the very parts of the plant in which many of the veteran, and more highly paid, workers labored.

Local 81359 offered many ideas to save the positions and prevent outsourcing, including work area flexibility (which would allow management to move workers around the plant), fewer supervisors, and lower starting wages for new hires.

"We did the math for them, showed them all types of business models," said Dominick Patrignani, the local's president. "But they had it all figured out ahead of time."

In late 2008, the company announced that production workers' pay would be slashed by 25 to 50 percent. The announcement came just as the recession hit, leaving the union with little leverage to hit back in a plant that suddenly had very few orders.

In a show of "shared sacrifice," in mid-2009 senior management took 8 to 10 percent cuts in pay—which were restored in 2010. Securities and Exchange Commission filings show that CEO John Rich made $1.6 million the previous year. When business picked up, rather than restore the pay cuts for production workers, Momentive outsourced forty-three jobs to non-union workers at $12 an hour, illegally changed job classifications to pile on work for the survivors, and started a job-posting system that decimated the seniority-based mobility of union members.

Local president Patrignani said the pay cuts were a "huge wake-up call." Workers initially expressed their outrage on an *Albany Times Union* blog, which drew thousands of angry comments. Here is a typical example, dated December 4, 2008:

> If any of you would have been at the big meeting when my so-called management team was telling me I had to take a 25% pay cut, and then laughed about it, tell me how you would feel. They had the nerve

to stand right in front of all of us and laugh and snicker when asked what kind of cut they were taking. I have been an employee for almost 20 years and have made a comfortable living, but have sacrificed more then you can know. Have you ever worked a continuous shift, 3 weekends a month, every holiday? Most workers don't. I choose to do this because I was well compensated, know after all these years they will take away what I rightfully earned. Also don't tell me about costs, those individuals were there at the end of quarter to make sure that materials were delivered to our customers, spending 16-20 hrs a day. All approved by management. The bottom line I feel is that they basically called me a servant, an uneducated servant at that. Did they ask for any giveback that was reasonable, no 25%, our union gave them many ways to save and cut cost, they listened to none.

Local 81359 counter-offered an equal percentage cut across the board, as long as everyone from the CEO down did it together. Given the lack of orders, the union decided to file charges with the National Labor Relations Board (NLRB) for the workers whose pay was cut. In a divide-and-conquer strategy, skilled maintenance workers were not affected, nor were seventy technicians at the plant represented by another IUE local.

In January 2010, the NLRB issued a complaint against Momentive. The violations included Momentive's implementation of substantial modifications, including wage reductions, to the terms of the labor contract with the IUE-CWA, the Industrial Division of the Communications Workers of America, and its Local 81359. The charges included that the company changed the wage scale, wage rates, and wage-step progression; changed the upgrading and job notification procedures and qualifications for bidding on new jobs; changed the job descriptions and job classifications; changed the practice of employees covering higher-paid positions and the overtime procedure; and bypassed the union and dealt directly with its bargaining unit employees.

The charge further stated that, by its conduct, the company failed and refused to bargain collectively and in good faith with the union. The NLRB sought restoration of the wage scale, wage rates, wage-step progression, job descriptions, job classifications, the upgrading and job notification procedure, and the overtime procedure. The NLRB also sought back pay and interest to compensate those who have suffered severe wage loss. This complaint was seen at the time as a strong validation of the union's position.

The NLRB scheduled the case for July 2010. Local 81359's contract expired in June 2010, creating a complicated scenario for the local's leaders to navigate.

The blog entries piled up on the *Times Unon* site. But the local broke out of the online world—and the traditional insularity of big IUE unions. Patrignani and his stewards became ubiquitous on picket lines and labor events in the Capital District of New York. The local joined virtually every labor council in the area, with particular emphasis on the Troy Area Labor Council, which in response voted to make the Waterford workers' struggle against pay cuts its major campaign for 2010.

Labor council leaders helped Local 81359 put out a flyer against the wage cuts over the 2009 holidays, which was distributed to thousands. A contract campaign to mobilize members and get support from other unions had begun. A contract campaign involves a union reaching out to the broader labor movement and community to organize pressure on an employer. This was a new concept for Momentive workers, but they soon embraced it eagerly.

The first big public protest took place on Tuesday, January 12, 2010, in freezing temperatures not far from the shore of the Hudson River. Scores of members of IUE/CWA 81359 picketed outside the plant, protesting the anniversary of the pay cuts imposed by Momentive Performance Materials in late 2008. Workers held up signs saying "Wage Cuts Don't Work," "John Rich, Me Poor," and "Honor the Contract." They were joined by representatives of other unions in the area, a fact that really impressed local members. At the same time, notably absent from this event and all subsequent actions organized by 81359, were any of the international leaders of the IUE, something that was resented by the local membership, and this would have serious repercussions down the line. The picket was followed by a rally at a nearby restaurant, the first of a number of such events there.

When the hotel workers of Workers United Local 471, who had been on strike for recognition at the Holiday Inn Express in nearby Latham, held a rally in the last days of January 2010, a busload of Momentive workers joined them. IUE/CWA members had been faithfully participating in weekly pickets at the hotel for the past year.

"For years we've been living in the GE world," Patrignani said. "It was like therapy helping others fighting for the right to unionize. We started to realize how good it could be for all of us to stand together and fight back. There's so much knowledge out there."

Local 81359 and the Troy Area Labor Council sponsored a meeting March 31, 2010, to hear labor activist, former CWA organizer, and author Steve Early discuss contract bargaining in tough times. More than a hundred Momentive workers and supporters came, including key leaders of locals and the Capital District Area Labor Federation (CDALF), and after giving Early a standing ovation, a big brainstorming session broke out, which left the participants ready to take up both the Momentive workers' battle and others developing in the region.

When the first big state workers' protest broke out in Albany in the spring of 2010, Local 81359 members showed up with their big inflatable rat, and president Patrignani was able to bring greetings of solidarity to the public employees from workers in the private sector.

With the contract expiration and NLRB hearing looming that summer, the local sought to build momentum, discussing both how to prepare for a possible strike and how to carry out in-plant strategies.

Members experimented with work-to-rule, doing exactly what the contract states and requiring engineers and supervisors to make decisions and corrections to process and work flows that were done in the past on the floor by the true experts, the union workers.

In April, Patrignani and local treasurer Mike Leon attended the *Labor Notes* biannual conference in Detroit, where they met with other CWA locals and labor activists from across the country. They had a memorable lunch with Teamsters leader Sandy Pope, who is now challenging James P. Hoffa for the leadership of that union. This trip cemented a relationship with *Labor Notes* that is ongoing at the time of this writing.

In early June 2010, Local 81359 workers in upstate New York came out in force for a rally to kick off contract talks. Wearing bright red shirts emblazoned with a cobra on the back warning "Will Strike if Provoked," the workers picketed along with representatives of nearly twenty other unions from the Capital District of New York. Three striking workers from the Mott's applesauce plant also made the four-hour trip from the shores of Lake Ontario to join the rally at the plant outside Albany.

The line of red-shirted workers stretched for a quarter-mile in front of the Momentive works.

Among the labor speakers on the picket line was Ed Bloch, a retired leader of the United Electrical Workers (UE). For Bloch, who walked his first picket line in 1946, coming together with this IUE local was sweet, after the bitter split of the UE during the 1950s McCarthy era, which he lived through.

"There are people over the past decades with whom we have disagreed," he said, "to our enormous cost. What we have to find is a way to stick together for what we believe in and fight until the damn thing is over and we are successful in fulfilling our demands."

This healing of old wounds was another aspect of what makes the struggle at Momentive notable. Another was the makeup of the rally after the picket, which was addressed by union leaders, single-payer health care activist Andy Coates, and Green Party candidate Howie Hawkins. A collection was taken up for striking Mott's workers, marking the beginning of a relationship between the two locals.

The Dr Pepper Snapple group, owners of the upstate New York Mott's applesauce plant, had just come off a year in which profits exceeded $500 million, but the company demanded that 305 workers at its subsidiary near Rochester accept a $1.50 per hour wage cut. The Mott's plant workers, who belong to RWDSU Local 220 and earned around $20 an hour, went on strike in early May 2010, citing unfair bargaining practices. When the leaders of Local 81359 went out to

Rochester for their contract negotiations in June, they made a point of going to the Mott's plant where they walked the picket line with the striking workers of RWDSU 220.

A joint mobilization committee between Local 81359 leaders, the Troy Area Labor Council, and the Capital District Area Labor Federation was set up to support the local during the negotiations. In addition, Local 81359 reached across the still-existing division between the IUE and CWA, and according to President Dominick Patrignani, "punched holes in the wall" that still exist between the two international unions.

Then came a stunning development. When the time came to vote on the new contract, it was ratified despite Local 81359 members voting it down.

Three unions were involved in the contract vote. The two others were a small unit of lab technicians in the Momentive plant and a small local from Ohio in the company's quartz division. The two small locals—whose pay was not cut—combined with enough votes from Local 81359 members to put the contract over the top 388 to 337.

As part of the settlement, the IUE International insisted on dropping the NLRB case. The Local 81359 members had on average $30,000 in back pay riding on the settlement. At information meetings held before the vote, an IUE-CWA attorney told workers they risked delaying the payout for up to five years by rejecting the deal—a threat that workers heavily criticized.

IUE national president Jim Clark hailed the agreement. "It is never easy to adjust to a new owner with a different structure and different needs," he said in a statement. "But this contract does give members a pathway to put the acrimony behind us and rebuild."

Patrignani had a different assessment. In a letter to members he said the contract was "a tough pill to swallow," noting that pension and medical costs would climb and the lower wages would now be locked in, as the union gave up its NLRB suit to gain the agreement.

While production workers received $2-an-hour wage increases, they did not get their old pay scale back, leaving them still far behind where they were in 2007. Senior workers at the plant previously made as much as $30 an hour. "I wish we could have resolved this differently, but this is the path the majority has decided to take," Patrignani wrote.

There is little question that Momentive's willingness to pay back the wage cuts in a lump sum was tough for many to turn down. Many who were attracted to this aspect of the agreement were close to retirement. The "no" vote came largely from the production workers, whose pay scales were not restored, along with a large portion of the local's maintenance workers—whose pay was not cut, but who have stood in support of the production workers despite Momentive's effort to drive a wedge between the groups over the past eighteen months.

Some of the members of Local 81359 were so disappointed in the outcome that they began a deauthorization campaign aimed at the IUE. Again from the *Times Union* blog, a typical comment on this issue:

> In the useless section called IUE CWA News stuck in the middle of the paper is an article called Momentive Contract Passes. Jimmy C, President of the useless IUE states that the contract passed but failed to state that the Local that was affected by the illegal actions of the company defeated the contract. He had the gall to state that this new contract lays the groundwork for growth and continued success in Waterford and Willoughby. There is no doubt that the growth he speaks of is more dues-paying members who work for cut rates and who cares about the members who have been paying dues for years.

According to a definition in USLEGAL.com: "The National Labor Relations Act (NLRA) permits employees working under a union contract to petition the National Labor Relations Board (NLRB) to hold a vote on whether to revoke any contractual requirement to join the union or support it financially as fee payers. This is known as a deauthorization election. Employees cannot fire their exclusive representative after a successful deauthorization vote, but they can withhold its pay. The deauthorized union still represents the employees, but it cannot legally force them to pay dues and fees."

After a contentious internal debate the deauthorization vote failed. The majority of the workers did not want to chance things without a union, even with an international leadership they deeply distrusted. In January of 2011, Local 81359 shut the plant down in a grievance strike. Despite the deep alienation of a section of the membership with the IUE international, the strike was 100 percent solid. With freezing weather jeopardizing complex plant processes, management quickly backed down from lockout threats, and the workers returned to work with the grim satisfaction of finally delivering a blow for their self-respect. Local president Patrignani was able to report the successful job action at a *Labor Notes* Troublemakers School in Burlington, Vermont, the day after it ended.

In a matter of weeks after the Local 81359 strike, the mass labor uprising in Wisconsin shook the country. Though the Wisconsin upheaval ostensibly revolved over the question of the right to collective bargaining, underlying the struggle was a rejection of austerity in the form of wage and benefit cuts, the very issues confronted by Momentive workers. Masses of working people took to the streets to defend their rights and interests against a right-wing assault.

Wisconsin started as a spontaneous rank-and-file rebellion against a union-busting agenda. After several weeks of statehouse occupation and huge demonstrations, this movement was shunted into an electoral effort to recall Republican state senators. Although the labor leadership rallied against attacks on collective bargaining, they did not seriously contest the notion that workers must sacrifice to "save" the Wisconsin state budget.

In an article for NewLeftProject.org, Paul Street noted: "Throughout the Wisconsin drama, American labor 'leadership' has shown itself remarkably ready to surrender on economic austerity and the broader plutocratic agenda. It has been willing to accept (on behalf of unconsulted rank-and-file workers) unnecessary wage and benefit rollbacks demanded by policymakers who are feeding government deficits with tax breaks for the rich and corporate few."

Much the same could be said for the private sector union leaders like those of IUE/CWA. Despite this, when given a chance, through a loophole found by a shrewd local leadership, in the case of Local 81359, a legal grievance strike, the workers will respond. As a younger generation begins to predominate in the workplaces of the United States, that will be the challenge they face: how to find the openings to take action, despite the inheritance of misleadership so often dragging them down.

In the wake of Wisconsin several insurgent labor candidates emerged, most notably Sandy Pope's campaign for general president of the Teamsters Union. As of this writing it definitely appears that her campaign is catching on with a rank and file tired of concessionary contracts negotiated by the incumbent Hoffa administration.

In the CWA, a local president, Don Trementozzi, waged a campaign for the union's number-two spot, secretary treasurer, and garnered 25 percent of the vote at the CWA convention. Just days after the convention ended, Trementozzi and the CWA leadership found themselves leading 45,000 Verizon workers out on strike. Verizon, a corporation awash in profits, is demanding huge concessions from its workforce.

On the first day of the strike, local IUE-CWA 81359's giant inflatable rat went up in front of a Verizon Wireless store being picketed by CWA workers.

Soon after the Verizon strike was put on hold, the Occupy Wall Street movement erupted. In New York City unions mobilized to support the occupiers, at one point providing key support when Mayor Bloomberg threatened to evict the protesters. Union members are participating in the General Assemblies of the occupations, and are getting a taste of "direct democracy." In Albany Dominick Patrignani and several leaders of CWA 1118, which represents Verizon workers, attended the General Assembly that called for an Albany occupation.

The occupation movement is demonstrating globally that mass mobilization does more to change the terms of the debate than all the money labor has spent on politicians, in lieu of mobilizing its members. As this document goes to press occupations are in full swing, here in the Capital District of New York as elsewhere. The lessons learned at a chemical plant on the banks of the Hudson are now being learned in new venues; we can fully expect that workers will be a critical part of the process.

EDITOR'S NOTE: James Hoffa, Jr. has since won reelection as president of the Teamsters.

14—Beyond Wisconsin: Seeking New Priorities as Labor Challenges War

MICHAEL ZWEIG

The attack on labor by Wisconsin Governor Scott Walker and that state's legislature in early 2011 appeared at first to be a response to the state's budget crisis. Two developments quickly contradicted this belief. First, the amount of money the governor said would be saved almost exactly matched the $140 million in tax cuts the legislature and governor had provided for Wisconsin businesses just a few weeks before. Also, within a few days of the proposal, Wisconsin's public employee unions announced that they would accept all the governor's proposed cuts in wages and benefits in collective bargaining negotiations. But the governor pressed on with the new legislation nonetheless. In the end, it passed only after Republicans in the legislature acknowledged that destroying public sector collective bargaining was *not* a budgetary matter, thereby avoiding the required quorum that Democrats in the legislature had prevented by escaping to Illinois for nearly three weeks.

Wisconsin was unusual in the ease with which it became apparent that the state's budget problems were not the actual basis of attacks on public sector services and the workers who provide them. Throughout the United States, in states with conservative governors, but also where liberals like Jerry Brown of California are chief executives, budget deficits continue to be the ever-present backdrop to cuts in public services and reductions in wages and benefits for public sector workers.

In 2011, almost every state in the country was running a deficit in its operating budget (not including capital budget items). At the federal level, too, addressing the deficit became the principal policy issue, requiring "painful cuts" despite persistently high unemployment, crumbling infrastructure, and education levels among young people far below those of other industrial countries with which our businesses compete.

Unions and other civic organizations dedicated to confronting this agenda emphasize the revenue side of the budget rather than reduced expenditures. Some have joined the New Priorities Network (NewPrioritiesNetwork.org) to coordinate and popularize this approach. The starting point for this work is a direct challenge to the proposition that "there is no money" when we address budget shortfalls.

Unions and others point to two main sources of funds: increasing taxes on corporations and wealthy individuals—often called the "millionaire's tax"—and redirecting money from the military by ending the wars and occupations in Afghanistan and Iraq, closing unnecessary weapons programs and overseas military bases, and ending other wasteful military practices. Funds freed by these changes could, if not swallowed by deficit reduction, then go to support critically important public programs and the workers who deliver them.[1]

Before considering these elements of labor's response to budget crises, it will be helpful to address directly the basic claim that government deficits and debt are urgent problems—in fact our highest priorities—that must be resolved if our economy is to thrive. This claim is not true.

One common assertion intended to make the problem intelligible to ordinary people claims that the government is just like a family. We hear this analogy over and over. Every responsible family knows that it has to pay its bills. (Never mind decades-long corporate efforts to get consumers to borrow evermore money on their credit cards and use their homes as ATMs based on supposedly ever-increasing house prices, a strategy that failed spectacularly with the collapse of the housing bubble and financial crisis in 2008.) In the tough economic times of 2011, as families are cutting back on spending and losing their homes, it seems reasonable to conclude that government has to tighten its belt too.

But as I have said elsewhere:

Federal government deficits and resulting debt are usually not a problem. The government is not like a family that must balance its budget. The government is more like a corporation that lives longer than its individual shareholders or citizens. If it borrows to support productive activity that will generate greater future wealth, from which the debt with interest can be repaid (as for education, public health, roads, ports, and rail transportation), the debt is benign.

Large deficits over an extended period can sometimes be a problem. If there is full employment and a booming economy, government borrowing may increase interest rates and make it more difficult for private businesses to borrow to expand their operations. But in a period of widespread unemployment and businesses not investing (as was the case in 2009–2011), government deficits do not create this problem. Instead they help to prevent deeper unemployment and more widespread bankruptcies. They save taxpayers money over time by securing and improving the economic activity that generates more wealth, growth, and taxes in the future.

The idea that the deficits burden our children and grandchildren who must repay it misses two important points: first, current borrowing may create a better world in which our children and grandchildren will live; second, the interest that our grandchildren will pay will go to other of our grandchildren who will own government bonds—through their private pension funds, in the Social Security

Trust Fund, or directly. Future interest payments are not a net burden on future generations, but a transfer of wealth from those who then pay taxes, but own few or no bonds, to those who own government bonds and may also pay taxes from which the interest is paid.

Interest paid to foreign businesses and governments who own U.S. government bonds does leave the U.S. economy (in 2010 amounting to 30 percent of total interest payments, up from 19 percent in 2000).[2] But foreign ownership of U.S. government bonds reflects the strength of the dollar as a reserve currency others wish to hold—a plus for the United States—and the large deficit in the U.S. balance of trade, which must be addressed with tools other than adjusting the levels of government debt.

All in all, government deficits in the early years of the Obama administration were not a real concern, but were used to scare people into believing that public services and living standards for public workers must be reduced.[3]

Tragically, in the political climate we face in 2011 there is no practical way to escape the deficit/debt mania that corporate elites, eager to shrink government and escape the social responsibility of paying taxes, have created. The debt-ceiling crisis of summer 2011 and its resolution requiring trillions of dollars in further spending cuts guarantees the continuation of this set of questions. If we have to take deficits seriously, however, there are many ways to address the issue through the revenue side of budgets and by changing the priorities that shape the expenditure side. There is no need to blame public sector workers or adjust budgets with cuts to wages, benefits, and social programs. Just reversing the 2001 and 2003 federal tax cuts that went to households with incomes greater than $450,000 per year (the top 1 percent) would generate $1.36 trillion to the federal treasury over ten years.[4] Reversing similar cuts enacted in states across the country would relieve most of the states' fiscal problems. Unions and community groups address this aspect of the question with demands to "Make Wall Street Pay," "Tax the Rich," "Make the Corporations Pay," and the like.

Budgets are not just arithmetic documents. Budgets are also moral documents. Budgets reflect the values and priorities that guide budget-makers as they choose among competing possibilities. These choices affect not only the tax burdens that different people and businesses experience, but also the types and relative scales of the activities the government pays for. U.S. military expenses dwarf the military budgets of all other countries in the world.[5] The 2012 budget proposed by the White House allocates 59 percent of all discretionary federal spending to military purposes, compared with 5 percent for housing and community development, 4 percent for the State Department and civilian international affairs, 4 percent for education, and 2 percent for transportation.[6] These priorities are subject to increasing challenge as budget crises heat up at all levels of government.

Since its founding in 2003 in the run-up to the Iraq war, U.S. Labor Against the War (uslaboragainstwar.org) has been a strong voice within the labor movement challenging the values and priorities in the federal budget by opposing the wars in Iraq and Afghanistan and calling for the redirection of war dollars to meet urgent domestic needs. USLAW now brings together over 190 union locals, central labor councils, state federations of labor, international unions, and other labor groups, united in opposition to the wars in Iraq and Afghanistan.

The initial growth of USLAW came during the tenure of George W. Bush. At that time USLAW, like the administration and the U.S. public, focused on Iraq and largely ignored Afghanistan. From the start, opposition to the Iraq war grew from labor's opposition to Bush in response to his hostility to unions and working people's interests. The fact that Iraq was Bush's war, and based on lies, opened the door to the possibility of union opposition.

But opposition to the war *as a labor issue* grew from three arguments, often debated heatedly as union members and leadership addressed resolutions opposing the war. First, union members and working people more generally were fighting and dying, so unions representing them had an obligation to express concern for their safety and call for their return home. Second was the question of money. Even in 2003 and 2004, it was clear that the war was a drain on resources that could better be used at home. Finally, unions opposed the war in the context of labor's vision of the kind of society we should have, championing values and policies that would give priority to human needs and guide the country away from militarism and violence as the dominant response to international affairs.

By the end of 2008, it was clear that the war in Afghanistan could no longer be ignored. Barack Obama had campaigned on the commitment to wind down Iraq (which won him much support in the peace movement). But he also promised to escalate the war in Afghanistan (a pledge the peace movement largely chose to ignore, but one of the campaign promises he kept). Early in 2009, President Obama dispatched 17,000 additional U.S. military personnel to Afghanistan. By the end of 2009, he had committed another 30,000, bringing the total in 2011 to nearly 100,000 soldiers, sailors, airmen and Marines deployed to Afghanistan.

Within the labor movement, bridging opposition to the war in Iraq to the one in Afghanistan presented new challenges. Unions had devoted enormous effort and resources to Obama's election, which made it much more difficult to oppose him on the war than it had been to oppose George W. Bush in Iraq. And the basic narrative supporting the war in Afghanistan—running back to the al-Qaeda attacks of September 11, 2001—had an apparent legitimacy that the Iraq war never had. To complicate matters further, the economic crisis following the 2008 financial meltdown brought jobs to the forefront of labor's agenda, together with the extended congressional battle over health care reform throughout 2009.

In this context, straight antiwar messages had little continuing resonance in union halls, nor in the broader population. Yet the reasons for union opposition to the wars continued. The wars were major impediments to progressive agendas of all sorts, especially as the budget crises intensified at the local, state, and federal levels. There was growing awareness that our government and military were presenting shifting rationales for continuing the war in Afghanistan and had no coherent strategy. But the key to continuing antiwar work in the labor movement became making connections between the wars abroad and labor's domestic economic agenda.

Table 1 shows the amount of money taxpayers in each state were budgeted to pay to the federal government for the wars in 2011, compared with the anticipated 2011 budget deficit in the state. In all but eleven states, the war costs, if redirected to the states, would have completely paid for the state shortfalls and ended the budget crises altogether. Taking the country as a whole, redirecting 2011 war costs could have solved the budget problem in all states, with $40 billion left over. School systems could have hired more teachers instead of laying them off by the tens of thousands in 2011.

Severe state budget shortfalls were postponed in the economic crisis that began in 2008 because the $787 billion stimulus package Congress passed in early 2009 included $150 billion in aid to states specifically to shore up their finances. That aid came to an end in 2011. But the anemic recovery had not by then promoted the economic activity necessary to generate significant new revenues based on higher incomes, sales, and profits. At the same time, government spending continued to be high for unemployment compensation, housing subsidies, Medicaid, and other supports for the poor and unemployed suffering through the long period of economic distress. Had the wars ended and the stimulus continued, including aid to the states, working people would have had better lives. Instead, the stimulus ended and the wars continued.

This line of argument gained greater traction in the labor movement as the economic crisis continued through 2009, 2010, and 2011 and as attacks on the public sector intensified. Over the same period, support for the war in Afghanistan eroded significantly and rapidly as people came to realize that we were in league with a corrupt Afghan government and that, in the words of a 2008 Rand Corporation study, "there is no military solution to terrorism."[7] Meanwhile, frustration with President Obama among labor leaders and rank and file continued to build because of continuing high unemployment, widespread home foreclosures, and perceived softness in his approach to banks and the wealthy, lessening resistance to criticism of his war policies.

Table 1. Comparing the Costs of War with State Deficits (2011)

	What Taxpayers Paid for the Wars in Iraq and Afghanistan in 2011 (Billions of $)	Deficit 2011 (Billions of $)	War Spending as Percent of State Deficit	Trade-off of Cost of War: Number of Elementary School Teachers
Alabama	1.60	0.59	273	28,414
Alaska	0.30	no data	n/a	3,998
Arizona	2.40	3.10	77	46,133
Arkansas	1.60	no data	n/a	30,948
California	21.80	26.10	84	283,672
Colorado	2.60	1.50	173	44,423
Connecticut	4.20	5.10	82	52,563
Delaware	1.10	0.38	292	16,993
District of Columbia	0.74	0.10	712	10,555
Florida	9.50	4.70	202	150,016
Georgia	5.00	4.20	119	78,012
Hawaii	0.56	0.59	94	9,454
Idaho	0.47	0.84	56	7,528
Illinois	9.30	13.50	69	126,536
Indiana	2.60	1.30	200	43,906
Iowa	1.30	1.10	118	27,272
Kansas	1.40	0.51	275	26,542
Kentucky	1.30	1.30	100	23,081
Louisiana	1.30	1.00	130	24,527
Maine	0.46	0.94	49	8,340
Maryland	3.30	2.00	165	46,788
Massachusetts	4.90	2.70	181	65,421
Michigan	4.60	2.00	230	64,092
Minnesota	4.10	4.00	103	66,230
Mississippi	0.68	0.72	95	12,897
Missouri	2.60	0.73	356	48,105

Source: Cost of war and trade-offs, National Priorities Project, www.costofwar.com; state deficits, Center on Budget and Policy Priorities, www. cbpp.org. Prepared by the Center for Study of Working Class Life, SUNY Stony Brook, www.workingclass.sunysb.edu.

	What Taxpayers Paid for the Wars in Iraq and Afghanistan in 2011 (Billions of $)	Deficit 2011 (Billions of $)	War Spending as Percent of State Deficit	Trade-off of Cost of War: Number of Elementary School Teachers
Montana	0.26	no data	n/a	5,314
Nebraska	1.20	0.33	365	22,823
Nevada	1.50	1.80	83	26,806
New Hampshire	0.70	0.37	193	11,532
New Jersey	7.90	10.70	74	104,892
New York	15.50	8.50	182	190,346
North Carolina	4.70	5.80	81	89,719
North Dakota	0.21	no data	n/a	3,901
Ohio	6.00	3.00	200	90,252
Oklahoma	2.60	0.73	359	52,021
Oregon*	1.40	0.29	483	21,993
Pennsylvania	6.60	4.10	161	101,448
Rhode Island	0.69	0.40	175	8,267
South Carolina	1.30	1.30	100	22,704
South Dakota	0.26	0.10	257	5,596
Tennessee	2.70	1.00	270	47,424
Texas	14.10	4.60	307	245,982
Utah	0.92	0.70	132	15,820
Vermont	0.25	0.34	74	4,072
Virginia	4.70	1.30	362	65,685
Washington	3.90	3.50	111	58,159
West Virginia	0.47	0.13	351	8,777
Wisconsin*	2.70	1.70	159	43,957
Wyoming	0.30	0.15	201	4,513
TOTAL ALL STATES	171.10	130.16	131	2,606,887

*Oregon and Wisconsin have two-year budget cycles; deficits shown for 2011 are half the projected state deficit for the two-year budget cycle.

In 2010, the national conventions of the Communications Workers of America (CWA) and the American Federation of Teachers (AFT) passed resolutions calling for the end of the war in Afghanistan, full care of returning veterans and their families, and redirection of war dollars to domestic needs. AFT delegates called on their union "to undertake an educational campaign on these issues among its membership and seek to involve members in the political tasks necessary to implement this resolution in public policy." In 2011, the International Executive Board of the American Federation of State, County, and Municipal Workers (AFSCME) approved a similar resolution that had been referred to it by the union's national convention. In 2009, two smaller unions, the International Longshore and Warehouse Union (ILWU) and the United Electrical, Radio and Machine Workers (UE), were the first to oppose the Afghanistan war and call for its immediate end.[8] On August 3, 2011, one day after meeting with President Obama to urge the creation of millions of new jobs as the highest priority for labor and the country, the AFL-CIO Executive Council for the first time directly confronted the wars in Iraq and Afghanistan, declaring: "There is no way to fund what we must do as a nation without bringing our troops home from Iraq and Afghanistan. The militarization of our foreign policy has proven to be a costly mistake. It is time to invest at home."[9]

These resolutions, and the many similar ones at local and regional levels of the labor movement, indicate a new labor attitude toward U.S. foreign policy compared with the Cold War years, when its critics sometimes referred to the AFL-CIO as the AFL-CIA. In part, this is due to the end of the Cold War twenty years ago. It also reflects the presence in union leadership of men and women influenced by the Vietnam War and that era's radical critiques of U.S. foreign policy and corporate power. Another contributing factor was labor's experience in solidarity work with Central America in the 1980s and 1990s. This solidarity was partly responsible for the AFL-CIO's reversal of its historic hostility to immigrants in 2000, and subsequent opening to worker centers and immigrant rights issues, which lessened the jingoistic nationalism that had so often been characteristic of twentieth century labor leaders.

USLAW contributed to this change in attitude through steady education on the issues in the context of hundreds of resolutions introduced to labor bodies at all levels. USLAW mobilized its affiliates for local and national demonstrations, bringing the working class directly into the mainstream peace movement. And it organized lobbying efforts that involved labor leaders and rank-and-file activists addressing politicians with demands that they implement peace policies.

As a central part of its activities, USLAW undertook solidarity work with Iraqi unions, beginning in 2003. In October of that year, two U.S. trade unionists traveled to Iraq as part of an international labor delegation. On their return to the United States, USLAW organized a national tour in which American workers could hear firsthand reports of the conditions under which Iraqi workers lived and worked as the U.S. occupation took hold. It was the first time most people had heard of the existence of trade unions in Iraq and their long history going back to the days of British occupation in the 1920s.

Picking up on the energy and interest the tour generated, USLAW, with the cooperation of the AFL-CIO's Solidarity Center, organized three subsequent tours that for the first time brought Iraqi labor leaders to the United States. They visited twenty-six U.S. cities in 2005, and returned for smaller tours in 2007 and 2009.[10] The Iraqis spoke to thousands of U.S. workers and met with union leaders in dozens of locals and central labor councils, and with AFL-CIO president John Sweeney. In their presentations, the Iraqis stressed three goals: the end of the occupation and sectarian violence in Iraq; the preservation of Iraqi oil from efforts to privatize it and other Iraqi economic resources; and the creation of legal protections in Iraq for independent trade unions as an essential ingredient of the democratic society they hoped to build once the war and occupation ended.

These messages resonated with audiences of U.S. workers. They, too, were battling privatization. They, too, were trying to organize without legal protections. And, when they heard from Iraqi workers directly what damage the war and occupation were doing to that country, they could join the broad U.S. antiwar movement and bring labor's voice into it. Working from the bottom up in the labor movement, by the time the AFL-CIO national convention met in Chicago in September 2005, USLAW affiliates had submitted eighteen resolutions from unions, central labor councils, and state federations across the country calling for the end of the war in Iraq and redirection of the funds to domestic needs. After a full debate on the convention floor, the delegates approved such a resolution, the first time in history that the mainstream labor movement had opposed an ongoing U.S. war. [11]

When the Afghanistan war heated up in 2009, USLAW already had broad ties in the peace movement. As the October 2, 2010, One Nation rally in Washington was being planned, USLAW joined many other organizations to push for inclusion of an antiwar message in the day's activity. Taking advantage of the presence in DC that weekend of people from around the country, CWA hosted an October 3 meeting of leaders of more than thirty labor, peace, community, religious, and racial and economic justice organizations to form the New Priorities Network.

In one example of work along these lines, the Long Island (NY) chapter of Jobs with Justice (an affiliate of USLAW) undertook in the spring of 2011 a campaign to save the public bus system in Nassau County, which the county government wanted to privatize in response to a severe budget crisis. Ending the public bus system would result in a 20 percent fare increase and cuts in services, which would place extraordinary burdens on low-paid workers and poor residents in the county. It would result in layoffs of unionized bus drivers and mechanics and reduced wages and benefits for those who remained. One aspect of the campaign involved getting the member organizations of the Jobs with Justice chapter and their allies in this battle to call for the end of the wars and redirection of funds to save local government services, like the bus line, and to call on the county legislature to do the same. In the process, the campaign raised the question of the wars and national priorities in the context of their implications for immediate local concerns.

On a larger scale, Code Pink initiated a campaign that led to the U.S. Conference of Mayors passing a resolution in June 2011 calling on Congress to end the wars and redirect the funds to help the nation's mayors meet the urgent needs they faced on behalf of their constituents. Resolutions by local city councils in Los Angeles, Baltimore, and Eugene, Oregon, led the way to the national resolution.

The New Priorities Network, and USLAW within it, seeks to reproduce this process in cities and towns across the country. Wherever a library has to close, a school has to end its arts program, a bus line is discontinued, and other public services erode because "there is no money," resistance needs to arise with demands to end the wars and move the money—together with demands from local governments and civic organizations directed to their federal representatives to tax the corporations and high-end incomes. The tasks of taxing corporations and ending the wars and moving the money emerged as priorities at the Jobs with Justice national convention in August 2011, recommended to JwJ chapters for initiatives toward the creation of a new economy in the United States.

In April 2011, thirteen labor leaders in Oregon sent a strongly worded letter to all Oregon representatives and senators. They said:

> As labor leaders dedicated to protecting the best interests of working Oregonians, we are writing to thank those of you who have gone on the record supporting an end to the war in Afghanistan and urge you to intensify your efforts to end this costly and unnecessary war.
>
> Oregonians have already spent more than $3 billion on the war, and there is no end in sight. President Obama's proposed 2012 budget includes devastating cuts that impact the poor and working class—from low-income home heating assistance to community service block grants to Pell grants—while allocating another $107 billion to continue the war in Afghanistan.
>
> Meanwhile, American soldiers and their families bear a costly burden to continue this war. More than 1,400 American soldiers have died in Afghanistan since 2001, and suicide and Post-Traumatic Stress Disorder rates for veterans have hit record highs.
>
> We have seen the outrage at this attack on the middle and working classes erupt in the streets of Madison, WI, and throughout the country. Our supporters and members cannot tolerate government

actions that prioritize continuing a war beyond the ten-year mark over building our communities at home.

This trade-off in spending is especially egregious given the lack of evidence that the war in Afghanistan contributes to improving American security. By all major indicators—US casualties, civilian casualties, corruption, security—the military strategy is failing. With fewer than 100 Al Qaeda members reportedly in Afghanistan, we are asking Americans to spend more than $1 billion per Al Qaeda fighter while they struggle to make ends meet at home.

There are much more cost-effective alternatives in Afghanistan that stand a better chance of success. The US should implement a nonmilitary strategy based on regional diplomacy, political negotiations, development and humanitarian aid and divert the saved resources toward economic opportunities in Oregon and around the country.

It is unconscionable to balance the budget on the backs of working people in order to fund a war that isn't making Americans safer. We urge you to take action to pressure the administration to end the war, including cosponsoring and voting for legislation to end the war and speaking out forcefully for a new approach.

The letter was signed by Tom Chamberlain, president of the Oregon AFL-CIO and officers of nine public and private sector unions and the Oregon chapter of Jobs with Justice.[12]

Connecting labor's opposition to the war in Afghanistan with events in Wisconsin is not just a recognition of the intense budget battle that erupted there. This international link also reflects the inspiration and sense of solidarity Wisconsin activists and others around the United States took from the "Arab Spring" in Tunisia and Egypt, which had captured the popular imagination in this country just as the events in Wisconsin reached their most intense peak. When Egyptian unions sent money to Madison for pizza delivery to people occupying the state capitol building, feelings of international labor solidarity arose among U.S. workers in return. "From Tahrir Square to Madison" was a common expression, carrying the sense that all were engaged in a common battle for democracy, as well as for material well-being.

Here we come back to the basic point arising from the budget battles in Wisconsin, Ohio, California, and elsewhere throughout the country: they are not just accounting contests over balance sheets. They highlight conflict over the most basic values required for a democratic society. In addressing these issues by linking the wars in Iraq and Afghanistan with the domestic needs of working people, the labor movement is helping to create a new direction in foreign policy as it helps to reorder the domestic balance of power as well.

15—Building Communities of Solidarity from Madison to Bend

Fernando Gapasin

At the 2011 Left Forum in New York City, in a discussion about building a workers' offensive, London-based labor economist Paul Mason spoke of the importance of creating new cultures of struggle and creating communities that actively support social justice. This means creating history, values, beliefs, and behaviors that reflect class consciousness, which is then transformed into action.[1] For example, historian Zoltan Grossman said in a recent article that the response of Wisconsin workers to the conservative assault on their rights is no surprise.

Milwaukee workers struck for an eight-hour day in 1886, and seven workers were lost in the infamous Bay View Massacre. Populist farmers took on the railroad companies during the 1890s depression, sparking the formation of a Progressive Republican movement that briefly took power in the 1900s, and dairy farmers launched "milk strikes" against creamery bosses who were skimming off their income.

Unemployment benefit and workers' comp laws, vocational schools, and the AFSCME public employee union all started in Wisconsin.

Ingrained in community cultures of solidarity is the expectation that the community will respond to injustice and hold itself accountable for defending social justice. Neoconservative cultural strategies create a formidable obstacle to cultures of solidarity. Manipulation of mass media is an important part of the neoconservative agenda. In the United States, a conservative overhaul of the Communications Act of 1934 enabled the corporate monopolization of the media and enhanced corporate manipulation of culture, making possible the monopolized media power we see today.[2] Neoconservative cultural strategies have played a major role in the reshaping of the cultural terrain of the U.S. working class. Consumerism, personal enrichment, privatization, and the diminishing social role of government, deteriorating public infrastructure, deregulation, increased poverty, deteriorating health care and education, immigrant-bashing racism, and no alternative worldview all breed hopelessness. National and local conservative community cultures have diminished the scope of civic responsibility along with notions of class solidarity. The building of local "cultures of solidarity," thus expanding the scope of civic responsibility, becomes an essential building block for making possible an alternative worldview.

At its essence, our labor movement is about democracy. It is only through collective action that regular working folks have a voice. As stated by the public sector workers in Wisconsin themselves, their willingness to fight on was inspired by the people's victory in Egypt over tyranny and for democracy. It is no accident that right-wing forces in the United States are currently trying to obliterate unions. For forty years the conservative political forces in North America have been experiencing a cultural and political resurgence. They have been spurred on by the theories of Milton Friedman and the conservative Chicago School of Economics.[3] Since the 1970s, conservative policymakers who influenced presidents have advanced a revised conservative economic and political agenda that transferred income and wealth upward and guided U.S. foreign policy. In the United States, this neoliberal strategy provided the means to reverse the reforms of the New Deal and the War on Poverty. This strategy has five major policy components that manifest themselves locally, nationally, and internationally. These are: implementing a regressive tax system (the rich and the corporations get a much lower tax burden), casualizing the workforce (more part-time work), reducing the political and economic role of unions, eliminating the role of government to regulate and redistribute resources to those who are poor, and the privatization of public services.

In order for this to be accomplished, the role of the public sector has to be dramatically reduced, and the burden of taxation has to be shifted onto the backs of working people. Data from the Tax Policy Center shows that in 1940 corporations paid 18.3 percent of the federal tax, while personal income accounted for 13.6 percent. In 2011, personal income accounted for 44 percent of the federal tax revenue, while taxes on corporations accounted for 9.1 percent.[4] A similar redistribution of the tax burden is reflected at the state level. In Oregon, 44.1 percent of tax revenue comes from personal income, and corporations pay 3.6 percent.[5] Because governments do not tax those with the largest incomes or corporations with high profits, governments find themselves strapped for revenues. The result is an unnecessary but universal fiscal crisis. What is left of the public sector in terms of its social welfare function is being stripped away through privatization and sale of public assets.

Our unions have difficulty forming a united front against this assault. They operate like competitive corporations instead of workers with a common enemy. The reason lies in an example from the book written by Bill Fletcher and myself, *Solidarity Divided*. In Johannesburg, South Africa, we were engaged in a dialogue between U.S. and South African unions. In a discussion about political action, a question was raised about the fundamental purpose of unions. A progressive union leader from SEIU responded in a manner that seemed obvious to him: that the role of a union is to represent the interests of its members. A South African union leader responded diplomatically: "Comrades, the role of the union is to represent the interests of the working class. There are times when the interests of the working-class conflict with interests of the members of our respective unions." [6] For example, in New York, Governor Andrew Cuomo successfully broke the solidarity of the state's union movement by offering needed jobs to the building trades with the money saved by eliminating public sector work. Fundamental notions of working-class solidarity gave way to the interests of particular unions and their members. On the other hand, in Wisconsin the police and firefighters were exempted from the draconian laws that would weaken or destroy the other public sector unions; however, when asked to support Governor Walker and his policies, they said they would rather stand together with their union brothers and sisters than support a tyrant like Walker.[7]

This essay is about turning the cultural tide in local communities by consolidating communities of solidarity and making the fight for social justice a cultural norm. I take my examples from Oregon, where I have been helping to build working-class solidarity for many years. In Oregon, there are wonderful examples of building communities of solidarity. Probably no better example is the twenty-year-old Portland Jobs with Justice Coalition, which was an inspiration for the work in which I participated in Central Oregon.[8] The difference in Central Oregon was that the social movement component of our labor movement, which became the Central Oregon Jobs with Justice Coalition (JwJ), and the traditional union-based institution, the Central Oregon Labor Council (COLC), were able to consolidate resources around the same goals and objectives with common leadership.

But before I can get to the details of the work in Central Oregon, I need to briefly discuss Central Labor Councils (CLC). A CLC is a voluntary federation of AFL-CIO local unions in a particular U.S. city, county, or region. CLCs represent the oldest federated structure in the U.S. labor movement and are independent of any particular union. They are subordinate only to the national AFL-CIO. They predate national labor federations, including the American Federation of Labor and the Knights of Labor. On a geographic basis, there are "many questions affecting the interest of working classes which cannot be dealt with in special and separate Trade and Labor Unions." Thus central labor organizations were formed for the purpose of organizing, educating, and mobilizing working people.[9]

Competition intensified between national unions and CLCs for the affiliation and resources of local unions. After the AFL constitution was changed in the 1890s to prevent CLCs from competing with national unions for members, CLCs became dependent on local affiliates of national and international unions for resources.[10]

In 1996, the AFL-CIO made a dramatic effort to jump-start the union movement when it embarked on "The Road to Union City." Then AFL-CIO president John Sweeney said:

> Today's AFL-CIO Central Labor Councils (CLCs) have a critical role in the revitalization of the American labor movement. By building real power and strength in communities, we are raising the voices of working families. Through our Union Cities campaign, labor councils are fulfilling their mission to organize our communities and fight for social and economic justice.[11]

The Union City program was the coming-out party for the New Voice coalition of the AFL-CIO, which took power in an unprecedented open election in 1995. In the late summer of 1996, the National AFL-CIO produced a glossy fold-out titled, "The Road to Union City: A Guide to Greatness for Local Unions and Their AFL-CIO Central Labor Councils." It prescribed eight steps for rebuilding the U.S. labor movement in cities, towns, and communities.

- Step 1 was "Organizing for Change, Changing to Organize." The idea was for CLCs to get half of their local unions to commit staff and at least 30 percent of their resources to organizing the unorganized.

- Step 2 was "Mobilizing against Anti-Union Employers." CLCs were to recruit 1 percent of the union members in their jurisdiction to "Street Heat," the AFL-CIO's rapid response team.[12]

- Step 3 was "Building Political Power and Community Coalitions." CLCs were supposed to establish a group of one hundred political activists to build community alliances and coalitions for legislation and candidates that championed working families. Candidates would also be held accountable for their promises.

- Step 4 was "Promoting Economic Growth, Protecting Our Communities." CLCs were to promote growth and economic development that advanced public health, improved the environment, increased employment, and promoted labor management standards.

- Step 5 was to "Educate Union Members in Pocketbook Economics." The "Common Sense Economics" training program developed by the AFL-CIO Education Department could be used to teach workers why working families were experiencing economic hardships and how education, political power, and organizing could improve their future.

- Step 6 was "Generating Support for the Right to Organize." CLCs had the responsibility to educate public officials and the general public about supporting union organizing and the need for labor law reform.

- Step 7 was "Making Sure Our Leadership Mirrors the Faces of Our Members." CLCs were charged with building an inclusive labor movement. This included emphasizing the importance of having union leaders who were as diverse as their members and creating solidarity with communities in the governance of the CLC.

- Step 8 was "Encouraging All Local Unions to Increase Their Membership." CLCs were given the goal of achieving a 3 percent growth rate in their jurisdictions by 2000. CLCs were instructed to create a culture of organizing, to employ multiple union organizing strategies, and to use their developing political clout to achieve greater union density.[13]

Using the Union City Program as their model, activists set out to build a community of solidarity in Central Oregon. For at least a generation, rural Oregon east of the Cascade Mountains has been a conservative stronghold. In 2002, the population of Bend (the largest city east of the Cascades) was about 48,000 (in 2010 it was nearly 85,000). It was rapidly becoming the second-largest city in Oregon. When I first moved to Bend, lifelong residents told me about the KKK in the 1930s and the old Sundowner law that persisted into the 1960s and how it required black people to be out of town by sundown. African American exclusion in Oregon is well documented in Elizabeth McLagan's *A Peculiar Paradise: A History of Blacks in Oregon, 1788–1940* (Georgian Press Company, 1980).

Central Oregon in the early 2000s was a boom economy with rapid growth and construction. It was also an agricultural region, and Mexican immigrant populations began to grow in agriculture, construction, and the service industry.

Bend is a pretty place. It is surrounded by a ring of volcanic mountains that remain covered with snow most of the year. The area offers loads of outdoor activities like skiing, golfing, kayaking, and fly fishing. Rivers and lakes that surround Bend provide excellent opportunities for fly fishing. In fact, the world-famous Deschutes River runs right through the center of town. Fly fishing was an industry that at one time supported eight fly shops. Many have since gone out of business because of competition from Internet vendors and big box stores. Bend also had the third-cleanest water in the United States. Since the logging mills in Bend closed in 1992, the city's leaders have attempted to reconstruct the image of Bend by focusing on the natural resources of the area and characterizing the city as a "destination resort location."

The low union density of Central Oregon (11.2 percent compared to 15.6 percent statewide) and the nearly invisible union movement was conducive to working people forgetting that cultures of union solidarity had existed in Bend since 1905 when almost all of the building trades were unionized and even clerks, printers, and barbers were union. The Central Oregon Labor Council (COLC) was founded in 1916. Labor Day picnics organized by the unions were the largest community events during most of Bend's history, and the AFL building in the town center was a focal point for social events. When the mills were organized in 1949 in the wave of AFL and CIO organizing after the Second World War, union power reached its pinnacle in Bend. And on two separate occasions during the 1950s, the president of the Woodworkers Union was also the mayor of Bend, with a majority of council people being union members or supporters. Although militant, Bend's union history was not necessarily enlightened. In the 1980s, a president of the COLC claimed fame for having sawed down a tree with an environmental activist still in it.[14] In other words, if we were going to build a culture of solidarity, we had to revitalize but also change local traditions.

The major newspaper, *The Bend Bulletin*, is conservative, overtly anti-union, and a strong advocate of the privatization of public services. It set the tone for the media in the area. Union organizing was nonexistent, and Labor Day picnics had not been organized for the better part of the previous decade.

Three events began to change this scenario. The Oregon School Employees Association (OSEA) represents classified school workers in 133 school districts in Oregon. The biggest threat facing the OSEA was the privatization of their members' work. In Bend, in 2000, the school board was about to take a vote to privatize student bus service. Second, in 2001, Cogentrix, a major power company, wanted to build a non-union power plant along the Deschutes River. Third, community activists organized an event to emphasize the economic plight of the area and the need to organize. With the help of the local community college and the local Chandler Foundation, they brought the author of *Nickel and Dimed*, Barbara Ehrenreich, to the town known for its "Poverty with a View."

Since most local unions in Oregon have their headquarters in "the Valley" (the I-5 corridor on the west side of the Cascade Mountains), union members on the east side of the Cascades, such as in Central Oregon, planned their own local actions and relied on other union members for support. In January 2000, OSEA , not a member of the AFL-CIO, reached out for help, and in the middle of a blizzard that blanketed Bend with several inches of snow, a hundred OSEA and other union and community activists marched in the freezing cold around the besieged Bend LaPine School District Office. Their march was later joined by the school board chair, Randy Gordon, and the measure to privatize Bend's school buses was defeated.[15]

In 2001, behind closed doors, Cogentrix negotiated a deal with Jefferson County commissioners to build a power plant along the Deschutes River near Madras. Neither Cogentrix nor the County commissioners would discuss the deal with community members, let alone organized labor. This covertness alienated large sectors of the community, including farmers, Native Americans, environmentalists, unions, and both the Republicans and Democrats. The Oregon Building Trades Council retained high-priced environmental lawyers to put up legal obstacles, while the Central Oregon Labor Council and the Central Oregon Building Trades Council formed a broad political coalition in Jefferson County, which was supported throughout Central Oregon. In November 2002, the Jefferson County commissioners were unseated and Cogentrix was forced to leave town and abandon its anti-union, anti-community project.[16]

Because of growing concerns about the low wages, low union density, and civil rights, the December 2002 Barbara Ehrenreich event drew 700 people together at Central Oregon Community College. She highlighted how companies like Wal-Mart intensify poverty by getting tax breaks and supplying only minimum wage jobs with no benefits and reducing the revenue of local communities. She also made clear that the most important thing workers could do to end poverty was unionize. This event linked union activists, housing activists, peace activists, environmentalists, and gay rights activists in a way that created ongoing interaction.

In 2002, as the population grew, new activists, people with previous union experience and with other social movements, moved to Bend. This helped to expand the "gene pool" of activist ideas. Clusters of activists began to meet and discuss the possibilities of creating a progressive agenda for Bend and possibly Central Oregon. Since many of these activists had a history of union action, they gravitated to a small but energetic COLC. They began to plan how the labor movement could be revitalized and how the organizing of workers could be accomplished locally.[17] Their planning process involved changing the political culture of the town and the region and creating a political power bloc. Two organizing attempts provided the impetus for planned action.

In 2003, the Communication Workers of America (CWA) started an organizing campaign at Bend Broad Band, a cable television company with about a hundred employees. COLC contacted CWA to see if it could render assistance. It was suggested that CWA and COLC create a joint strategy that would include community activists. CWA organizers agreed that they would need such a campaign, but only after they won an NLRB election. Unfortunately, the company moved faster and employed a union-busting firm that isolated the workers in captive audience meetings and one-on-one interrogations. CWA was trying to organize the workers from the other side of the Cascades, and the workers felt isolated. One worker said, "We felt like we were on an island and alone." What had been an 80 percent majority dwindled to less than 50 percent within two weeks. CWA staffers realized they could not win and withdrew their petition for an election.

Soon after, a group of Head Start workers asked the COLC for organizing help. Head Start in Central Oregon was run by a highly visible nonprofit corporation known as the Central Oregon Community Action Agency Network (COCAAN). Some of the workers had a memory of a previous OSEA campaign that failed, but most wanted a union because they had no voice about working conditions and because discipline was arbitrary. It became the campaign of the COLC.

The COLC leadership wanted to build a broad-based organizing campaign that would incorporate the community forces that put on the Barbara Ehrenreich event. Because the COLC constitution included only AFL-CIO unions, activists needed to build an organization that combined other social movements with union activists. They created a social map of Central Oregon to determine how to work with the different social forces in the region. In the course of their investigation, they learned about the key economic and social issues facing workers in the region.

The COLC invited the various organizations to participate in an organizing conference in the fall of 2003. The guest speaker was the president of Seattle-based UNITE HERE Local 8, who was also a national vice president of UNITE HERE. The newly elected president of the COLC had previously worked with the president of UNITE HERE Local 8 in a large California city and through their CLC had built a labor/community coalition and organized downtown hotels and businesses. The conference had two major components. First, the participants had to identify the most important issues to working people in Central Oregon. Second, they had to build an organization to address these issues. The primary concerns of working people involved: public transportation, affordable housing, affordable health care, fair trade as it was related to immigrant rights (End NAFTA), and family-wage jobs (accomplished mainly through union organizing).

The conference participants were committed to the idea that no worker who was trying to organize would be without support in Central Oregon and that the model for organizing workers should involve making whole communities stakeholders in the success of workers organizing. The Head Start workers' campaign became the labor movement's campaign. The consensus reached by the fifty-plus participants was to build a chapter of Jobs with Justice to facilitate the organizing of the entire community.

After meeting the requirements to become one of the forty-two chapters of Jobs with Justice, a steering committee was elected that included community activists, union members, and COLC leaders. The steering committee was evenly divided between men and women. Its demographic weaknesses were that, with the exception of two Latinos, it was all white, and it lacked faith-based membership and youth activists. Its events, however, included a diversity of activists.

The COLC developed a strategic plan that focused on addressing the social and economic concerns brought forward at the organizing conference. They also adopted the slogan "Workers in Central

Oregon stand shoulder to shoulder for social justice." Because of the lack of organizing activities by unions in Central Oregon and because the AFL-CIO's Union City program guided it, the COLC was committed to the idea that if workers needed organizing then the CLC would do it.[18] Care was taken by the CLC leadership to always balance the broad interests of social justice with the practical concerns of each union affiliate. Leadership always included private and public sector workers, service, and building trades workers. Care was taken to make sure that all of the unions participated in the decision-making process. Public sector unions were always alert to contracting opportunities for the building trades, helping to establish a fair bidding process, and if possible creating favorable project labor agreements for the building trades unions. An ongoing process of education and reciprocation became a habit for the COLC, and in this process, more often than not, the unions supported each other's projects, including those advocated by social movement organizations. This was critical in Central Oregon because of the hegemony of right-wing conservative politics and culture.

Together, the COLC and JwJ raised money because of growing union participation in the COLC and the writing of grants for JwJ projects. They were able to get seed grants from progressive foundations like the McKenzie River Foundation, the Social Justice Fund Northwest, and CAUSA. They established coalition partners with organizations like the Oregon-based Rural Organizing Project, the Human Dignity Coalition, Basic Rights Oregon, and *Pineros y Campesinos Unidos del Noroeste* (PCUN), Sweatshop Watch, Oregon Fair Trade Coalition, and the Oregon Center for Public Policy (OCPP, a research-based nonprofit). In later years, especially as the work among Latino immigrants increased and as they attempted to expand organizing to the service sector, they reached out to *Enlace* (a cross-border workers' rights nonprofit) and Restaurant Opportunities Centers United (a nonprofit for organizing restaurant workers).

The two groups planned annual events that focused on education and organizing. They reestablished a Labor Day event that was renamed Solidarity Day. It served as an event to celebrate workers' struggles throughout the year. They helped organize and create a racial justice curriculum for the annual celebration of Dr. Martin Luther King Jr.'s birthday. They used the opportunity to bring activists and cultural workers to Central Oregon. Maya Angelou, Dolores Huerta, and David Bacon were among the guests. They did annual educational events around May Day, Cinco de Mayo, and Mexican Independence Day and supported other events like Earth Day and Gay Pride. They did the annual press release for the OCPP report on the economic state of Oregon. They did regular events about labor history, labor cultural events, immigrant rights, living wage, and worker rights. Curriculum-based labor education was regularly taught by the University of Oregon Labor Research and Education Center (LERC) in Bend. The COLC and JwJ helped to fund and produce a theatrical production of Barbara Ehrenreich's book *Nickel and Dimed*. And activists became regular contributors and commentators in the local media on television, radio, and in both the mainstream conservative *Bend Bulletin* and the alternative weekly, *The Source*. They helped to fund and support the creation of a local progressive radio station, KPOV, and utilized popular Spanish language radio stations, like KRDM *La Bronca*, to discuss campaigns and progressive issues.

But most of all they were dedicated to the notion of organizing working people's struggles and responding to injustice. This meant organizing workers into unions and supporting union organizing, but it also meant organizing workers around pay and health and safety issues. It also meant fighting for workers' civil rights and fighting to achieve affordable housing, public transportation, medical care, and creating family-wage jobs. If the unions were not the appropriate organization to help people fight back, they helped to create new organizations for struggle and they built an identifiable progressive bloc that participated with, but was separate from, the local Democratic Party.

From 2004 to 2008, the coalition organizations were able to help hold together a progressive majority on the Bend City Council, and activists participated on city commissions. During that time they were able to advocate and create progressive legislation for their strategic issues. For example, an unprecedented equal rights ordinance that protected civil rights of all Bend residents, a public transit system in the largest city west of the Mississippi without one was built, an ordinance that created funds for affordable housing from development taxes was created, and legislation locally and statewide was enacted that protected tenants of manufactured home parks from property loss due to developer speculation and land grabs. During that same period, the expansion of Wal-Mart in Bend was stopped, the privatization of public school bus services throughout Central Oregon was halted, and one large private contractor was completely driven out of the region.

All of the legislative changes they helped pass were preceded by identifying a need and the mobilization of mass action. The equal rights ordinance occurred because of assaults on African American and gay people. The passage of the ordinance was vehemently opposed by right-wing Christian zealots. In fact, the groups opposing the ordinance were so large that the City Council meeting venue had to be changed to a local theater on two occasions. The COLC vigorously supported a coalition led by the Human Dignity coalition.

Public transit was achieved when a broad coalition of working people, small business, and disabled people (Citizens for Bend Area Transit) demanded it and forced the City Council to create a public transit system out of its general fund. The measure for manufactured home park tenants came about when land developers began to evict manufactured home tenants from their homes and Jobs with Justice and hundreds of tenants formed a coalition called Tenants United for Fairness (TUFF) that jammed the council chambers for months until it and eventually the state legislature passed legislation that protected the property rights of tenants.

When Wal-Mart bought a huge tract of land to build a superstore, JwJ organized another coalition of organized labor, property owners, small business owners, and mall owners (Community First) to fight its creation. With the help of the City Council, the coalition has fought and defeated multiple appeals by Wal-Mart, and after seven years of struggle the lot remains empty.

Since 2003, the COLC and JwJ have recognized the importance of incorporating the struggle for the civil rights of immigrant workers into the labor movement. Regular educational events have linked the scapegoating of immigrant workers to free trade policies and the retrograde immigration policies of the United States. JwJ helped form different coalitions to organize immigrant workers in Central Oregon. Success occurred when JwJ received grant money that was earmarked for the purpose of immigrant organizing and targeted the churches as sites for this organizing. The catalyst for the creation of a multiethnic coalition and mass movement in Central Oregon was a 2008 tour organized by JwJ that featured labor journalist and photographer David Bacon and his new book, *Illegal People: How Globalizaton Creates Migration and Criminalizes Immigrants.*[19] The tour occurred during the MLK celebrations, and by May Day 300 workers, immigrants, and union members from Central Oregon marched with 2,000 other workers on the state capital demanding justice for immigrants. The immigrant rights group in Central Oregon eventually merged into a statewide immigrant rights group organized by CAUSA.

Central Oregon played a role when the whole Oregon labor movement showed the nation how to create and pass "tax the rich" legislation when they united to pass Ballot Measures 66 and 67 in 2009.

After three and a half years of organizing weekly solidarity events inside the bargaining unit and with community support built on the outside, Head Start workers with OSEA achieved a collective bargaining agreement. Similarly, after helping to create the transit district, the COLC and JwJ set out to organize the workers of ParaTransit Inc. into a union. After forming an organizing committee, the workers picked ATU as their union. Authorization cards were collected by the COLC and JwJ, and when ParaTransit tried to change the venue of the election to a distant location, the Bend City Council ordered ParaTransit to hold the election at the work site. The union won. ParaTransit hired anti-union consultants and tried to break the union, but mass demonstrations helped win back the jobs of transit workers that ParaTransit illegally fired. Eventually, the workers received a significant wage increase and some benefits. Unions have begun to pick up the pace of organizing in Central Oregon, in no small part due to the continued efforts of the COLC and JwJ. The Oregon Nurses Association has had successful organizing drives and contract fights in Redmond and Prineville, and SEIU organized the rest of the largest employer in Bend, St. Charles Hospital, when 600 hospital workers successfully organized in 2011. And Bend workers brag that they have been able to turn out more support for the struggle in Wisconsin than in Portland, the largest city in Oregon.

At some point, building communities of solidarity has to be a conscious process, and the values and behaviors that promote social justice have to be reinforced over time. The leadership of the labor movement in Central Oregon has changed, but so far, though new leaders do things differently, the social movements continue to be supported and workers are still getting organized. And if the right-wing promoters of regressive anti-people culture want a fight, they will find one in Central Oregon, where workers stand shoulder to shoulder for social justice.

16—Class Warfare in Longview, Washington: "No Wisconsin Here"

MICHAEL D. YATES

We have passed by Longview, Washington, many times on our way to Seattle or Mt. Rainier. We never knew about its rich labor history, and we would never have guessed that it would become the center of a struggle that is as important for the future of the labor movement as the uprising in Wisconsin.

Longview is a town of 36, 000 people, located along Interstate 5, forty-eight miles north of Portland, Oregon, and 128 miles south of Seattle. It was established in 1921, built privately by Robert A. Long, president of the Long-Bell Lumber Company. A company town, it was constructed originally to support a population of 50,000, including the 14,000 workers Long needed for his operations. About two miles southwest of the center of Longview is the Port of Longview, which was also established in 1921, by the state, as a locally run Port Authority.

Today both Longview and the Port are staunchly pro-union strongholds. The Wikipedia entry for the Port tells us that

The Port manages and operates a marine terminal complex where domestic and international ships and barges arrive and depart, and bulk, break bulk and project cargos are loaded or unloaded by local labor union workers. Union workers operate lifting and moving equipment including cranes, forklifts and reach stackers. These workers belong to the International Longshore and Warehouse Union Local 21.

The International Longshore and Warehouse Union (ILWU) has had a presence at the Port since the late 1930s, after the famous San Francisco general strike of 1934. Longshore workers, led by Harry Bridges and other radicals, including many Communists, defeated the shipping companies and forced them to accept a union hiring hall. This would dispatch workers, according to union rules, to any employer on the docks that needed them. Such a hiring hall arrangement, operated by ILWU Local 21, is in force at the Port of Longview. The Port has an agreement with the union that all of the shipping businesses using the port will utilize ILWU members to load and unload cargo. The ILWU also has a collective bargaining agreement with all of the owners of export grain terminals at ports along the Pacific Coast, an agreement that spells out the wages, hours, and terms and conditions of employment of the ILWU members who work at grain terminals.

In June 2009, three multinational corporations created a joint venture, EGT Development (hereinafter, EGT), to build a new, state-of-the-art, export grain terminal at the Port. The three companies are

- Bunge Limited: from its beginning in the Netherlands in 1818, Bunge has spread its tentacles around the globe and is today an agricultural giant, with operations in every aspect of food production, processing, storage, shipping, and finance.

- Itochu Corporation: this company was born in 1858 in Japan and is now a conglomerate with interests in textiles, machinery, aerospace, electronics, multimedia, energy, metals, chemicals, forest products, food, finance, realty, insurance, and logistics.

- STX Corporation: this South Korean business is involved in the provision of trading services (cargo management, crew management, insurance, etc.), shipbuilding, and a host of other shipping-related activities.

The grain terminal would be the first one built in the Pacific Northwest in more than thirty years. EGT used the promise of good union jobs as a tactic to obtain generous tax and land lease concessions from the state and the Port. However, non-union workers from the United States and from Guatemala were employed in the construction of the $200 million grain terminal. Then, prior to the planned opening, EGT made known its intentions to operate with non-union labor, in violation of the agreement the union had with the Port and in disregard of the ILWU's grain terminal contracts. [Judge Ronald B. Leighton (see below) ruled in October 2011 that the agreement between the ILWU and the Port was valid but its exact meaning was to be determined by a federal labor arbitrator.] While the number of jobs is small (probably less than fifty), the union saw EGT's actions as nothing less than an attempt to break the union, since if EGT succeeded in running its facility non-union, every other company would seek to do the same.

Unlike so many unions today, the ILWU has maintained its tradition of militant opposition to any employer actions that threaten its members' hard-won rights. And unlike nearly all contemporary unions, the ILWU can still mobilize its rank-and-file simply by invoking the principle of solidarity, that an injury to one is an injury to all. So, as soon as EGT's position became clear, the ILWU went to war, one that began more than a year ago but heated to the boiling point over the past five months. It should be noted that the unions and EGT have negotiated, but that the company has refused to endorse the industry-wide agreement. EGT argues, as well, that it cannot be legally compelled to honor the agreement the ILWU has with the Port.

Union protests have escalated from informational pickets to invasion of terminal property to blocking of trains trying to deliver grain to the terminal to—on September 8—storming the EGT terminal and dumping grain onto train tracks and destroying some property. To deflect the ILWU assault, in July, EGT agreed to use union labor, but it hired a contractor to do the hiring, and the contractor employed members of the Portland local of the International Union of Operating Engineers (IUOE). This achieved two purposes for CGT. It allowed it to claim that it had no direct relationship with the ILWU and was therefore not obliged to bargain, and it gave it cover for arguing that the ILWU dispute was really a jurisdictional disagreement with the IUOE.

The decision of the IUOE local to do work traditionally done by ILWU members has not sat well with most of organized labor, including some leaders within the IUOE itself. The AFL-CIO has decided that its jurisdictional dispute resolution machinery should be applied here, but, given that operating engineers have never done this work at grain terminals on the West Coast, this is a questionable ruling. As ILWU president Robert McEllrath put it in a letter to AFL-CIO president Richard Trumka: "I have never seen an Operating Engineer working in a grain facility before or since my time as a Longshoreman. This is 'historically' ILWU jurisdiction any way you cut it!"

As the ILWU escalated its response to EGT"s defiance of the rights of the workers, those perennial allies of the employers, the police and the courts, sprang into action. Local police began to make arrests and escort scabs and trains into the Port. Union members and supporters were sought out and arrested—forced from their homes in front of young children who were left to fend for themselves, dragged roughly from their cars, and even taken from their churches. While the community has solidly supported the ILWU, which is a key contributor to the local economy and whose members are friends and neighbors, the same cannot be said for the police. In these post-9/11 times, police forces are flush with federal funds and swat teams and seem to enjoy denying citizens their right to protest.

The courts became involved in the EGT-ILWU war as a result of steps taken by the National Labor Relations Board (NLRB). The NLRB was originally established by the National Labor Relations Act (NLRA) of 1935 to investigate employer activities that violated the act and set penalties for employer tactics that denied workers their rights under the NLRA to unionize and bargain collectively with employers. However, under the draconian amendments to the NLRA added by Congress in the 1947 Taft -Hartley law, the NLRB must seek an injunction whenever a union commits certain, newly-defined, "union unfair labor practices." One such unfair labor practice occurs when a union tries to force a third party from dealing with the employer with which the union has a dispute. If the NLRB has even superficial evidence that a union has done this, it must, according to another Taft-Hartley amendment, petition a court for an injunction to stop the union's pressure on the third party. So when ILWU workers tried to prevent a railroad company from delivering goods to the EGT terminal, they violated the National Labor Relations Act's Section 8(b)(4) and the NLRB had to seek an injunction. The board also sought an injunction to end what it considered to be illegal picketing by the ILWU. The board argued that this violated another Taft-Hartley amendment, 8(b)(1), whose provisions make picketing that keeps other workers (including scabs) from getting to work illegal. In this case, the NLRB did not have to seek an injunction, but it had the power to do so. It decided to exercise this power, and it asked the court to ban all ILWU picketing at the Port. Note that besides the requests for court-issued injunctions, the NLRB also filed unfair labor practice charges, which will be prosecuted in the near future.

All of this put the union in a precarious position. It had to make bail and arrange for the defense of its arrested members. And if the court issued injunctions and the union continued to do the things the injunction orders it to stop doing (blocking trains, engaging in mass or violent picketing, entering EGT property), it would be held in contempt of the injunction and face stiff fines and possible imprisonment of those who defied the injunctions. This would be especially problematic for the union if the court said that all picketing had to stop. A union that cannot picket is unlikely to prevail in a labor dispute. In addition, if the union were found guilty of the unfair labor practices, the NLRB could also issue harsh penalties.

In response to the NLRB's petition for an injunction, in early September, Federal Judge Ronald B. Leighton, of the Western District of Washington, issued a Temporary Restraining Order (TRO) and then, after the union ignored the TRO, issued a Preliminary Injunction. In his order, Judge Leighton prohibited the union from "picket line violence, threat and property damage, mass picketing and blocking of ingress and egress at the facility of EGT." He made one concession to the union by refusing to prohibit all picketing as the NLRB had requested. The judge set a hearing for September 15 to determine whether the union, by its actions after the issuance of the TRO, was in contempt.

At the September 15 hearing, Judge Leighton found the union in contempt and asked the NLRB to provide the court with estimates of the costs EGT, the NLRB, the police, and injured third parties had to bear as a result of the union's defiance of the TRO. The NLRB set an estimate of $293,000. At a hearing on September 30, Judge Leighton ordered the union to pay damages of $250,000 and threatened to levy harsh fines on anyone who continued to disobey the injunction order.

The ILWU, which will appeal the damage ruling, responded to the fines with a statement that said in part:

> Accountability goes both ways. The workers faced the judge today, but so far there has been no accountability for multinational EGT, which has created chaos in the community by taking millions in a special tax exemption, breaking their agreement to hire ILWU workers, suing the port, and trying to destabilize the grain industry in the Northwest. If union members stand on a train track exercising their First Amendment rights, it is a crime. But, if a major corporation plunders an entire community, it matters not.

The union also sharply criticized the calculations made to justify the fine, pointing out that

> The damage amount of $250,000 imposed by the court includes the July 2011 purchase of law enforcement uniforms, the purchase of various forms of weaponry to arm public and private police forces, the

overtime pay associated with the unnecessary overuse of law enforcement by Cowlitz County Sheriff Nelson, the reimbursement for travel and salary of EGT lawyers some of whom make over $400 an hour and fly first class, and the reimbursement of NLRB lawyers at corporate attorney hourly rates exceeding $450.

It is difficult to face a combination of large multinational corporations, a hostile labor law climate, the courts, and the police. Most unions won't do it. Their leaders are often afraid of the consequences for themselves, and even when they are not, they do not know how to effectively mobilize their members to combat such powerful adversaries. The ILWU will have to wage a legal war appealing NLRB and court rulings, knowing that the labor laws are stacked against its members. This will cost the union a great deal of time and money. Most unions would have weighed these costs and never have engaged in illegal actions in the first place. They would just complain that the laws were bad and had to be changed. But they would never do anything but try to elect sympathetic Democrats who promise to support labor law reform. This strategy has never worked. The ILWU comes out of a different tradition, one that understands that workers must, through solidarity, develop enough power to directly challenge the power of employers and the government. When you do this, you might get what you want, including better labor laws.

The ILWU has begun a petition campaign to recall the local sheriff. [This has since been rejected by a judge, on the grounds that the union did not present one of the reasons required by Washington state law for a recall effort to go forward. The union has not decided whether to appeal this ruling to the Washington Supreme Court.] It is organizing rallies and demonstrations and building solidarity support with transport workers around the world. I don't doubt that we will see solidarity strikes and boycotts here and abroad against the three corporations that own the grain terminal. And I don't doubt that as longshoremen and women meet each day at the hiring hall, they will talk about this conflict and develop new tactics that will ultimately defeat their class enemies.

At one of support-the-union rallies in Longview, a protester had a sign that read "No Wisconsin Here." One commentator said that this referred to the attempt by Wisconsin governor Scott Walker to take away collective bargaining rights from public employees. The longshore workers were not going to let Walker's Washington counterparts—EGT, the police, and the courts—do the same to them. However, the sign might have another meaning. The leaders of the public employee unions in Wisconsin ultimately decided to withdraw their support for mass demonstrations and the occupation of the state capitol and instead moved their organizations toward a campaign to recall the Republican politicians who supported Walker's plans to destroy the unions. They agreed to make economic concessions as well. Perhaps the sign signifies the ILWU's more aggressive stand. It won't make concessions, and it won't rely on political campaigns that do not (and cannot) directly challenge the power of the forces arrayed against it. Instead, it will rely upon and try to strengthen its own power to shut down the flow of commerce. It will make life so difficult for its enemies that they will be compelled to negotiate a settlement that will keep the ILWU a potent force at the grain terminal. It will also set an example for the rest of organized labor—that what workers have that capitalists don't is numbers, and when these numbers cohere into a single force, then what IWW songwriter Ralph Chapin said will be true:

> When the union's inspiration through the workers' blood shall run,
> There can be no power greater anywhere beneath the sun;
> Yet what force on earth is weaker than the feeble strength of one,
> But the union makes us strong.

Afterword

MICHAEL D. YATES

Most of the material in this book stands on its own. That is, it either describes what happened on the ground in Wisconsin and in different parts of the country or it offers lessons that we might learn from what happened in these places. Most of the essays do both. However, there are references to possible future developments, and since Wisconsin certain things have happened that need to be discussed and, if possible, connected to Wisconsin and the U.S. labor movement.

The most important thing that has taken place since Wisconsin is another uprising, the phenomenal Occupy Wall Street (OWS). It began in Manhattan's Zuccotti Park in September 2011 and spread rapidly to more than 2,600 towns and cities around the world. With OWS, the anger over growing inequality and the political power of the rich that has been bubbling under the surface for the past several years has finally burst into the open. Suddenly, everything seems different, and a political opening for more radical thinking and acting is certainly at hand.

One especially important opening is the possible alliance between those who are organizing OWS efforts and the labor movement. Workers are the 99 percent, and their organization as workers within the OWS framework could help to transform an uprising into a movement for a radical transformation of what is a sick and dehumanizing social system. Most OWS organizers, participants, and supporters are members of the working class, and thousands of rank-and-file union members have participated in and offered material aid to OWS. No doubt, the Wisconsin uprising helped prepare working people for OWS. Jon Flanders, one of the authors in this book, tells us that "A leading young trade union activist from this area went out to Madison, slept on the floor, and came back inspired. Now he is marching to NYC from Albany with a group of Communication Workers of America (CWA)."[1] What Wisconsin helped do was make workers less afraid to take action and better aware that much of the public shares their frustrations and anger. Now that OWS, which is broader than the labor movement in terms of the groups and individuals who support and have participated in it, has erupted, workers have seen that they have a place to go to vent their grievances and others who will support them in their struggles.

OWS encampments in various places have taken up specific labor struggles. New York City OWS protested on behalf of the International Brotherhood of Teamsters workers who handle the art that is auctioned at Sotheby's. The art handlers perform a variety of tasks, which can include packing and crating valuable works of art, driving the trucks that deliver the art to galleries and auction houses, preparing condition reports, and photographing artworks. Sotheby's, which has made record profits but wants major concessions from the handlers, locked the employees out in August 2011 and hired temporary replacements. The workers and their OWS supporters joined forces on Wednesday, November 9, when a major auction took place. The contrast between the picketers and the rich patrons could not have been more striking; it was a real-world juxtaposition of the 1 percent and the 99 percent.

So far, the most dramatic labor-OWS alliance took place in Oakland, California, where a massive march on November 2, part of a call for a general strike, shut down the Port of Oakland, one of the nation's busiest. The International Longshore and Warehouse

Workers (ILWU) has strongly supported the OWS uprising, and the occupiers have reciprocated. One of the demands the marchers made was in support of the ILWU dispute with the companies that own the new Export Grain Terminal at the Port of Longview in Washington:

> The historic blockade of the Port Of Oakland on November 2nd by thousands of people is our response to what EGT has done to Longshoremen in Washington—we feel that an injury to the livelihood of the Longshoreman and their families who have been adversely impacted by your practices is an injury to all of us in the Occupy Oakland movement.
>
> As EGT continues to move forward with union busting practices as well as repression and recriminations against the Longshoremen in Washington, we want you to know that Occupy Oakland will still be watching. We have done research on EGT and we know who you are. We know about a range of destructive capitalist ventures your company is involved in as the 1% both here in the United States and in countries like Argentina.
>
> Let the shut down of the Oakland Ports by tens of thousands of protesters on Wednesday November 2nd be a strong message to you—when we stand in solidarity with Longshoremen, we mean it.
>
> Hands off the Longshoremen in Longview Washington![2]

There is another "shut the port" march set for December 12, 2011. In an interesting sidebar, ILWU Director of Organizing Peter Olney suggested that union hiring halls be tied to protests against foreclosures. Olney put it this way:

> The New Bottom Line reports that in California alone there are 2,107,984 mortgages under water. Many of those drowning in debt and in danger of losing their homes are our union members. When our building trades leaders say that 40% of their members are on the bench they are talking about the 40% of their members most likely to face foreclosure. The link can be graphically made between unemployment and foreclosure by using our hiring halls for mortgage

workshops and mobilizing centers for home defense. The dispatcher announces to the hall: "If you do not go out on a job you go out to a home defense."[3]

The "Out of the Park and Into the Streets" demonstration called by Occupy Wall Street in New York City for November 17 was endorsed by scores of unions, and union members were enthusiastic participants. And around the country, students protesting conditions at their schools have been allying themselves with college employees and immigrant workers. In California, where campus police have responded to student occupiers with violence, including the infamous pepper spraying at the Davis campus of the University of California, students have begun to argue that campuses should become "sanctuaries" for undocumented immigrants, most of whom are workers.

A very heartening aspect of the developing OWS-labor bond is the active participation of young workers. In Baltimore there is a group called the Young Trade Unionists. One of its founders, Cory McCray, marched in the OWS actions in New York City on November 17 and was a part of the Maryland and District of Columbia AFL-CIO Biennial Convention that passed a resolution stating that its members should consider OWS sites the same way they treat picket lines and refuse to do work that undermines OWS, such as hauling away tents, equipment, and books when public officials decide to close OWS encampments. When asked about OWS and labor working together, he said:

> I think they go hand in hand because the labor movement has always fought against the foreclosures, the high cost of education, the workplace violations, the large corporations . . . So many of the things that OWS are bringing to attention and putting to the forefront are always things that labor has taken action on. But right now it's such a visible one because it's very strategic and placed all across the country. Right now, the labor movement has a great possibility of having something come to fruition with the OWS movement. But I think that this is probably the beginning, that's what it looks like. And it's ready to

come to something big. And when we do these types of things, we always are going to need partners. It's definitely not only going to be labor. It's also going to have to be the communities, the churches, LGBT, the minority factor. I think that it takes everyone as a whole to lift up the workers.[4]

On November 8, 2011, elections and referendums in various states seemed to confirm that the spirit of the Wisconsin uprising, energized by OWS, is bearing still more fruit. In Ohio, a bill that took away collective bargaining rights for the state's public employees was overturned by referendum, by an astounding 61 to 39 percent margin. A virulent immigrant-bashing legislator in Arizona was defeated in a primary election, and in Iowa a special election saw the victory of a labor-friendly legislator, a victory that denied Republicans control of the Iowa senate.

Workers, simply as a function of their daily activities on the job, can do what no one else can—stop production and the flow of profits that are the lifeblood of capitalist economies. Nothing would shake the powers that be more than the threat of a militant, organized working class, ready to demonstrate, picket, strike, boycott, and agitate against every manner of corporate and political outrage, from unconscionable bank fees to unbearable student loans to the super exploitation of immigrants to wars to, well, you name it. And if students, the unemployed, the homeless, retirees, and other disenfranchised groups build alliances with workers, the 1 percent will be shaken to their foundations.

However, if the embrace of OWS by the labor movement is an exciting prospect, it is not without its problems. United Auto Workers dissident Gregg Shotwell put it bluntly and directly when he said,

Occupiers should be wary of trusting union leaders who have consistently undermined, sold out, and betrayed every militant uprising or cry for more democracy in the labor movement. Most union leaders in the U.S. are wedded to the prostitution of social ideals. Every union in the United States is in thrall to the number one pimp on Wall Street, the Democratic Party.

Concession and compromise to the One Percent is the M.O. of U.S. unions. Rank-and-file workers should be able to see themselves in the bloody skull of Iraq War veteran Scott Olsen, struck dumb by Oakland police. Every day workers make heroic sacrifices to provide a dignified life for their families. Every day union leaders shoot down workers' aspirations and incapacitate any chance workers have to shield their families from the latest act of economic terrorism.

Where is the union leader in the United States today who has the temerity to defy the capitalist oligarchy? For the most part, we don't have genuine union leaders, we have corporate servants with union titles and six figure salaries. When U.S. corporations invested profits "Made in America" overseas, labor unions in the U.S. cut wages for new hires and blamed foreign competition. When U.S. corporations underfunded pensions, U.S. labor leaders forced retirees to make sacrifices.

The operable word for rank-and-file workers isn't competition, concession, or compromise. The operable word is Occupy.[5]

One possibility is that labor leaders will try to co-opt OWS and fold it into the Democratic Party politics that Shotwell deplores. Already the SEIU, which predictably gave an early endorsement to President Obama, has begun an Occupy Congress effort. Blogger Greg Sargent describes the SEIU plan in a recent post:

One of the enduring questions about Occupy Wall Street has been this: Can the energy unleashed by the movement be leveraged behind a concrete political agenda and push for change that will constitute a meaningful challenge to the inequality and excessive Wall Street influence highlighted by the protests?

A coalition of labor and progressive groups is about to unveil its answer to that question. Get ready for "Occupy Congress."

The coalition—which includes unions like SEIU and CWA and groups like the Center for Community Change—is currently working on a plan to bus thousands of protesters from across the country to Washington, where they will congregate around the

Capitol from December 5–9, SEIU president Mary Kay Henry tells me in an interview.

"Thousands of people have signed up to come to Capitol Hill during the first week in December," Henry says, adding that protesters are invited to make their way to Washington on their own, too. "We're figuring out buses and transportation now.". . .

One goal of the protests, Henry says, is to pressure Republicans to support Obama's jobs creation proposals. More generally, the aim is to highlight Congress's misguided obsession with the deficit and overall inaction on unemployment.

"We're talking about it as an effort to take back the Capitol," Henry says. "It would be great if we could build pressure that goes beyond the jobs act."

Of course, Occupy Wall Street is distinguished by its organic, bottom-up nature and its critique of both parties' coziness with Wall Street. Does a coordinated effort by labor and liberal groups to channel the movement's energy into pressuring one party risk compromising the essence of what's driven the protests?

Henry said she wasn't worried about that happening, noting that Occupy Wall Street had created a "framework"—which she described as "we are the 99 percent"—within which such activities would fit comfortably.

"The reason we're targeting Republicans is because this is about jobs," she said. "The Republicans' insistence that no revenue can be put on the table is the reason we're not creating jobs in this country. We want to draw a stark contrast between a party that wants to scapegoat immigrants, attack public workers, and protect the rich, versus a president who has been saying he wants America to get back to work and that everybody should pay their fair share."

But Henry added she salutes Occupy Wall Street for finding fault with both parties, adding: "We agree that on domestic social programs, we have not won the day with either party. And we are applying pressure to both."[6]

Journalist Glenn Greenwald puts his disgust with SEIU in pointed terms. "Having SEIU officials—fresh off endorsing the Obama reelection campaign—shape, fund, dictate and decree an anti-GOP, pro-Obama march is about as antithetical as one can imagine to what the Occupy movement has been."[7]

Besides co-optation, another problem is that organized labor has to confront legally binding collective bargaining agreements and a hostile labor law that usually prohibits various kinds of strikes and solidarity action. The ILWU, for example, has issued a statement saying, "To be clear, the ILWU, the Coast Longshore Division and Local 21 are not coordinating independently or in conjunction with any self-proclaimed organization or group to shut down any port or terminal, particularly as it relates to our dispute with EGT in Longview [Wash]." Members were advised as well that a public demonstration was not a picket line as defined by the collective bargaining agreement.[8]

Despite any and all caveats, there are many hopeful things going on that will keep the spirit of Wisconsin alive for the foreseeable future. This is especially true when we note that labor revolts are now worldwide and spreading. Those of us who have written for this book have, to use Gramsci's memorable phrase, always had an "optimism of the will." It might be time for an "optimism of the intellect" as well.

About the Contributors

MARK BRENNER is the director of *Labor Notes,* the independent monthly magazine and website for workers looking to "put the movement back in the labor movement" (www.labornotes.org). *Labor Notes* sponsors Troublemakers Schools in cities around the country. Its 2012 national conference will be May 11–13 in Chicago.

CONNOR DONEGAN is an activist, a graduate student of human geography at the University of British Columbia, and a member of Solidarity: A Socialist, Feminist, Anti-Racist Organization. He was raised in Wauwatosa, Wisconsin.

STEVE EARLY worked as a New England–based organizer and international representative for the Communications Workers of America between 1980 and 2007. He is the author of *Embedded With Organized Labor* (Monthly Review Press, 2009) and *The Civil Wars in U.S. Labor* (Haymarket Books, 2011).

FRANK EMSPAK is a labor educator, activist, journalist, and scholar. He is manager and executive producer of WINS, the Workers' Independent News Service.

JON FLANDERS is a railroad machinist, past president of his IAM local, co-chair of Railroad Workers United, a cross-craft caucus of railroaders, and Trustee of the Troy Area Labor Council, AFL-CIO.

FERNANDO GAPASIN has led several local unions and Central Labor Councils. He is a union organizer, labor educator, author, and former professor of Industrial Relations and Chicana/o Studies. He is the co-author with Bill Fletcher Jr. of *Solidarity Divided: The Crisis in Organized Labor and a New Path toward Social Justice.*

SAM GINDIN is a retired former assistant to the president of the Canadian Auto Workers (CAW). He is a member of the Greater Toronto Workers' Assembly. The GTWA aims to develop a new form of working-class organization, creating an activist organizing space that crosses workplaces, unions, and communities and bridges workers' lives inside and outside their working lives. This article was first published in Socialist Project's e-bulletin, *Bullet* 516 (14 June 2011).

MICHAEL HURLEY is president of the Ontario Council of Hospital Unions, a division of CUPE, and is a member of the Greater Toronto Workers' Assembly. The GTWA aims to develop a new form of working-class organization, creating an activist organizing space that crosses workplaces, unions, and communities and bridges workers' lives inside and outside their working lives. This article was first published in Socialist Project's e-bulletin, *Bullet* 516 (14 June 2011).

DAN LA BOTZ is Adjunct Professor of History at the University of Cincinnati. He is co-founder of the Teamsters for a Democratic Union and the author of *Rank and File Rebellion: Teamsters for a Democratic Union* (Verso Books, 1990).

ELLY LEARY, a former autoworker whose plant closed, retired as vice president and chief negotiator of UAW 2324 at Boston University. She currently lives in Florida where she participates in a wide range of labor solidarity and education activities.

STEPHANIE LUCE is an Associate Professor at the Murphy Institute, City University of New York. She was a founding member of Progressive Dane/New Party and the Student Labor Action Coalition in Madison, Wisconsin, and active in the Teaching Assistants Association. She is the author of *Fighting for a Living Wage*, and co-author of *The Living Wage: Building a Fair Economy* and *The Measure of Fairness* as well as many articles and book chapters on low-wage work, globalization, and labor and community organizing. This essay is based on a piece that first appeared in the web magazine *Organizing Upgrade*.

ROBERT W. McCHESNEY teaches at the University of Illinois at Urbana-Champaign and writes periodically for *Monthly Review*.

ANDREW SERNATINGER is a baker and journalist based in Madison, Wisconsin. He has written for *Labor Notes, Against the*

Current, and *Democracy and Socialism.* Andrew is a member of Solidarity: A Socialist, Feminist, Anti-Racist Organization.

JANE SLAUGHTER a staff writer at *Labor Notes,* the independent monthly magazine and website for workers looking to "put the movement back in the labor movement" (www.labornotes.org).

LEE SUSTAR is the labor editor of the website SocialistWorker.org and a frequent contributor to the *International Socialist Review, Counterpunch, Znet,* and other publications on labor, the economy, international affairs, and other topics. He is co-editor, with Aisha Karim, of *Poetry & Protest: A Dennis Brutus Reader* (Chicago: Haymarket, 2006) and is a member of the National Writers Union, UAW Local 1981.

RAND WILSON has worked as an organizer for many unions. He has helped workers build non-traditional organizations at a number of companies, most recently at Comcast. He now works for an SEIU local in Boston, Massachusetts.

MICHAEL D. YATES is Associate Editor of *Monthly Review* and Editorial Director of Monthly Review Press. He is the author of *Why Unions Matter,* second edition (Monthly Review Press, 2009). His essays in this book are based upon posts on his blog: blog.cheapmotelsandahotplate.org.

DAVE ZIRIN is in the sports department of *The Nation* magazine and is author of *The John Carlos Story* (Haymarket, 2011). He is also the host of Sirius/XM radio's *Edge of Sports.* See more of his work at www.edgeofsports.com.

MICHAEL ZWEIG is a professor of economics and director of the Center for Study of Working Class Life at the State University of New York at Stony Brook. He represents his union, United University Professions (AFT Local 2190), on the national steering committee of U.S. Labor Against the War and is a national co-convenor of USLAW.

Notes

Foreword

1. I want to thank John Nichols for talking about all things Wisconsin with me, and John Bellamy Foster for reading and commenting on this foreword.
2. On this see Al Sandine, *The Taming of the American Crowd* (New York: Monthly Review Press, 2009).
3. This point is developed in Jacob S. Hacker and Paul Pierson, *Winner-Take-All Politics* (New York: Simon and Schuster, 2010).
4. John Nichols , "AFL's Trumka on Pols Selling Out Workers: 'I've Had a Snootful of This S**t!'," http://www.thenation.com/blog/161208/afls-trumka-pols-selling-out-workers-ive-had-snootful-st (June 8, 2011).
5. See John Maynard Keynes, *Essays in Persuasion* (New York: Harcourt, Brace, 1932), 372; John Bellamy Foster, "The End of Rational Capitalism," *Monthly Review* 56/10 (March 2005): 1–13.
6. Alexander Cockburn, "The Waste Land," *CounterPunch*, September 10-11, 2011. http://www.counterpunch.org/2011/09/09/the-waste-land/.
7. Mike Davis, "How Obama Became the Curator of the Bush Legacy," TomDispatch.com, September 13, 2011; www.tomdispatch.com/post/175440/tomgram%3A_mike_davis%2C_how_obama_became_the_curator_of_the_bush_legacy/#more.

1—Disciplining Labor, Dismantling Democracy

Special thanks to Rebecca Kemble and Adam Chern for your generosity as my hosts in Madison. My reporting on and participation in this struggle would not have been possible without it. Thank you also to Stephanie Schneider for answering my questions on the Educator's Network for Social Justice and the struggle against mayoral control, the sickouts and organizing efforts of Milwaukee teachers, and the late-night MTEA meeting described in this article.

1. "Koch Whore: Wisconsin Governor Scott Walker," *The Beast*, Feb. 23, 2011. http://buffalobeast.com/?p=5045

2. Quoted in Hal Draper, *Karl Marx's Theory of Revolution*, vol. 1 (New York and London: Monthly Review Press, 1977), 273.

3. Institute for Wisconsin's Future, "Wisconsin's Revenue Gap: An Analysis of Corporate Tax Avoidance," Dec. 2007, www.wisconsinfuture.org.

4. For more analysis, see Connor Donegan, "Taking Stock and Moving Forward in Wisconsin: Reflections of a Struggle," *Solidarity*, www.solidarity-us.org.

5. "For black Milwaukeeans, however, a 'stealth depression' in the region's labor market has been under way for decades. . . . [In 2007] a staggering 51.1 percent of metro Milwaukee's working-age African American males were out-of-work." Marc V. Levine, "The Crisis Continues: Black Male Joblessness in Milwaukee," UWM Center for Economic Development, Oct. 2008, http://www4.uwm.edu/ced/.

6. Patti Wenzel, "Walker to propose $1 billion cut to education: MPS would lose up to 25% of its funding," *Third Coast Digest*, Feb. 16, 2011, http://www.thirdcoastdigest.com.

7. Barbara Miner interviewed by Todd Price, "Vouchers for the Wealthy," http://www.youtube.com/user/tprice1963#p/u/17/x5MnDYk9RRY. Miner has been reporting on Milwaukee's voucher program for *Milwaukee Journal Sentinel* and Rethinking Schools since 1990.

8. Barbara Miner, "Distorting the Civil Rights Legacy" (Spring 2004); "Keeping Public Schools Public: Free Market Education" (Fall 2005); and "Who's Bankrolling Vouchers?" (Fall 2001), in *Rethinking Schools*, http://www.rethinkingschools.org. In "Keeping Public Schools Public" Miner examines the results of a *Milwaukee Journal Sentinel* investigation into these recently opened, private voucher schools. "Overall, the *Milwaukee Journal Sentinel* estimated that 10 percent of the 115 voucher schools demonstrate 'alarming deficiencies' without 'the ability, resources, knowledge or will to offer children even a mediocre education.'"

9. "Madison Capitol MTEA Rally," www.youtube.com/watch?v=tgaXyzJv7OY.

10. Personal communication with Stephanie Schneider, May 15, 2011.

11. Andre Gunder Frank, *Crisis: In the World Economy* (New York: Holmes & Meier, 1980), 102.

12.   Quoted in ibid., 123.
13.   David McNally, *Global Slump* (Oakland, CA: PM Press, 2011), 36.
14.   Ibid.
15.   Wisconsin Department of Administration, *State of Wisconsin 2011–13 Executive Budget*, "Budget in Brief," 2; http://www.doa.state.wi.us.
16.   Ibid., 3.
17.   Heather Sawaski, "GB teachers Have New 2-Year Contract," WFRV-TV, March 8, 2011, http://www.wfrv.com.
18.   For more on capitalism and crisis, see McNally, *Global Slump,* or David Harvey, *The Enigma of Capital and the Crises of Capitalism* (Oxford and New York: Oxford University Press, 2010).
19.   Quoted in Kim Moody, "Two-Sided Class War at Last? Wisconsin and Beyond," *Against the Current* 152 (May/June 2011): 13; http://www.solidarity-us.org/current/atc.

2—Capitalist Crisis and the Wisconsin Uprising

1.   This essay isn't really the place to chart the particulars of the crisis, but suffice to say that there is agreement among just about all schools of thought on the Marxist left that there was a deeper crisis underneath the bank meltdowns. See David McNally, *Global Slump: The Economics and Politics of Crisis and Resistance* (Oakland, CA: PM Press, 2010); Robert Brenner, *The Economics of Global Turbulence* (New York: Verso, 2006); and John Bellamy Foster and Fred Magdoff, *The Great Financial Crisis: Causes and Consequences* (New York: Monthly Review Press, 2009).
2.   Jack Rasmus,"The Unfolding Epic Recession," *Against the Current 147* (July–August 2010).
3.   I must point out here that nothing was natural about the state's crisis. It was seemingly real insofar as state budgets are largely dependent on the private economy, but in actuality it was largely artificial due to the state's own policies that took on bank debt and accepted budget cuts as opposed to taxing the country's vast wealth.
4.   Editorial, "Walker Gins Up 'Crisis' to Reward Cronies," *Cap Times*, February 16, 2011.
5.   One Wisconsin Now, "Walker Concocts 'Scoop and Toss' Borrowing Scheme to Pay for $140 Million in Special Interest Spending," February 11, 2011, www.onewisconsinnow.org/press/walker-concocts-scoop-and-toss-borrowing-scheme-to-pay-for-140-million-in-special-interest-spending.html.

3—Who Were the Leaders of the Wisconsin Uprising?

Many Wisconsin activists generously shared their experiences with me to help write this article. I would like to thank in particular the following individuals for their comments on an earlier draft: Eric Cobb, Joe Conway, Mike Imbrogno, Sam Jordan,and Eric Robson.

1. Elizabeth Schulte and Lee Sustar, "Solidarity City," February 28, 2011, http://www.www.socialistworker.org/2011/02/28/solidarity-city.
2. Interview with Ben Gall and Ron Moore, March 1, 2011.
3. Interview with the author, March 1, 2011.
4. Phil Gasper, "What Comes Next in Wisconsin?" March 7, 2011, wwww.socialistworker.org/2011/03/07/what-comes-next-wisconsin.
5. Mark Pitsch, "Labor's Last Stand? Unions Appear to Be on Life Support as Memberships Dwindle," *Wisconsin State Journal,* April 17, 2011.
6. Leslie Wirpsa, "Briggs & Stratton Layoffs Tear Family Hopes," *National Catholic Reporter*, December 2, 1994.
7. Rick Romell, "Briggs Contract Boosts Pay, but Health Insurance Costs also Grow," *Milwaukee Journal Sentinel,* October 22, 2010, http://www.jsonline.com/business/105529283.html.
8. Ronald Cox, "The Milwaukee Plants—End of an Era," http://history.gmheritagecenter.com/wiki/index.php/The_Milwaukee_Plants_-_End_of_an_Era.
9. Roger Bybee, "Obama and the Heartland: The Good, the Bad, and the Very Ugly (Part 2)," *In These Times,* July 6, 2010, http://www.inthesetimes.com/working/entry/6177/.
10. Jim Leute, "Local Union Membership Declines," *Janesville Gazette,* September 6, 2009, http://gazettextra.com/news/2009/sep/06/local-union-membership-declines/.
11. Roger Bybee, " Paper Chase: Struggle Underscores Larger Pattern of Hurt in the Heartland," *Isthmus Daily Page,* October 17, 2008, http://www.thedailypage.com/isthmus/article.php?article=24051.
12. Matt McKinney, "Hormel Union Lauds Terms of New Contract," *Minneapolis Star-Tribune,* September 12, 2007, www.startribune.com/business/11224696.html. For the wage comparison, see also "Tentative Pact Reached in Lengthy Hormel Strike," August 28, 1986.
13. Judy Newman, "Kraft/Oscar Mayer, Union Reach Tentative Deal," *Wisconsin State Journal,* January 11, 2010, http://host.madison.com/wsj/business/article_fb58f6ea-9019-5000-9681-20cdfda17053.html.
14. Madeleine Baran, "Almost Six Months Later, Aftershock of Tyson Strike Still Felt in Small Town," July 6, 2004, www.scfl.org/?ulnid=42&highlight=strike.
15. Eric Ruder, "Taking on Tyson," *Socialist Worker,* September 3, 2003.

16. Baran, "Almost Six Months Later."
17. Jim Leute, "Union Rejected by Woodman's," *Janesville Gazette,* December 16, 2009, www.GazetteXtra.com/news/2009/dec/16/union-rejected-woodmans//.
18. "BNA Daily Labor Report: Local 200 Teamsters Approve Agreement," October 1, 2008, http://tdu.org/node/2417.
19. Roger Bybee, "Mercury Plant Shutdown Will Torpedo Town's Future," *In These Times,* August 25, 2009, www.inthesetimes.com/working/entry/4800/.
20. Rick Barrett, "Did Mercury Marine Trio Save Jobs or Betray Union?" *Milwaukee Journal Sentinel,* September 5, 2009.
21. Rick Barrett and Joe Taschler, "Harley Workers OK Deal," *Milwaukee Journal Sentinel,* September 13, 2010.
22. LaToya Dennis, "Kohler Union Accepts Contract," WUWM (Milwaukee), December 20, 2010, www.wuwm.com/programs/news/print_news.php? articleid=7419.
23. "Sub-Zero Workers Reach Agreement with Company," January 22, 2011, http://www.channel3000.com/money/26573821/detail.html.
24. Bureau of Labor Statistics, "State and Area Employment, Hours, and Earnings," July 30, 2011, http://data.bls.gov/timeseries/SMS55000002 000000001? data_tool=XGtable.
25. Don Behm, "Labor Unions Voice Support of Lake Michigan Plan," *Milwaukee Journal-Sentinel,* July 26, 2011.
26. Bureau of Labor Statistics, " Local Area Unemployment Statistics," July 30, 2011, http://data.bls.gov/timeseries/LASST55000003.
27. Robert D. Krause, "The Short, Troubled History of Wisconsin's New Labor Law," *Public Administration Review* 25/4 (December 1965): 302–7.
28. Robert J. Lavigna, "Best Practices in Public Sector Human Resources: Wisconsin State Government," *Human Resource Management* (Ann Arbor, Mich.) (Fall 2002): 379.
29. Wisconsin Education Association Council, "WEAC History Book," chapter 5, www.weac.org/about_weac/history/history_book_chp5-1.aspx.
30. Ron Seely, "Ending Collective Bargaining Would Risk Return to Teacher Strikes," *Wisconsin State Journal,* February 21, 2011, http://host. madison.com/wsj/news/local/govt-and-politics/article_bbadeb 74-f33e-5360-9d6f-ceebdd64ebc0.html.
31. Lindsay Fiori, "Madison Events Call to Mind Infamous 1977 Racine Teachers' Strike," *Racine Journal-Times,* February 26, 2011.
32. Greg Bond, "Solidarity City in 1977 & Walkerville in 2011," June 8, 2011, posted on Facebook at http://www.facebook.com/notes/greg-bond/soli-darity-city-in-1977-walkerville-in-2011-united-by-a-common-cause-on-capitol-/210514775653386.
33. Lavigna, "Best Practices in Public Sector Human Resources," 380–82.
34. Steven Greenhouse, "Union Leader Minces No Words When Labor Issues Are at Stake," *New York Times,* February 22, 2011.

35. Tom Sheehan, "State Workers Protest Proposed Job, Benefit Cuts," *Wisconsin State Journal*, March 29, 2002.

36. Phil Brinkman, "State Panel OKs Labor Contracts," *Wisconsin State Journal*, May 6, 2003.

37. Steven Walters, "3 Unions Plan to Run Radio Ads Critical of Doyle," *Milwaukee Journal Sentinel*, September 7, 2002.

38. Jason Stein, "Budget Plan Brings State to Square One," *Wisconsin State Journal*, February 15, 2007.

39. Matt Pommer, "Doyle Plan Hit for Effect on Lowest-Paid Employees," *Capital Times*, May 6, 2003.

40. Patricia Simms, "State Advances Tentative Labor Deal," *Wisconsin State Journal*, June 26, 2005.

41. Wisconsin Office of State Employee Relations, *Agreement between the State of Wisconsin and AFSCME Council 24 Wisconsin State Employees Union, AFL-CIO*, 171, http://oser.state.wi.us/docview.asp?docid=6865.

42. "Former Wisconsin Gov. Jim Doyle Says He Imposed Tougher Cost Controls on State Employees than Any Previous Governor," December 19, 2010, www.politifact.com/wisconsin/statements/2011/jan/11/jim-doyle/former-wisconsin-gov-jim-doyle-says-he-imposed-tou/.

43. Larry Sandler, "No Layoffs Promised in Tentative City Union Agreement," *Milwaukee Journal Sentinel*, September 15, 2009.

44. Craig Gilbert, "Measuring the Union Vote in Wisconsin," *Milwaukee Journal Sentinel*, February 18, 2011.

45. Jason Stein and Patrick Marley, "Walker Budget Plan Would Limit State Unions to Negotiating only on Salaries," *Milwaukee Journal-Sentinel*, February 10, 2011.

46. PolitiFact Wisconsin, "Gov. Scott Walker says public-employee unions falsely told members that they would have to pay up to 13 percent of incomes for health insurance," July 10, 2011, www.politifact.com/wisconsin/statements/2011/jul/10/scott-walker/gov-scott-walker-says-public-employee-unions-false/.

47. PolitiFact Wisconsin, "Group says Wisconsin state workers 'haven't had to sacrifice,'" February 18, 2011, www.politifact.com/wisconsin/statements/2011/feb/18/club-growth/group-says-wisconsin-state-workers-havent-had-sacr/.

48. Lee Sustar, "The Lessons of Wisconsin's Labor Revolt," *International Socialist Review* 77 (May–June 2011), www.isreview.org/issues/77/analysis-wisconsin.shtml.

49. Aongus Ó Murchadha, "Workers Draw the Line in Wisconsin," February 16, 2011, www.socialistworker.org/2011/02/16/workers-draw-line-wisconsin.

50. Lee Sustar, "Class War in Wisconsin," February 18, 2011, www.socialistworker.org/2011/02/18/class-war-in-wisconsin.

51. Daniel Bice, "5 Firefighters on Union Board Resign Amid Expense-Report Scam," *Milwaukee Journal-Sentinel*, January 13, 2011, http://www.jsonline.com/watchdog/noquarter/113433394.html.

52. Lee Sustar, "Wisconsin Unions Turn Up the Heat," February 17, 2011, www.socialistworker.org/2011/02/17/wisconsin-unions-turn-up-heat.

53. TheUpTake, "Madison Firefighters Prez Calls for General Strike," March 9, 2011 http://www.youtube.com/watch?v=i_Z_TVrBUtw.

54. Joe Conway's comments at "Chicago: Lessons from Wisconsin" forum, University of Chicago, May 25, 2011.

55. Interview with Mahlon Mitchell, Madison, March 12, 2011.

56. Interview with Phil Neuenfeldt, Madison, March 12, 2011.

57. Matthew Rothschild, "We Need More Mass Protests in Madison," April 23, 2011, http://www.progressive.org/wx042311.html.

58. Jason Stein, Patrick Marley, and Steve Schultze, "Assembly's Abrupt Adjournment Caps Chaotic Day in Capitol," *Milwaukee Journal Sentinel,* February 18, 2011, www.jsonline.com/news/statepolitics/116470423.html.

59. Kill the Whole Bill Coalition, "Why We Demand to Kill the Whole Bill," February 24, 2011, http://www.facebook.com/groups/KillTheWholeBill/.

60. Robin Gee, "Madison Labor Raises the Stakes," February 22, 2011, wwww.socialistworker.org/2011/02/22/madison-labor-raises-the-stakes.

61. Eric Cobb, opening plenary, Labor Notes Troublemakers School, Chicago, May 21, 2011.

62. Rose Ann DeMoro, "Just Say No—No More Cuts for Workers," February 21, 2011, www.nationalnursesunited.org/blog/entry/just-say-no-no-more-cuts-for-workers/.

63. Interview with Ben Manski, Chicago, May 25, 2011.

64. "Madison, AFSCME Local 60 Reach Labor Agreement," March 15, 2011, http://www.channel3000.com/politics/27205771/detail.html.

65. Scott Bauer, "In Recall Campaigns, Union Is a Dirty Word—on Both Sides," August 1, 2011, http://host.madison.com/wsj/news/local/govt-and-politics/elections/article_f7a30ee6-bb8b-11e0-8532-001cc4c03286.html.

66. Interview with Mike Imbrogno of AFSCME Local 171, Madison, March 9, 2011.

67. See Aaron Brenner, Robert Brenner, and Cal Winslow, eds., *Rebel Rank and File: Labor Militancy and Revolt during the Long 1970s* (Verso: London and New York, 2010).

68. Public Policy Forum, "Tracking Local Government: Monitoring Performance Data Trends," Milwaukee, October 2010.

5—The Wisconsin Uprising

1. Workers Independent News producers were initially denied access to the capitol on the same basis as reporters working for the so-called mainstream media. WIN fought this restriction on free access and respect for independent media. Eventually WIN secured permanent press passes for our

reporters. We could do so because of the unstinting support of the IBEW and the OPEIU.

6—Back to the Future:
Union Survival in Open Shop America

1. Editorial, "Wisconsin Unions Get Ugly," *Wall Street Journal*, February 9, 2011.
2. Steve Greenhouse, "In Indiana, Clues to Future of Wisconsin Labor," *New York Times*, February 27, 2011.
3. See Steve Early, "GOP Targets Fragile Gains of Home-Based Caregivers," *Working In These Times*, April 9, 2011.
4. Jane Slaughter, "Judge Blocks Wisconsin Law as Unions Scramble to Beat Bargaining Deadline," *Labor Notes*, March 18, 2011.
5. Stephen Meyer, as quoted by Roger Bybee in "What Wisconsin Means," *Dollars & Sense*, May/June 2011, 16. Bybee, one of the best reporters on the scene in Madison, describes in detail the public sector labor law changes won by Walker that were aimed at "making union representation futile."
6. See news analysis by Stephen Greenhouse, *New York Times*, April 1, 2011.
7. Shira Schoenberg, "N.H. Closing In on a Repeal of Union Dues Rule," *Boston Globe*, June 18, 2011.
8. Email to authors from Martin Morand, longtime labor activist and retired professor of Labor Studies and Industrial Relations at Indiana University of Pennsylvania.
9. Editorial, "Union-Bashing, Now in Ohio," *New York Times*, April 5, 2011.
10. Aronowitz is a professor of sociology at City University of New York and a union activist since the 1960s. See his article, "One, Two, Many Madisons: The War on Public Sector Workers," *New Labor Forum* (Spring 2011): 15–21.
11. Leah Fried, "No Bargaining Is No Cure for Budget Ills," *Labor Notes*, April 14, 2011; http://labornotes.org/2011/04/no-bargaining-no-cure-budget-ills.
12. Steve Bader, "Pre-Majority Public Workers Union Makes Gains in North Carolina," *Labor Notes*, September 1, 2002.
13. Tom Smith, "What Happens If We Lose Dues Check-Off?" *Labor Notes*, March 30, 2011; http://labornotes.org/2011/03/what-happens-if-we-lose-dues-check-check-other-means. For an interesting account of a state university faculty union campaign to build membership in open shop Florida, see Paul Ortiz, "An Organizing Drive that Doubled the Union," *Labor Notes*, July 2011.
14. For a good case study in private sector union dues collection in the absence of check-off, see David Cohen, "Hand Collecting and Thriving," *Labor Notes*, http://labornotes.org/2011/03/what-happens-if-we-lose-dues-check-hand-collecting-and-thriving.

15. William Rogers, "Collective Bargaining Loss Not Necessarily the End to Voice on the Job," May 2, 2011, http://leftlaborreporter.wordpress. com/2011/05/02/collective-bargaining-loss-not-necessarily-the-end-to-voice-on-the-job/. In addition to backing TSEU, CWA has also supported 3,000-member Mississippi Alliance State Employees (MASE) for the last twenty-two years. For more on MASE's "non-majority union" representation of state, county, municipal employees, see http://masecwa.org/ masecwa.

16. Mike Elk, "The Good News in Wisconsin that the Media Isn't Reporting," *Working In These Times,* June 7, 2011.

17. Jane Slaughter, "Wisconsin Reacts as Anti-Union Bill Is Rubber-Stamped," *Labor Notes,* June 17, 2011. See also Steven Verburg, "Public Unions Make Push for Membership Dues as Automatic Payments End," *Wisconsin State Journal,* July 30, 2011, which reports on the results of initial union efforts to "ramp up drives to sign members up to pay dues directly to their unions."

18. Jason Stein, "Unions Might Drop State Status," *Milwaukee Journal Sentinel,* May 6, 2011. As Stein reported, under Walker's union recertification requirement, "unions would have to get 51 percent of the vote of all the potential union members in their bargaining unit, not just the ones who actually cast ballots."

19. AFT-Wisconsin, www.aftwhighered.org.

20. Stein, "Unions Might Drop State Status."

21. "One, Two, Many Madisons: The War on Public Sector Workers," *New Labor Forum* (Spring, 2011): 20.

9—Potholes and Roadblocks on "The Roads Not Taken"

Here are some useful references, all of which were used in researching this article: on the sugar beet workers see Tomas Almaguer, *Racial Fault Line: The Historical Origins of White Supremacy in California* (Berkeley: University of California Press, 1994); Philip Foner, *Organized Labor and the Black Worker, 1619–1973* (New York: International Publishers, 1976); on the Lawrence mills strike see Philip Foner, *History of the Labor Movement in the United States,* vol. 4 (New York: International Publishers, 1965); Barbara Griffith, *The Crisis of American Labor: Operation Dixie and the Defeat of the CIO* (Philadelphia: Temple University Press, 1988); Michael Goldfield, *The Color of Politics: Race and the Mainsprings of American Politics* (New York: New Press, 1997); Michael Honey, *Southern Labor and Black Civil Rights, Organizing Memphis Workers* (Champaign: University of Illinois Press, 1993); Robert Korstad, *Civil Rights Unionism: Tobacco Workers and the Struggle for Democracy in the Mid-Twentieth Century South* (Chapel Hill: University of North Carolina Press, 2003); Jon

Quaccia, "National Endowment for Death Squads?" The AFL-CIO and the NED," *Against the Current,* 2004; Peter Rachleff, *Black Labor in Richmond: 1865–1890* (Philadelphia: Temple University Press, 1984); Deborah Rosenfelt, "Ideology and Structure in *Salt of the Earth*," *Jump Cut: A Review of Contemporary Media* 12/13 (1976), http://www.ejumpcut.org/archive/ onlinessays/jc12-13folder/saltofearth.html.

14—Beyond Wisconsin: Seeking New Priorities as Labor Challenges War

1. Difficult questions often arise for workers and communities in the conversion from military to civilian production. Jobs are at stake, and state and local tax revenues. There is a substantial literature on the subject going back to the writings of Seymour Melman and U.S. Department of Defense base-closing studies in the 1990s. In 2011, Miriam Pemberton at the Institute for Policy Studies was working with unions and communities facing the end of weapons systems to design specific conversion strategies to "green manufacturing." See Seymour Melman, *Pentagon Capitalism: The Political Economy of War* (New York: McGraw Hill, 1971); and Seymour Melman, *The War Economy of the United States: Readings in Military Industry and Economy* (New York; St. Martin's Press, 1971).

2. "Ownership of Federal Securities," *Treasury Bulletin*, December 2010, http://www.fms.treas.gov/bulletin/index.html.

3. Michael Zweig, *The Working Class Majority: America's Best Kept Secret*, 2nd ed. (Ithaca, NY: Cornell University Press, 2012) 184.

4. Calculated from Center on Budget and Policy Priorities data, http://www.cbpp.org/cms/index.cfm?fa=view&id=2705.

5. The Stockholm International Peace Research Institute reports that the United States accounts for 43 percent of global military spending, with China in second place at 7.3 percent; www.globalissues.org/article/75/world-military-spending. The CIA has a much higher estimate for China's military spending, amounting to almost 18 percent of the world's total, reducing the U.S. share to 34 percent; http://www.globalsecurity.org/military/world/spending.htm.

6. National Priorities Project analysis of the Budget of the U.S. Government, Fiscal Year 2012, http://nationalpriorities.org/resources/federal-budget-101/budget-briefs/federal-discretionary-and-mandatory-spending/. The "discretionary budget" includes items that Congress must decide each year, as opposed to the "mandatory budget" or "entitlements," such as Social Security, Medicare and Medicaid, interest on the national debt, Supplemental Nutrition Assistance Program (SNAP, formerly known as Food Stamps), and other items whose expenditures each year are governed

by eligibility standards and payment levels determined by Congress and that remain unchanged from year to year unless Congress acts to change them.

7. Seth Jones, *How Terrorist Groups End: Lessons for Countering Al Qaeda* (Santa Monica, CA: RAND Corporation, 2008), www.rand.org/pubs/monographs/MG741-1.html.

8. The full texts of these resolutions and many more passed by labor bodies opposing the wars in Afghanistan and Iraq can be found at www.uslaboragainstwar.org/section.php?id=51.

9. See www.aflcio.org/mediacenter/prsptm/08032011.cfm.

10. The 2005 tour is documented in *Meeting Face to Face: The Iraq-U.S. Labor Solidarity Tour*, DVD produced by the Center for Study of Working Class Life, www.workingclass.sunysb.edu.

11. The full convention debate is available in ibid.

12. See http://blog.peaceactionwest.org/2011/04/18/2802/.

15—Building Communities of Solidarity from Madison to Bend

1. Examples: Rick Fantasia, *Cultures of Solidarity: Consciousness, Action, and Contemporary American Workers* (Berkeley: University of California Press, 1988); Bill Fletcher Jr. and Fernando E. Gapasin, *Solidarity Divided: The Crisis in Organized Labor and a Path toward Social Justice*, (Berkeley: University of California Press, 2008).

2. Examples: Telecommunications Act of 1996 (47 U.S.C. 51); Michael Parenti, "Monopoly Media Manipulation," May 2001, www.michaelparenti.org/MonopolyMedia.html.

3. Naomi Klein, *Shock Doctrine: The Rise of Disaster Capitalism* (New York: Metropolitan Books/Henry Holt, , 2007), 14–15.

4. See http://www.taxpolicycenter.org/taxfacts/displayafact.cfm.

5. See http://www.taxfoundation.org.

6. Gapasin, *Solidarity Divided*, ix.

7. Speech by Mahlon Mitchell, a Wisconsin member of the Fire Fighters Association, at Portland Rising, April 16, 2011.

8. The work in Central Oregon was also inspired by the numerous examples in our book *Solidarity Divided*, in particular the AFL-CIO's Union City Program, the discussion of the Los Angeles County Federation of Labor, and the case study in Appendix B.

9. Stuart Eimer, "The History of Labor Councils in the Labor Movement: From the AFL to New Voice," in Immanuel Ness and Stuart Eimer, eds., *Central Labor Councils and the Revival of American Unionism: Organizing for Justice in Our Communities* (Armonk, NY: M. E. Sharpe, Inc., 2001), 57.

10. Ibid., 58.

11. Immanuel Ness and Stuart Eimer, eds., *Central Labor Councils and the Revival of American Unionism: Organizing for Justice in Our Communities* (Armonk, NY: M. E. Sharpe, 2001).
12. As Jobs with Justice has done since 1987.
13. Fernando Gapasin, "The AFL–CIO's Road to Union City: A Bold Plan to Move Unions to the Left," *Working USA: The Journal of Labor and Society* 13 (September 2010): 425–432.
14. I found out a lot about the history of Central Oregon by becoming a member of the Deschutes County Historical Society. Old newspapers and phone books in which personal information like occupation were included were very helpful.
15. Linda Bradetich, president OSEA/AFT Local 6732, Chapter 6.
16. Jerry Fletcher, organizer for IBEW 280 and president of the COLC in 2001.
17. Service Employees International Union Local 503 was involved in a statewide organizing campaign to organize Fish and Wild Life workers in Central Oregon.
18. As other CLCs had done, e.g., Santa Clara County Labor Council.
19. David Bacon, *Illegal People: How Globalization Creates Migration and Criminalizes Immigrants* (Boston: Beacon Press, 2008).

Afterword

1. http://mrzine.monthlyreview.org/2011/cy151111.html.
2. http://www.occupyoakland.org/.
3. http://www.beyondchron.org/news/index.php?itemid=9663.
4. http://mrzine.monthlyreview.org/2011/nowak221111.html.
5. Gregg posted this as a comment on a members' only Listserv.
6. http://www.salon.com/2011/11/19/.
7. Ibid.
8. http://transportworkers.org/node/2026. But see http://socialistworker.org/ 2011/12/08/organizing-for-the-port-shutdown for evidence that many ILWU members support a proposed port shutdown by Occupy Oakland.

Index